RELIGION WITHIN THE LIMITS OF LANGUAGE ALONE

Religion Within the Limits of Language Alone provides a critical examination of the Wittgensteinian philosophers of religion who claim that the word "God" cannot be understood as referring to a metaphysical being who may or may not exist. McCutcheon traces the arguments offered by these philosophers of religion back to Wittgenstein's own criticisms of speculative metaphysics, arguing that in its religious usage the concept of God does not fall under Wittgenstein's anti-metaphysical gaze. In presenting a detailed account of Wittgenstein's own philosophical method, including his criticisms of metaphysics, McCutcheon shows that it is possible to accept Wittgenstein's criticisms of metaphysics whilst retaining the metaphysical content of religious language.

This book offers a fresh understanding of Wittgenstein's philosophical method and a new critique of religious discourse for those studying philosophy and religious studies.

HEYTHROP STUDIES
IN CONTEMPORARY PHILOSOPHY, RELIGION & THEOLOGY

Series Editor
Laurence Paul Hemming, Heythrop College, University of London, UK

Series Editorial Advisory Board
John McDade SJ; Peter Vardy; Michael Barnes SJ; James Hanvey SJ;
Philip Endean SJ; Anne Murphy SHCJ

Drawing on renewed willingness amongst theologians and philosophers to enter into critical dialogues with contemporary issues, this series is characterised by Heythrop's reputation for openness and accessibility in academic engagement. Presenting volumes from a wide international, ecumenical, and disciplinary range of authors, the series explores areas of current theological, philosophical, historical, and political interest. The series incorporates a range of titles: accessible texts, cutting-edge research monographs, and edited collections of essays. Appealing to a wide academic and intellectual community interested in philosophical, religious and theological issues, research and debate, the books in this series will also appeal to a theological readership which includes enquiring lay-people, Clergy, members of religious communities, training priests, and anyone engaging broadly in the Catholic tradition and with its many dialogue partners.

Religion Within the Limits of Language Alone

Wittgenstein on Philosophy and Religion

FELICITY McCUTCHEON

Routledge
Taylor & Francis Group

LONDON AND NEW YORK

First published 2001 by Ashgate Publishing

Published 2016 by Routledge
2 Park Square, Milton Park, Abingdon, Oxon OX14 4RN
711 Third Avenue, New York, NY 10017, USA

Routledge is an imprint of the Taylor & Francis Group, an informa business

British Library Cataloguing in Publication Data
McCutcheon, Felicity
    Religion within the limits of language alone : Wittgenstein
    on philosophy and religion. - (Heythrop studies in
    contemporary philosophy, religion and theology)
    1. Wittgenstein, Ludwig, 1889-1951 2. Religion - Philosophy
    I. Title II. Heythrop College
    210

Library of Congress Cataloging-in-Publication Data
McCutcheon, Felicity.
    Religion within the limits of language alone : Wittgenstein on philosophy and religion /
Felicity McCutcheon.
        p. cm. -- (Heythrop studies in contemporary philosophy, religion and theology)
    Includes bibliographical references.
    ISBN 0-7546-1442-5
        1. Wittgenstein, Ludwig, 1889-1951 --Contributions in philosophy of religion. 2.
Religion--Philosophy. I. Title. II. Series.

    B3376.W564 M36 2001
    210'.1'4--dc21
                                                                        2001022055

ISBN 13: 978-0-7546-1442-5 (hbk)

For Oscar

In the elder days of art,
Builders wrought with greatest care
Each minute and unseen part,
For the gods are everywhere

Longfellow

Contents

Preface

My first encounter with Wittgenstein's work was as an undergraduate studying philosophy of religion at King's College, London. Importantly, that initial introduction came via the work of Wittgensteinian philosophers writing about the nature of religious belief and religious language. I knew nothing about Wittgenstein or his work apart from what these philosophers (D.Z. Phillips, Peter Winch, Rush Rhees and others) told me. As a young philosopher and a religious believer, I found their position deeply threatening to the way I had always understood the nature of religious language and yet also somehow compelling. The threat was most significant in relation to the Wittgensteinian philosophers' account of what it means to talk about God and their denial that the word "God" is taken by believers to stand for an object or being that may or may not really exist. Clearly this denial was not the same as the denial of the atheist. It was the stronger and more subtle claim that an examination of the meaning of the language showed us that talk of God existing could not be understood as talk about *some thing* existing; that when the believer and the atheist disagree about the existence of God, this disagreement isn't about the existence of something, but a disagreement about how to see the world or what to hold important and so on.

It was my inability to reconcile the tension between the seemingly revisionary consequences of the Wittgensteinian philosophers' position and their insistence that they were doing nothing more than *describing* how religious language is used, that motivated my research. This naturally took me to Wittgenstein's own work. The more I read of Wittgenstein, the less happy I was with the account of religious belief and language being offered by these Wittgensteinian philosophers. I could not see how the gap between the way ordinary believers understand their beliefs and the interpretation offered of those beliefs could arise from a philosophically descriptive stance. It became a mystery that I had to solve. This book is the result of my detective work. My central claim is that Wittgenstein's own philosophical method, when applied to religious belief and language, will not license the conclusions drawn by the

Wittgensteinian philosophers of religion. For this reason, they are referred to throughout as Neo-Wittgensteinians. I wanted to highlight the fact that whatever merit their work may have, it is misleading in the extreme to believe that their conclusions follow from applying Wittgenstein's philosophical insights to religious language.

To those who have helped me in my philosophical endeavours, special thanks must go to Dr. John Hawthorne, not only for his support and patience in his role as supervisor of the thesis from which this book has developed, but also for his philosophical integrity and expertise, the example of which has had an enormous influence on my own philosophical development.

Thanks are also due to Dr. Brian Clack, Dr. Peter Vardy and Mr. Peter Bennett who have all provided invaluable comments on earlier drafts and given their personal support to the project. My philosophy students at Lowther Hall Anglican Grammar School fuelled my passion for philosophy, and the honesty they displayed in their own philosophical pursuits has been a source of inspiration to me.

I also wish to acknowledge my deep gratitude to members of my family who have remained contant in their love and support; particularly to my sister, Lucy, who has given extensively of her time in helping with editorial details. For the gift of their friendship I would like to thank Eva Deligiannis, John Adam and Josie Wakim.

Finally, for his encouragement, criticisms and understanding of my particular philosophical needs I would like to thank Emeritus Professor David Pears. Without his unwavering support I doubt whether I would have taken up the challenge of producing this book.

Chapter One

Wittgenstein's Philosophical Ambition

"Philosophical dissatisfaction disappears by our *seeing* more."[1]

The Pursuit of Perspicuity

Wittgenstein was a remarkable philosopher. The depth and breadth of his philosophical project is simply breathtaking. Wittgenstein is also a notoriously difficult philosopher to read and understand. This is not because he writes in difficult, jargon-laden language. Rather, it is because his fundamental philosophical insights are impossible to state outright. In order to learn what Wittgenstein has to teach us we have to embark on a philosophical journey whose final destination cannot be known until it has been reached. This means that when you pick up any philosophical text written by Wittgenstein, you cannot remain passive in your philosophical reading of it. You will either find yourself involved in an entirely new kind of philosophical adventure or you will be bemused and ultimately reject the text before you. Wittgenstein knew that he would have two kinds of readers. He also knew that what type of reader you turn out to be is ultimately up to you. No one can make another person embark on a journey of thought unless they are willing to do so.

The reason Wittgenstein's philosophical texts are so demanding is because Wittgenstein believed that philosophy was an activity and not simply a kind of knowledge. Further, he maintained that philosophical insights cannot be stated but have to be *shown*. The emphasis in all of his work is on clear showing or what he calls *perspicuity*.

The concept of perspicuous representation (*Ubersichtlichen*) lies at the centre of Wittgenstein's philosophical purpose and is intimately connected with his proposed philosophical method. It is not an easy idea to explicate and yet

---

[1] Wittgenstein, L., *Remarks on the Foundations of Mathematics*, Oxford, Blackwell, 1978, p. 218

there can be no doubt that without a clear understanding of exactly what Wittgenstein was after in his pursuit of perspicuity and what motivated the pursuit, we will fail to see the point of Wittgenstein's remarks and in failing to see their point, we will fail to see what Rush Rhees has called "the *philosophy of Wittgenstein*".[2] In whatever way one characterises the changes that took place in Wittgenstein's thinking, the concept of perspicuity and the need for clarification are continuous themes. They are central to Wittgenstein's first treatise and clearly evident in his last.[3] Not only are they continuous themes, but their content or target remains unchanged, suggesting that the point of Wittgenstein's remarks was also unchanging; that his purpose in doing philosophy was essentially the same throughout his life. Our central aim in this section is to develop a deeper sense of what that purpose was and show how it was, for Wittgenstein, connected to the concept (and pursuit) of perspicuity. What we are after is an understanding of the philosophy of *Wittgenstein*.

As a member of the Krausian tradition,[4] Wittgenstein's constant emphasis on the fact that understanding his work was only possible if one understood what he was trying to do and what he considered important is less perplexing. Kraus had connected the writer with their work in such a way that the work had no meaning when considered apart from the moral identity of the writer. Both were fused together and so genuine appreciation or criticism of a piece of work could itself only be genuine if the work was considered as the essential expression of the writer. The difficulty facing the polemicists of the late nineteenth century and early twentieth century such as Kraus and Adolf Loos (another acknowledged influence on Wittgenstein), was that general criticisms of culture, philosophy and art could not be made without implying a doctrinal standpoint which itself required that one occupy or belong to the standpoint under critique. Thus to provide an ethical critique of the way a culture employs categories of thought or artistic expression, one cannot simply provide a rational argument to show one's opponent where you think they are wrong. For Kraus and Loos, such an enterprise would miss its mark anyway because it

---

[2] Rhees, R., *Discussions of Wittgenstein*, London, Routledge & Kegan Paul, 1970, p. 37

[3] See Wittgenstein, L., *Tractatus Logico-Philosophicus*, London, Routledge, 1961, §§4.003, 6.54 and Wittgenstein, L., *Philosophical Investigations*, Oxford, Blackwell, 1958, §§122, 133

[4] See Janik, A. and Toulmin, S., *Wittgenstein's Vienna*, New York, Simon and Shuster, 1973, especially Chapter Three; Bouveressee, J., *The Darkness of this Time: Wittgenstein in the Modern World* in Griffiths, A., [ed] *Wittgenstein Centenary Essays*, Cambridge, Cambridge University Press, 1991, and Wittgenstein's own remarks in *Culture and Value*, Oxford, Blackwell, 1980, especially p. 19

wasn't the categories of thought that needed to be criticised as unethical. In themselves, the categories of reason and thought are morally neutral.[5] The human being is the moral individual and so criticism needs to be directed not at the idea but at the individual who misuses the idea. Janik and Toulmin[6] point out that in keeping with this stance, Kraus in particular never launched a general attack on an intellectual or artistic movement. His criticisms were directed firmly at individuals who were lacking the integrity that Kraus considered essential to genuine artistic expression.

It is important to see in Wittgenstein these central Krausian ideas.[7] They enable us to see that an individual's philosophy can reflect their ethical world view. The necessary connection between the moral identity of the artist and their work was also appealed to by Spengler who made explicit the distinction between great thinkers of the past who were great men, and modern philosophers of whom he was ashamed because they were no longer human beings writing for the human world. Of the latter Spengler uncompromisingly writes:

> How poor their personalities, how commonplace their political outlook! . . . I look around in vain for an instance in which a modern philosopher has made a name by even one deep or far-seeing pronouncement on an important question of the day. . . . We must allow ourselves no illusions as to the gravity of this negative result. It is palpable that we have lost sight of the final significance of effective philosophy. We confuse philosophy with preaching, with agitation, with novel writing, with lecture-room jargon . . . It has come to this, that the very possibility of a real philosophy of today and tomorrow is in question.[8]

And he goes on to lament that instead of philosophers we now have "professionals". An identical sentiment was expressed by Wittgenstein, who remarked that instead of philosophers we now had skilful thinkers for whom philosophy could become a profession.[9]

---

[5] Kraus and Loos (and Wittgenstein) were clearly committed to the idea that ethical categories are only applicable to subjects and not to things unconnected with motive, integrity etc.

[6] Janik and Toulmin, *Wittgenstein's Vienna*, p. 88

[7] For example, "the greatness of what a man writes depends on everything else he writes and does",Wittgenstein, L., *Culture and Value*, p. 65 and "the greatness, or triviality, of a piece of work depends on where the man who made it was standing." (Wittgenstein, L., *Culture and Value*, p. 49)

[8] Spengler, O., *Decline of the West: Form and Actuality*, London, George Allen and Unwin, 1926, p. 43

[9] Moore, G.E., *Wittgenstein's Lectures 1930-33* in Klagge and Nordmann [eds] *Ludwig Wittgenstein: Philosophical Occasions 1912-1951*, Indianapolis, Hackett Publishing Company,

The connection between Spengler and Wittgenstein is interesting and important. It is difficult not to see the direct influence of Spengler on how Wittgenstein perceived the possibilities for his own work in relation to the times in which he was writing. Because of his central idea that historical/cultural development contained some inbuilt necessity (the Hegelian influence on Spengler never clearer), Spengler regarded the paucity of great thinkers a necessary consequence of the decline of a great civilisation. What we had to do was to accept the time to which we belonged and the limitations it placed on the possibilities available to us:

> We cannot help it if we are born as men of the early winter of full-Civilisation, instead of on the golden summit of a ripe Culture. Everything depends on our seeing our own position, our destiny, clearly, on our realising that though we may lie to ourselves about it, we cannot evade it.[10]

Although Wittgenstein rejected Spengler's doctrine of historical necessity he showed allegiance to the idea that the spirit of the time shaped the possibility of thought and its appropriate expression. He also thought that one needed to face that fact with honesty and courage. His references to the way culture constrained him as a thinker are numerous. To Bouwsma he remarked, for example, that it was because this was the age of science that it could not be the age of philosophy.[11] He admitted that his own disillusionment with art and value would not have been possible for someone 100 years ago,[12] and that although he would have liked to have dedicated one of his books "to the glory of God", he didn't because to do so would be misunderstood by the age: "Nowadays this would be the trick of a cheat i.e. it would not be correctly understood."[13] Drury remembers him applauding the architects of some

---

p. 113

[10] Wittgenstein, L., *Culture and Value*, p. 66

[11] Bouwsma, O.K., *Wittgenstein: Conversations 1949-51*, Indianapolis, Hackett Publishing Company, 1986, p. 28

[12] Wittgenstein, L., *Culture and Value*, p. 79

[13] Wittgenstein, L., *Philosophical Remarks*, Oxford, Blackwell, 1975, Foreword. I am convinced that the following remarks from *Culture and Value* are autobiographical, reflective of how out of place Wittgenstein himself was in the modern world: "Put a man in the wrong atmosphere and nothing will function as it should. He will seem unhealthy in every part. Put him back into his proper element and everything will blossom and look healthy. But if he is not in his right element, what then? Well, then he just has to make the best of appearing before the world as a cripple." p. 42

Georgian houses in Dublin that "the people who built these houses had the good taste to know that they have nothing very important to say; and therefore they didn't attempt to express anything".[14] Wittgenstein's belief that one's cultural surroundings in some sense determined the possibility of what could be expressed also helps explain why he could defend metaphysicians of the past as great thinkers and at the same time criticise metaphysics as a confusion. In an age where the spirit lives in earnest, metaphysics, like architecture, "glorifies something. Hence there can be no architecture (or metaphysics?) where there is nothing to glorify".[15] In Krausian terms, metaphysics could be a genuine expression of an individual's integrity, and in Spenglerian terms, it could be a genuine expression of the spirit of the time. Thus Wittgenstein could both criticise metaphysical thinking and consider it as "among the noblest productions of the human mind".[16] This also helps explain why to the Positivist's surprise, Schopenhauer's metaphysics could be defended by Wittgenstein.[17]

It would be wrong to conclude from this that Wittgenstein didn't think that speculative metaphysics, even in earlier ages, was inextricably tied up with grammar and a confusion concerning the limits of language. There is good reason to think otherwise. Bouwsma, for example, recalls him talking about serious thinkers of the past as "deep" men, who *although mistaken*, "gave their lives and hard labour" to the problems of metaphysics. They were very earnest. The contemporary philosopher on the other hand, although they were not likely to make the same mistakes,

> are hollow men sounding . . . they have nothing but this show to put on. What a clever boy I am! . . . Very well, these other philosophers made mistakes, in earnest, but what now are you doing in earnest? There you are crowing over the mistakes of earnest men. So you will never make an important mistake, for nothing is important to you. Wonderful! Crow![18]

Wittgenstein's identification between culture, thinker and forms of thought clearly affected the way he perceived the appropriate form for his own philosophical activity. If metaphysical thinking was an expression of something

---

[14] Drury, M., *Some Notes on Conversations with Wittgenstein* and *Conversations with Wittgenstein*, in Rhees, R., *Recollections of Wittgenstein*, Oxford, Oxford University Press, 1981, p. 152

[15] Wittgenstein, L., *Culture and Value*, p. 69, brackets mine

[16] Drury, M., *Conversations*, p. 120

[17] Carnap, R., in Schliff [ed], *Intellectual Biography: the Philosophy of Rudolf Carnap*, p. 26

[18] Bouwsma, *Conversations*, pp. 67-8

important in one age, the new age (the "modern" world) required a different kind of philosophical activity. The thinker with integrity would realise this and not succumb to the temptation to say what could no longer even be expressed. Wittgenstein acknowledged that it might require a "heroic effort to give up" metaphysics[19] and he also seemed to think that it was something the thinker with integrity must do. "The difference between a good and a poor architect (thinker) is that the poor architect (thinker) succumbs to every temptation and the good one resists it."[20]

Wittgenstein explicitly separated what he did as "philosophy" from what had been done in the past. In his 1930-33 lectures, for example, he discussed extensively the relationship of his own philosophical activity to that of previous times.[21] He conceded that the way he did philosophy was "new", but also thought that it bore enough resemblance to the way philosophy was done in the past to warrant being called "philosophy". If we take on board the Spenglerian influence, we can understand why philosophy needed to find a new form of expression and why Wittgenstein must not be understood as suggesting that he was providing a new method to be used once and for all. G.H. von Wright makes the point:

> It is a well-known saying of his that what he did was a 'legitimate heir' related by family resemblance to what philosophers of the past had done . . . his way of seeing philosophy was not an attempt to tell us what philosophy, once and for all is, but expressed what for him, in the setting of his times, it had to be.[22]

In the light of this, real questions can be asked about developments in a Wittgensteinian philosophy, especially those that have seen the subject of philosophy become linguistic analysis. Moore recalls him emphasising that he was not interested in language for any other reason than that philosophical questions were symptomatic of linguistic confusions and he wanted to give peace to those perplexed by such confusions:

> He did discuss at great length . . . certain very general questions about language; but he said, more than once, that *he did not discuss these questions because he thought that language was the subject-matter of philosophy*. He did not think that it was. He discussed

---

[19] Drury, M., *Conversations*, p. 120

[20] Wittgenstein, L., *Culture and Value*, p. 3, brackets mine

[21] Moore, G.E., *Lectures*, p. 51 and pp. 113-114

[22] von Wright, G.H., *Wittgenstein in relation to his Times*, in McGuiness, B. [ed], *Wittgenstein and his Times*, Oxford, Blackwell, 1982, p. 119

it only because he thought that particular philosophical errors or 'troubles in our thought' were due to false analogies expressed by our actual use of expressions.[23]

So although Wittgenstein confessed that his preferred expression of philosophical thought was poetry,[24] accepting Spengler's dictum that "only a very few of the problems of metaphysics are, so to say, allocated for solution to any epoch of thought . . . a whole world separates Nietzsche's time . . . from our own",[25] meant that he couldn't express himself in the form which in another age might have been possible. Echoing Spengler's sentiments, Wittgenstein writes, "there are problems I never get anywhere near, which do not lie on my path or are not part of my world".[26] Despite his concessions to cultural constraints however, Wittgenstein never accepted Spengler's historical necessity. Rather, he took a more fatalistic attitude towards the development of culture and history.[27] Although the loss of value, the degeneration of the human spirit and the death of a language (metaphysics?) is not inevitable, it is "tragic" and there may be nothing you can do to stop it.[28]

We have seen some of the influences at work on Wittgenstein and the particular ways in which they might have affected his own understanding of his work and the method appropriate for him to achieve his goal. We must now examine how Wittgenstein's method can be better understood in connection with his goal of perspicuity. It is time to look more closely at the details of his work in order to develop a picture of the kind of philosophical understanding Wittgenstein sought to provide. It was, in fact, the only kind of philosophical understanding that he thought was genuinely possible.

The Goal of the "Tractatus"

It is well known that Wittgenstein was, from the start, preoccupied with the limits of thought and of language and that he somehow thought that philosophy was about showing these limits whilst at the same time clarifying the logic of language. Why was Wittgenstein preoccupied with language and its limits? Why did he think that philosophical questions were to be answered by

---

[23] Moore, G.E., *Lectures*, p. 51 (italics mine)

[24] Wittgenstein, L., *Culture and Value*, p. 24

[25] Spengler, O., *Decline*, pp. 44-5

[26] Wittgenstein, L., *Culture and Value*, p. 9

[27] Wittgenstein, *Culture and Value*, p. 60

[28] Drury, M., *Conversations*, p. 152

clarifying the logic of our language? These questions take us to the heart of Wittgenstein's philosophical project. They also lead into a more general question, one that is not often asked and is extremely difficult to answer. The question is this: what is the nature of philosophy? What is going on when human beings philosophise? What kind of knowledge or understanding is being sought? How might it be attained? These are the questions that Wittgenstein has in view. Coming to understand the answers that he gives to these questions is what it means to understand his philosophical project. And it all began with the *Tractatus*.

The central claim of the *Tractatus* is breathtaking in its boldness. In the Preface, Wittgenstein tells us that he believes himself "to have found, on all essential points, the final solution of the problems [of philosophy]". The main contention of the *Tractatus* is the idea that philosophical problems are posed because "the logic of our language is misunderstood" and so in clarifying the logic of our language, Wittgenstein believes he has solved the problems of philosophy.

What kind of claim is this and why might anyone be tempted to make it? Underlying Wittgenstein's bold claim that the *Tractatus* has solved all the questions of philosophy lies an assumption about the nature of philosophical questions. This assumption is never defended or explained by Wittgenstein but understanding it is crucial to a genuine understanding of Wittgenstein's philosophy. First, we must note that although Wittgenstein claims that philosophical questions are posed because we misunderstand the *logic of language*, this does not mean that philosophical questions are simply *about* language. We have already seen that Wittgenstein explicitly rejects the idea that language itself is the subject matter of philosophy. Secondly, we can note that understanding the logic of language (as opposed to misunderstanding it) brings about the solution on *all essential points* to the problems of philosophy. This is a quite remarkable claim. What might Wittgenstein mean by it? Is it an obscure interpretation of Wittgenstein's on the nature of philosophy or does it have a more general and objective validity? We can attempt to answer those questions when we have more fully understood the nature of Wittgenstein's claim.

What *is* the nature of a philosophical question? What is it that a philosopher seeks when he asks a philosophical question? Wittgenstein claims both in the *Tractatus* and his later work that philosophers are after a very special kind of understanding that cannot be provided by science. He was adamant that philosophical questions were different *in kind* from scientific questions. In what ways they are different will be explored more fully as we proceed. In the context of the *Tractatus* the ideas of Schopenhauer can help us begin to understand and appreciate Wittgenstein's position. Schopenhauer's ideas helpfully illuminate the distinction between scientific and philosophical questions and also give us insight into Wittgenstein's diagnosis of the reasons why we seek such understanding.

According to Schopenhauer, "a man becomes a philosopher by reason of a certain perplexity from which he seeks to free himself". This perplexity, Schopenhauer claims, is grounded in wonder "concerning the world and our own existence inasmuch as these press upon the intellect as a riddle".[29] The solution to the riddle of the world must come from an understanding of the world itself but it cannot be found in science because scientific explanations are restricted to particular phenomena. Referring to science, Schopenhauer tells us that "such an explanation can only be relative, i.e. cannot be the method of explanation of the difficult riddle of things and to the true understanding of the world and existence".[30] He makes the same point when he writes "with the purely physical way of looking at things, we shall never attain our end; it is like a sum that never comes out". [31]

So the philosopher seeks to understand the world but will not be satisfied with the explanations provided by science. For Schopenhauer it was also out of the question for the philosopher to indulge in speculative flights of metaphysical fancy in attempting to understand the world. Schopenhauer had learnt well from Kant that speculative metaphysics was illegitimate and so according to Schopenhauer the task of metaphysics "is not to soar above the experience in which the world is presented but to understand it thoroughly". "Philosophy's theme must restrict itself to the world; pronouncing in all aspects *what* the world *is*."[32] This will of course be an understanding of the *essence* of the world rather than knowledge of its contingent configuration, which is the province of science. The task of philosophy is to provide an understanding of the essence of the world that is neither scientific nor speculative. How is this to be achieved?

Schopenhauer offered his own answer to this question, one that is itself rather speculative. In the *Tractatus* Wittgenstein uses the essence of language

---

[29] Schopenhauer, A., *The World as Will and Idea, Volume II*, London, Routledge & Kegan Paul, 1964, p. 372
[30] Schopenhauer, A., *The World as Will*, Vol II, p. 376
[31] Schopenhauer, A., *The World as Will*, Vol II, p. 380
[32] Schopenhauer, A., *The World as Will*, Vol II, p. 612

as a clue to the essence of the world. Like Schopenhauer, Wittgenstein's philosophical heritage is Kantian critical philosophy. Where Kant offered a critique of reason (or thought), Wittgenstein is attempting a critique of the expression of thought in language. In the wake of Hume's dramatic scepticism, the question that motivated Kant was not whether knowledge was possible. Kant could see that there were plenty of things we could legitimately claim to know. What became the pressing task for philosophy was to show *how* this knowledge was possible. Kant's brilliant solution was to give an account of the relationship between the workings of the mind and the workings of the world, thereby drawing a limit to what we could legitimately claim to have knowledge of. Science, it turns out, rests on a basic metaphysics which is not itself a mere extension of science.

Wittgenstein's philosophical enterprise is remarkably similar. Given we can think about the world and express those thoughts in propositions that can be either true or false, Wittgenstein asks the Kantian question: how is this possible? What is the basic metaphysic that underlies the possibility of scientific knowledge or factual language?

The assumption on which Wittgenstein's method is based is that language matches the world at the deeper level of meaning and essence and it is this fundamental match that makes it possible for language to match the world at the empirical level of truth and facts. The world of facts floats in a space of possibilities, and true propositions, reporting those facts, are surrounded by a space of meaningful but false propositions. The central difficulty facing Wittgenstein was finding a way to express these insights without falling into speculative metaphysics. The problem is that if one is giving an account of the possibility of factual language, it is not possible, if one is being philosophically rigorous, to express the view in factual language itself. It was in his attempt to avoid that error that Wittgenstein developed his saying/showing distinction. He can use language to *show* how language matches the world but he cannot *say* how it does this in factual language.

The difficulty caused by this problem of being unable to state in factual language how factual language is possible is a significant one. It requires that Wittgenstein not succumb to speculative metaphysics but it also requires his reader to be led to see something rather than to come to know something. The frustration that many people experience on reading Wittgenstein is in part caused by this problem. We want to be told things whereas Wittgenstein refuses to do anything but set up a picture for us to view and we have to come to understand its details for ourselves. What adds to the frustration is that it is extremely difficult to see why Wittgenstein has to be so dialectical and obscure. It looks as if he should be able to come right out and say how the relation between language and the world operates. The key to understanding Wittgenstein's philosophy, whether it be early or later work, is to see why he cannot explain the relationship between language and the world through which meaningful language is experienced:

> It is relatively easy to see that we have no standpoint from which to assess the relation between the experienced world and a reality which is supposed to lie behind it. But it is far less easy to see that we have no standpoint from which to assess the relations between our words and the things to which we apply them. [33]

Given the fundamental match he assumes between meaning and essence, Wittgenstein can use the limits of language as a guide to the limits of the world's possibilities and so he can determine the essence of the world. As he rather strikingly puts it in a remark from the early notebooks: "my *whole* task consists in explaining the nature of the proposition. That is to say, in giving the nature of all facts, whose picture the proposition is. In giving *the nature of all being*."[34]

In the preface to the *Tractatus* Wittgenstein claims to have solved the problems of philosophy. This assertion makes perfect sense if we treat Wittgenstein as a Schopenhaueran metaphysician who understands the nature of philosophical perplexity as a desire to understand non-empirical essence in non-speculative terms. He takes himself to have provided just this kind of understanding in the *Tractatus* and so believes himself to have provided the solution to the problems of philosophy.

It is worth pointing out that the philosophical tools that Wittgenstein uses to build his picture theory of language come from Russell and Frege rather than Schopenhauer. But the Schopenhauer influence helps us appreciate the purpose and the tone of Wittgenstein's work. The importance of coming to understand the essence of the world is two-fold. First, if a person genuinely feels philosophical perplexity then, according to Wittgenstein, the only way to satisfy this perplexity is to come to see something essential or fundamental about the world. This is what he takes himself to have shown in the *Tractatus*. The second and according to Wittgenstein the more important point of the book, is an ethical one. Understanding it is notoriously difficult but a glance

---

[33] Pears, D., *The False Prison, Volume One*, Oxford, Clarendon Press, 1987, p. 13

[34] Wittgenstein, L., *Notebooks 1914-1916*, Oxford, Blackwell, 1961, p. 30, italics mine

back at Schopenhauer's ethics is also illuminating here. According to Schopenhauer the difference between a good and a bad character is that the former lives in homogeneity with the essence of the world. The good character (who for Schopenhauer is the artistic genius or the saint) contemplates reality from a standpoint that transcends ordinary empirical understanding. Importantly, for Schopenhauer, they are at one with the world. The bad character, on the other hand, feels a firm barrier between itself and everything outside it. Wittgenstein does not adopt Schopenhauer's analysis of the nature of the transcendental will but he clearly held the view that to live a happy (or good) life in a deeply ethical sense requires one to transcend everyday worries and concerns, famously claiming that to be concerned about one's own death was the surest sign of a bad life.[35] If the *Tractatus* enables the philosopher to see the limit of the world, it also enables the ethical individual to transcend the contingent particularities of the world and so live a happy (good) life. The "transcending" referred to here is not, of course, a getting *outside* the world in a geographical sense (how could that be achieved?) but a way of seeing the world and its limits. Wittgenstein writes:

> The good life is the world seen sub specie aeternitatis . . . the usual way of looking at things sees objects as it were from the midst of them, the view sub specie from outside. When one is frightened of the truth…then it is never the whole truth that one has an inkling of. Don't get involved in partial problems but always take flight to where there is a free view over the whole, single, great problem, even if this view is still not a clear one.[36] The facts all contribute only to the setting of the problem, not to its solution".[37]

So combining our understanding of Wittgenstein's early philosophy and his ethics we see how he could say of the *Tractatus* that it has two parts. Logic mirrors the structure of the world without concern for particular facts. In adopting this logical standpoint towards the world as a whole, without preference for one fact over any others, I can come to see the world aright in a profoundly ethical sense. "The problems of life (philosophy) are insoluble on the surface and can only be solved in depth. They are insoluble in surface dimensions."[38] Science can have nothing to say about philosophy or ethics because "one cannot speak in science of a great essential problem".[39]

---

[35] Wittgenstein, L., *Notebooks*, p. 75
[36] Wittgenstein, L., *Notebooks*, p. 83, p. 13, p. 23
[37] Wittgenstein, L., *Tractatus*, 6.4321
[38] Wittgenstein, L., *Culture and Value*, p. 74, brackets mine
[39] Wittgentein, L., *Culture and Value*, p. 10

The Transition

Wittgenstein believed that the *Tractatus* had provided the definitive solution to philosophical problems and so gave up philosophy and turned his attention to other things. He came to see, however, that his early work contained a fundamental flaw. His later work in philosophy is concerned with explaining and correcting this flaw. The problem he came to recognise concerned the key assumption he had made in the *Tractatus* about the nature of meaning. Only by correcting this flaw could Wittgenstein provide a genuine solution to the problems of philosophy. The *Tractatus* had merely appeared to do so.

There are three features of the philosophical system of the *Tractatus* that I need to emphasise in order to properly track the nature of Wittgenstein's philosophical transition.

1. Wittgenstein draws the limit of language from a standpoint within meaningful language because outside it there is only meaninglessness, just as outside the essence of the world there is only impossibility. It is difficult to gain a philosophical understanding of the essence of the world because it lacks a contrary "there is nothing that contrasts with the form of the world",[40] and so it is impossible to describe it factually. What is essential cannot be described but only shown. The understanding achieved in this way is to be sharply contrasted with factual information.[41]

2. In his closing remarks, Wittgenstein claims that the only correct method in philosophy is to show the metaphysical philosophers that they have failed to say anything legitimate. But he also claims that his propositions, when properly understood, will enable the philosopher to "see the world aright".[42] The philosopher will have a non-empirical, non-speculative understanding of the essence of the world.

3. In the *Tractatus* Wittgenstein adopts a very special kind of philosophical ontology: the ontology of simple objects in immediate combination with one another in elementary states of affairs. Elementary propositions are correlated with these states of affairs and all other propositions are constructed truth-functionally out of elementary propositions. In this way, the limit of language and the world is fixed.

---

[40] Wittgenstein, L., *Philosophical Grammar*, Oxford, Blackwell, 1974, p. 47

[41] Wittgenstein, L., *Philosophical Remarks*, p. 54

[42] Wittgenstein, L., *Tractatus*, 6.54

If we bring these points together we can draw the following conclusion. In his early work Wittgenstein is attempting to do two things. First, by providing an analysis of language Wittgenstein was attempting to show the true essence of the world ("the nature of all being"). Secondly, (and relatedly), in showing the essence of the world Wittgenstein was attempting to produce a solution to philosophical problems. The *Tractatus,* then, does not reject the metaphysical desire for transcendence but seeks to satisfy it. The strictly correct method in philosophy is to show the philosopher why they have failed to say anything legitimate because in genuinely seeing that this is so the philosopher must have properly understood the limit of meaning, and in so doing, understood the essence of the world. An understanding of the essence is what the metaphysician is seeking (insofar as metaphysics isn't science), hence Wittgenstein's claim that in coming to see that there are no questions left, "this itself is the answer".[43]

In the *Tractatus* Wittgenstein was trying to produce an understanding of essence that is seen *through* language but which cannot be stated *in* language. It is neither scientific nor speculative. It can only be shown and to come to see it depends somehow on seeing the contrast between meaningfulness (or possibility) and meaninglessness (or impossibility) from within meaningful language. In his later work we find Wittgenstein not rejecting but completing what he originally set out to do, namely, to provide a philosophical understanding of essence that is not scientific or speculative and which cannot be stated in language but can be shown through the analysis of the logic of language. The continuity between the early and later projects is difficult to see because of the changes in Wittgenstein's view of language and meaning.

Wittgenstein came to reject the Tractarian system on two counts. It wrongly assumed, first, that meaningful language has a uniform structure[44] and secondly, that meaning is both determinate and precisely demarcated.[45] The first assumption is mistaken because the way in which language is meaningfully applied to the world turns out to be immensely complicated.[46] So there is no such thing as a generalised propositional form that can be identified as that which shows, once and for all, the essence of language and the world. The determinacy of meaning, Wittgenstein's second assumption, had been one

---

[43] Wittgenstein, L., *Tractatus,* 6.52
[44] Wittgenstein, L., *Tractatus,* 6.124
[45] Wittgenstein, L., *Tractatus,* 3.23, 4.12
[46] Wittgenstein, L., *Philosophical Investigations,* §65

of the premises of the *Tractatus*' argument for the existence of simple objects. So its rejection led to the elimination of logical atomism.

The precise details of Wittgenstein's view of language and meaning will be given in chapter three. At the point we are simply attempting to get a general overview of the transition that took place in his thinking. The assumption that meaning is determinate and hidden is based on the assumption which Wittgenstein later described as the idea that our [actual] language is somehow crude, that it is an imperfect presentation of states of affairs. Given this assumption, it becomes the task of philosophy to improve and refine it in order to be able to understand the structure of the world. The philosophically significant point in giving up the idea of the exact and ethereal sense is that, just because it is an illusion, it is of absolutely no use to the philosopher who wants to understand the structure of language and the world. Such an understanding must be of actual language not an imaginary one. Wittgenstein had, in the *Tractatus*, avoided the confusion of speculative metaphysics by showing rather than speaking about the structure of language (the relationship between language and the world), but the structure he had supposed was not the actual structure but an idealised (and illusory) one. As he later admitted, "it became clear of course that I didn't have a general form of propositions and of language" yet "logical analysis [must be] the analysis of something we have, not of something we don't have".[47]

So with Wittgenstein's eye now firmly on the world as he finds it, rather than on the world as he imagines it to be, what happens to the possibility of providing a philosophical understanding of the world? Wittgenstein does not reject his original idea that language provides the clue. Philosophy is still concerned with the limit of language and the world but showing this limit now becomes more difficult because of the idea that there are many different systems of application, each with its own limits. This difficulty is further increased by the recognition that meaning is not precise or exact and so a transition from meaningfulness to meaninglessness at the limit of any application will not be sharp or sudden. This makes the limit more difficult to establish.

Wittgenstein's apparent shift from displaying the structure of the world, to the elimination of philosophical misunderstanding, suggests a radical transition: from believing in the early work that it was possible to understand the essence of language and the world to declaring this impossible and

---

[47] Wittgenstein, L., *Philosophical Remarks*, p. 53

attempting to rid philosophers of the desire to do so. However, if in his later work the goal is still to display the essence of the world through language, then it should come as no surprise to find Wittgenstein's focus entirely on philosophical questions and legitimate answers for them. This was, after all, the main goal of the *Tractatus* but because of his mistaken view of meaning, it was also part of his task to purify language. Now that he recognises that such purity is neither possible nor necessary, Wittgenstein is left with the task of satisfying philosophical puzzlement. The *Philosophical Investigations* becomes a philosophically rich text once you realise that Wittgenstein is not trying to show that philosophy is impossible but is still attempting to provide a non-empirical, non-speculative account of essence. How is he able to do this?

The Goal of the "Philosophical Investigations" (the Elimination of Philosophical Puzzles)

Acquiring a philosophical understanding of limits is difficult for two reasons. The first reason has something to do with the nature of limits and the second has something to do with our relationship to language. To put it another way: the first reason is a logical one and has been evident in Wittgenstein's work from the beginning; in order to draw a limit to thought (or language) one would have to think both sides of the limit. We cannot think both sides of the limit of thought and so establishing the limit has to be done from within by bumping up against the limit. The second reason has to do with the phenomenology of being language users. We are embedded in the language in which limits find their expression. We cannot step outside our language (or thought) in order to gain a clear view of its limits and so we must come to see them *within* language and thought. We will see that Wittgenstein's later method, which he describes in the Preface to the *Investigations* as that which "compels us to travel over a wide field of thought criss-cross in every direction"[48] is designed to make perspicuous the limits of thought in language. Because we can't step outside thought, we must draw a contrast between the limits of meaningful and meaningless thought from within meaningful thought and language.

A philosophical understanding of the limits of meaningful thought does not require a depth analysis of language in the way Wittgenstein had originally thought in the *Tractatus*. He writes critically of his Tractarian assumptions:

---

[48] Wittgenstein, L., *Philosophical Investigations*, p. vii

My notion in the *Tractatus Logico-Philosophicus* was wrong: 1) because I wasn't clear about the sense of the word 'a logical product is *hidden* in a sentence' (and suchlike), 2) because I too thought that logical analysis had to bring to light what was hidden (as chemical and physical analysis does).[49]

So "if we in our investigations are trying to understand the essence of language…this means something that already lies open to view".[50] The task for philosophy is still to bring something that is hidden to light but the notion of what it means to be hidden undergoes a transformation. What we need to see is not hidden beneath a surface but it is hidden because we are too familiar with it. The limits of meaning and thought are right before us but for just that reason we don't see them. "The aspects of things that are most important for us are hidden because of their simplicity and familiarity. (One is unable to notice something – because it is always before one's eyes.)"[51] This means that limits have to be *actively* demonstrated. Wittgenstein trains the eye to follow the play of surfaces.[52]

The need to *actively* demonstrate limits drives Wittgenstein's later philosophical method although we can see that the showing of limits was also the goal of the *Tractatus*. The assumption in that earlier document was that the limit of language was fixed and so had only to be shown. In the later work, the limits aren't fixed and so the philosopher has to do more than merely point them out. The philosopher has to present language in such a way as to "show" the relevant features – but the difficulty is that the "relevant" features (the criteria of relevance) is not given a priori – is not set; it is not "out there" to be gazed at but rather it has to be carved out, hence the crucial idea that philosophy is an *activity*.

The later method is notoriously difficult to understand and the insights Wittgenstein is trying to provide are extremely difficult to see. Wittgenstein's method is to demonstrate the limits of a language-game (which is an application of language within a specific context of use) by showing what happens when the limits are transgressed. There is no precise line that is crossed (no such thing as exactness) but rather, a zone of increasing absurdity. His use of real and imaginary language-games is not designed to eliminate the possibility of a philosophical understanding, rather, "giving [the examples]

---

[49] Wittgenstein, L., *Philosophical Grammar*, p. 210

[50] Wittgesntein, L., *Philosophical Investigations*, §92

[51] Wittgenstein, L., *Philosophical Investigations*, §129

[52] Staten, H., *Wittgenstein and Derrida*, Oxford, Blackwell, 1984, p. 85

effects that analysis" or provides the understanding.

How does such a method produce philosophical understanding? In this preliminary attempt to get an overview of Wittgenstein's work we can do no more than examine a few examples. Our attention will be turned to the specific details in later chapters. Wittgenstein's method of demonstrating the limits of different applications of language (in order to produce clarity for the philosopher who has transgressed the limits) is clearly seen in the following example from *Zettel* where Wittgenstein is dealing with the philosophical assumption that knowing is a state of consciousness.[53] He asks the philosopher to imagine a game in which we have to measure the duration of an impression or a state of consciousness. In other words, Wittgenstein is examining the actual relationship between our concept of knowledge and our concept of mental states. Being able to measure the duration of a mental state is part of our concept of being in such a state. ("How long have you had this pain?" "How long have you been hearing the sound?") If the philosophical assumption that knowing is a state of consciousness is correct then we should be able to record the duration of our knowing *in just the same way*. But we can't. Knowing, therefore, is not straightforwardly a state of consciousness although of course there will be points of similarity between the two. It is the apparent similarity that leads the unwary philosopher into the trap.

Here the philosopher's assumption that knowing is a mental state is taken seriously. Wittgenstein then makes a comparison, which brings out what he considers to be the source of the assumption; the surface similarity between the expressions "to know" and "to hear". The comparison shows that knowing and hearing are anything but similar, (it picks up on both similarities and differences), but the philosophical assumption that they are the same is given up in the light of the facts. The philosopher has acquired a better understanding of the nature of knowledge by bumping up against the limits of the related concepts. This is done by looking at applications of our use of the language in which these concepts find their expression and meaning:

> Our investigation is therefore a grammatical one. Such an investigation sheds light on our problem by clearing misunderstandings away. Misunderstandings concerning the use of words, caused, among other things, by certain analogies between the forms of expression in different regions of language. – some of them can be removed by substituting one form of expression for another; this may be called an 'analysis' of our forms of expression, for the process is sometimes like one of taking a thing apart.

---

[53] Wittgenstein, L., *Zettel*, Oxford, Blackwell, 1981, § 82

But now it may come to look as if there were something like a final analysis of our forms of language and so a *single* completely resolved form of every expression. That is, as if our usual forms of expression were, essentially, unanalysed; as if there were something hidden in them that had to be brought to light. When this is done the expression is completely clarified and our problem solved. It can also be put like this: we eliminate misunderstandings by making our expressions more exact; but now it may look as if we were moving towards a particular state, a state of complete exactness; and as if this were the real goal of our investigation.

This finds expression in question as to the *essence* of language, of propositions, of thought. – For if we too in these investigations are trying to understand the essence of language – its function, its structure, - yet *this* is not what those questions have in view. For they see in the essence, not something that already lies open to view and that becomes surveyable by rearrangement, but something that lies *beneath* the surface. Something that lies within, which we see when we look *into* the thing, and which an analysis digs out.[54]

Another example will help illustrate the method. It comes from the *Philosophical Investigations* and Wittgenstein's target is the philosophical theory that understanding is a mental state. This looks like a perfectly innocent assumption for surely understanding takes place in our minds and is therefore a mental state. Wittgenstein writes:

'Understanding a word': a state. But a mental state? – Depression, excitement, pain, are called mental states. Carry out a grammatical investigation as follows: we say
'He was depressed for the whole day'.
'He was in great excitement the whole day'.
'He has been in continuous pain since yesterday'. –
We also say 'since yesterday I have understood this word'. 'Continuously' though? – To be sure, one can speak of an interruption of understanding. But in what cases? Compare: 'when did your pains get less?' and 'when did you stop understanding that word?'[55]

Why can't Wittgenstein just *say* that knowing is not the same as hearing or that understanding meaning is not a mental state? First, because just stating this will not bring out the ways in which knowing is different from hearing and understanding is different from the mental states of depression and excitement. Secondly, because there is nothing fixed and determinate about the meanings of our concepts of knowing or understanding, there will, no doubt, be positive comparisons to make between knowing and hearing, understanding and mental states. "The language-games are set up as objects of comparison to throw light

---

[54] Wittgenstein, L., *Philosophical Investigations*, §§90-2
[55] Wittgenstein, L., *Philosophical Investigations*, p. 59, footnote

on the facts of language by way not only of similarities but also of dissimilarities."[56] The similarities and dissimilarities (and hence the limits) can only be *shown* through comparison and contrast. They cannot be *stated* because there is no "final analysis of our forms of language and so a single completely resolved form of every expression".

The philosopher who claims that knowing or understanding is a mental state and who then examines how we use the language of mental states, does not come to a new understanding of how we merely use the *words* "knowing" or "understanding". They come to see more clearly the nature of knowing or understanding, which is, after all, what they are seeking. The assumptions that philosophers bring to their enquiries actually *prevent* them from gaining a proper understanding. And so Wittgenstein must wrestle the assumption from them, bring it to light and then show what is right and what is wrong with it. This is why he describes his work as that of a therapist:

> We must begin with the mistake and transform it into what is true. That is, we must uncover the *source* of the error; otherwise hearing what is true won't help us. It cannot penetrate when something is taking its place. To convince someone of what is true, it is not enough to state it. We must find the road from error to truth. [57]

We will be examining the idea of philosophy as therapy in the next chapter. Our task here is simply to understand Wittgenstein's central claim that we cannot access a reality independent of the concepts we use to think about it. Furthermore, these concepts themselves find their meaning through their application in contexts of use. A philosophical question that seeks to understand the nature of something, call it x, can only be answered by examining how x is spoken of or thought about. This speaking or thinking occurs in language and so the philosopher must examine the use of language if an understanding of the nature of x is to be attained. The method is described by Wittgenstein thus (where "x" here stands for the imagination):

> One ought to ask, not what images are or what happens when one imagines anything but how the word 'imagination' is used. *But that does not mean that I want to talk only about words.* For the question as to the nature of the imagination is as much about the word 'imagination' as my question. And I am only saying that this question is not to be decided – neither for the person who does the imagining, nor for anyone else – by pointing; nor yet

---

[56] Wittgenstein, L., *Philosophical Investigations*, §130

[57] Wittgenstein, L., *Remarks on Frazer's Golden Bough*, Doncaster, Brynmill Press, 1979, p. 1e

by a description of any process. The first question also asks for a word to be explained; but it makes us expect a wrong kind of answer. [58]

Wittgenstein's insistence that questions about the nature of x can only be answered by thinking through the language that forms our concept of x has been greatly misunderstood. It is most often seen as a denial that we can get outside language and access Reality. So it is Realist metaphysicians in particular who find Wittgenstein's claims about the limits of language most troublesome. In the next section we will look at the nature of their criticisms. It is important to do so, not simply to gain a proper understanding of Wittgenstein's philosophy but more specifically because Wittgenstein's emphasis on the limits of language is appealed to by certain philosophers of religion in order to rule out the possibility of language about God being referential in a realist sense. It is this claim that we are ultimately interested in examining but we cannot do this with intelligibility until we have properly understood the nature of Wittgenstein's central philosophical claims.

Objectivity and the Limits of Language

Wittgenstein's claim that you can't think meaningfully about reality except through meaningful concepts sounds innocent enough. Unfortunately, it arouses the suspicion of many philosophers who think that Wittgenstein is claiming that there is nothing outside language or that there is no objective reality. Roger Trigg here describes what realist philosophers are after when he writes: "'metaphysical' need imply nothing more than a claim to objective validity detached from any particular language-game. The metaphysical urge is precisely the desire to break free of language and speak of reality."[59] Trigg and fellow realist metaphysicians do think that the goal in philosophy is to "break free of language" and find out how things really are, or as he puts it "to speak of reality".

Now this claim must be taken seriously and examined slowly. First, I do not know what anyone means if they claim that there is nothing outside language. If this means that there are only words and not things, then it is completely nonsensical. As if there is the word "chair" but not the object I am sitting on

---

[58] Wittgenstein, L., *Philosophical Investigations*, §370, italics mine

[59] Trigg, R., *Wittgenstein and Social Science* in Griffiths, A.P. [ed], *Wittgenstein Centenary Essays*, Cambridge, Cambriedge University Press, 1991, p. 127

as I write this sentence. Or perhaps the thing I am sitting on it just the word "chair" and not a physical object that holds my weight. If there are people who can make sense of claims like this then I would like to meet them.[60] It is certainly not what Wittgenstein is claiming when he draws the limit to meaningful language and thought and so any attempt to reduce his position to this kind of absurdity easily misses the point of his remarks.

Is there a more viable interpretation of Wittgenstein's claim that we cannot access reality except through language? What might Trigg have in mind? He wants to be able to break free of language altogether but he then wants to be able to speak of the reality he finds. Wittgenstein will then simply ask what Trigg will use to "speak" of reality when he has broken free of language. It is surely obvious that anything "free" of language cannot be spoken of and that anything spoken of is, therefore, not free of language. Only by imagining some sort of ideal language, which our own imperfectly gestures at, can we make any sense of the idea that we can break free of our own language and speak of things truly - we are almost tempted to say - to speak *in another tongue*.

What is going on here for Trigg? What is he imagining he can do here in his attempt to break free of language and speak of reality? Perhaps in his mind he can see the distinction between words and things and he thinks that he can also see reality without words. He imagines he sees the beyond of language and so can speak about what he sees beyond language and miraculously, without language! Part of the problem here is that in using the term "language" instead of "meaningful thought" it seems easier to step beyond the limit because we can, in ordinary life, distinguish between words and objects. It is not so easy to imagine getting outside our thinking and conceptualising reality in a way that is completely independent of our concepts. The paradox that Trigg is apparently unaware of becomes more explicit when we put it this way; he is attempting to think the unthought. He is apparently breaking free of thought in order to think reality. (Alternatively, he is breaking free of language in order to speak about reality.) The dilemma is well described by Henry Staten:

> We give ourselves the impression that we are indicating the beyond of language – when all we are doing is making signs. And there is no sign whose signification is 'that which is beyond signification'. Isn't this so in principle? How could it even occur to us to think that it is possible to signify what lies beyond signification?[61]

---

[60] I do not mean people from other tribes with completely different sets of concepts. I am talking about those who share my concepts

[61] Staten, H., p. 71

Why does Trigg think that Wittgenstein's view entails a denial of objective reality? Wittgenstein certainly maintains that this concept has to be clearly understood before it can do any useful philosophical work. Trigg does not address Wittgenstein's criticism by showing that his way of construing the concept (namely as that which is free of language) does make sense. This he assumes. In his mind he has an idea of what he means by objective reality and does not think that he has to explain what he means. But is it at all clear what he means? Staten again:

> You might say 'Nevertheless reality is reality', and perhaps no one will want to quarrel with that - but do we understand what is being said here?. . . It is as though a concept like 'objective reality' provides a clear boundary only when it is looked at from a distance, and then as we approach closer and closer, the boundary becomes fuzzier and fuzzier and finally disappears altogether. [62]

Wittgenstein puts the point another way in the *Investigations*:

> 'You understand this expression don't you [objective reality]? Well then – I am using it in the sense you are familiar with'. – As if the sense were an atmosphere accompanying the word, which is carried with it into every kind of application. [63]

It is important to realise the nature of Wittgenstein's criticism. He is not claiming that we don't know what Trigg means but that he himself obviously does. According to Wittgenstein, Trigg himself does not know what he means by "objective reality". The meaning of this concept is not "an atmosphere accompanying the words", nor can it possibly be self-evident to Trigg except in the play of his imagination. Insisting that something is so does not make it so:

> When philosophers use a word – 'knowledge', 'being', 'object', 'I', 'proposition', 'name' – and try to grasp the essence of the thing, one must always ask oneself: is the word every actually used in this way in the language-game which is its original home? – what we do is to bring words back from their metaphysical to their everyday use. [64]

The point is so difficult to see that it is worth repeating it in different words:

---

[62] Staten, H., *Wittgenstein and Derrida*, p. 158

[63] Wittgenstein, L., *Philosophical Investigations*, §117, brackets mine

[64] Wittgenstein, L., *Philosophical Investigations*, §116

When the metaphysician tries to find the right words to express his vision of reality, Wittgenstein reminds him, rather meanly, of the ordinary use of those words and of their place in human life. Worse, he points out that when they are transplanted they will not necessarily take their meanings with them and may even end up without any meanings at all.[65]

When Trigg insists on an objective reality all that he has in mind, according to Wittgenstein, is a philosophical chimera, a *paper draft* of objective reality and not objective reality itself. So rather than denying that there is such a thing, Wittgenstein is actually trying to show philosophers how they might develop an understanding of it, as opposed to their imagining that they have done so simply by using the words "objective reality".

The Struggle with Language

Words like "reality", "objectivity", "truth" and so on are words like any other. Like all other words, they are used in many different ways in a variety of different contexts. When philosophers ask about the nature of reality they are using the word "reality" (although as we have already seen, this does not mean that their question is about the *word* "reality"). What philosophers are seeking when they ask their questions is not clear because what they take "reality" to mean is not yet specified. Of course they can overcome this problem by specifying a meaning but in doing so they have conceptualised reality first and not accessed it without language or thought. In specifying a meaning or picking a particular model of reality, philosophers are simply insisting that one model be given priority over another. There may be nothing wrong with this but the philosopher needs to recognise and be honest about what they have done. It is no use dismissing other contenders and then insisting that your definition was the only one on offer in the first place. Such behaviour is rather like the child who covers his face with his hands and who then believes that because he can't see, no one can see him.

The philosophical desire to break free of language was one that Wittgenstein understood well. The desire for purity and simplicity are real (and perhaps even noble) but in order to satifsy this desire we must recognise the kind of purity and simplicity that are possible. That is the only hope a philosopher actually has of finding answers to his questions. The nature of their questions must be better understood.

---

[65] Pears, D., *False Prison*, Vol I, p. 16

Wittgenstein acknowledges the influence of Hertz for the idea that philosophical questions express mental *discomfort* due to the multifarious ways in which the same word gets applied and that these applications resist ordering. Hertz was particularly interested in the confusions that arise in theoretical science but his central ideas are taken up by Wittgenstein and applied to philosophy. In his fullest statement of how he perceives the difficulty, Hertz writes:

Why is it that people never . . . ask what is the nature of gold or what is the nature of velocity? Is the nature of gold better known than that of force? Can we by our conceptions, by our words, completely represent the nature of anything? Certainly not. I fancy the difference must lie in this. With the terms 'velocity' and 'gold' we connect a large number of relations to other terms; and between all these relations we find no contradictions which offend us. We are therefore satisfied and ask no further questions. But we have accumulated around the terms 'force' and 'electricity' more relations than can be completely reconciled amongst themselves. We have an obscure feeling of this and want to have things cleared up. Our confused wish finds expression in the confused questions on the nature of force and electricity. But the answer which we want is not really an answer to this question. It is not by finding out more and fresh relations and connections that it can be answered: but by removing the contradictions existing between those already known, and thus perhaps by reducing their number. When these painful contradictions are removed, the question as to the nature of force will not have been answered, but our minds no longer vexed, will cease to ask illegitimate questions.[66]

The parallels between Hertz and Wittgenstein on the entanglement of language is striking. The very nature of the confusion identified by Hertz, that different uses which cannot be reconciled make us uneasy, is mirrored exactly in Wittgenstein's own remarks. A clear example is found in the following passage from the *Blue Book*:

The man who is philosophically puzzled sees a law in the way a word is used, and trying to apply this law consistently comes up against cases that lead to very paradoxical results. Very often the way the discussion of such a puzzle runs is this: First the question is asked 'What is time?'. . . The question is then answered 'Time is the motion of celestial bodies'. The next step is to see that this definition is unsatisfactory. But this only means that we don't use the word 'time' synonymously with 'motion of celestial bodies'. However in saying that the first definition is wrong, we are now tempted to think that we must replace it by a different one, the correct one. . .the puzzlement which we interpret to be one about the nature of a medium is a puzzlement caused by the mystifying use of our language.[67]

---

[66] Hertz, H., *The Principles of Mechanics*, New York, Dover, 1956, p. 8
[67] Wittgenstein, L., *The Blue and Brown Books*, Oxford, Blackwell, 1969, p. 27 and p. 6

Look back at the remarks made by Hertz. We ask about the nature of force because "we have accumulated around the term 'force' more relations than can be completely reconciled amongst themselves. We have an obscure feeling of this and want to have things cleared up. Our confused wish finds expression in the confused questions on the nature of force". Wittgenstein's version would read something like this: "We have accumulated around the terms 'reality' and 'objectivity' more relations than can be completely reconciled amongst themselves. We have an obscure feeling of this and want to have things cleared up. Our confused wish finds expression in our questions on the nature of reality or objectivity. But the answer that we want is not really an answer to these questions. It is not by finding out more connections that they can be answered; indeed, more connections will only add to the confusion. We need to more clearly understand the connections and then these contradictions will be removed." Wittgenstein's method is precisely to present the existing connections in such a way as to produce perspicuity. Hence his claim that "philosophical dissatisfaction disappears by our *seeing* more".[68]

In his notes in the early 1930's Wittgenstein wrote: "the philosophical problem is an awareness of a disorder in our concepts and can be solved by ordering them."[69] The disorder spoken of here is simply the tensions and contradictions that arise because of the many uses to which a word is put. The ordering that Wittgenstein undertakes to do is not that of a language policeman or of a radical reformer. Indeed he explicitly rejects this interpretation of his work in the following remarks:

> We want to establish an order in our knowledge of the use of language . . . this makes it look as if we saw it as our task to reform language. Such a reform for particular practical purposes, an improvement in our terminology designed to prevent misunderstandings in practice, is perfectly possible. *But these are not the cases we have to do with.* The confusions which occupy us arise when language is like an engine idling, not when it is doing work.
>
> We want to establish an order in our knowledge of the use of language: an order with a particular end in view; one out of many possible orders; not *the* order. To this end we shall constantly be giving prominence to distinctions which our ordinary forms of language easily make us overlook.[70]

---

[68] Wittgenstein, L., *Remarks on Foundations of Mathematics,* p. 218

[69] Wittgenstein, L., *Philosophy (Sections 86-93 of the 'Big Typescript')* in *Philosophical Occasions 1912-1951*, Indianapolis, Hackett, 1993, p. 181

[70] Wittgenstein, L., *Philosophical Investigations,* §132, italics mine

What does this mean for Trigg and philosophers interested in the nature of reality or of reason? It means that any appeal to Reality or Reason is done in and through language. If I want to define Reason, I am going to have to carve out a definition from the various ways in which we use the word "reason" and "rationality". This will, of course, mean that I give one definition favour over others. Wittgenstein has no objection to this. What he objects to is the denial that this is what has gone on. Appealing to reality to justify one's definition of reality, or appealing to Reason in order to justify one's definition of reason is hopeless. A philosopher can certainly argue for one definition over another but they must accept that they cannot justify their definition by appealing to some independent reality that matches their definition. Reality is precisely what they understand through their definition. The definition itself cannot therefore be justified by appealing to reality. No particular concept can be justified by an appeal to reality or claim absolute legitimacy although this does not prevent people from claiming such legitimacy. Wittgenstein insists that:

> Nothing we do can be defended absolutely and finally. But only by reference to something else that is not questioned. I.e. no reason can be given why you should act (or should have acted) like this, except that by doing so, you bring about such and such a situation, which, again has to be an aim you accept.[71]

It is easy to misunderstand the claim Wittgenstein is making here. He is not denying the ordinary, everyday sense in which we make statements about reality that turn out to be true because they match reality. I can make a claim about the chair I am currently sitting on that will be true if the chair I am sitting on is the way I describe it to be. (It has 4 legs, a wooden frame and a brown cushion on it for example.) It is ludicrous to think that anything Wittgenstein says is supposed to undermine the ordinary ways in which we make statements about the way the world is. Wittgenstein's target is the philosophical attempt to justify the concepts we apply to the world by appealing to the way the world is. I may make certain claims about the chair I am sitting on which can be checked against the facts. I may claim, for example, that the chair I am currently sitting on has 3 legs and no cushion. This is false (you will just have to trust me on this). Wittgenstein is interested in what makes it possible to make true and false claims at all. I can speak about chairs and cushions because I have learnt the concept "chair" and the concept "cushion". As such, I can apply these concepts to the world as I find it and make true and false claims

---

[71] Wittgenstein, L., *Culture and Value*, p. 16

about it. What I cannot do, according to Wittgenstein, is to claim that the concept of a "chair" and a "cushion" can meaningfully be checked against reality and assessed for their truth or validity. I cannot claim that I am justified in using the concept "chair" because in reality there are chairs. This is a claim of an entirely different order. Showing what is wrong with it will be the goal of future chapters where Wittgenstein's account of the relationship between our concepts and reality will be examined in closer detail.

In the next chapter we will examine the broader consequences of Wittgenstein's view before focusing, in the following chapter, on the very specific details of his account of meaning.

Chapter Two

Perspicuity, Justice and Peace

Philosophical Explanations and Justice

In his notes on "Philosophy" (1933), Wittgenstein wrote that "the goal of philosophy is Justice". In the same set of notes, he wrote that "the method of philosophy [is] the perspicuous presentation of grammatical/linguistic facts".[1] Although we find the emphasis on peace rather than justice (as the goal of philosophy) in his post 1933 work, it is clear that taken either way, Wittgenstein is not here defining philosophy as it is traditionally done. This lends support to my earlier point that he conceived of his own work as new. No orthodox philosopher would naturally perceive a connection between justice/peace and linguistic perspicuity, nor would they conceive it as their philosophical task to pursue the goal of justice or peace via the method of perspicuity. How might we understand his remarks?

How can justice be achieved by the arranging of linguistic facts? To answer this we must have a better sense of what Wittgenstein took an injustice to be. Wittgenstein was primarily concerned to combat essentialist and reductionist forms of explanation. His principal target was the growing scientism of his day, although as we shall see, Wittgenstein's philosophical remarks were not merely directed against scientific reductionism but any form that promised to give *the* explanation of phenomena. Injustices occur when one particular method elbows all the others aside or when it implies a necessity without justification.[2] Wittgenstein writes:

> The insidious thing about the causal point of view is that it leads us to say: 'Of course it had to happen like that'. Whereas we ought to think: it may have happened like that - and also in many other ways ... what I am opposed to is the concept of some ideal exactitude; and none of them is supreme.[3]

---

[1] Wittgenstein, L., *Big Typescript*, p. 171
[2] Wittgenstein, L., *Culture and Value*, p. 60
[3] Wittgenstein, L., *Culture and Value*, p. 37

Our tendency to accept essentialist explanations, the "naturalness" with which we do so is something we need to become aware of according to Wittgenstein, because it can lead to injustices. We are particularly attracted to explanations of the form: "this is *really* only this." Wittgenstein cites the easy acceptance of Darwin's theory as an example: "One circle of admirers who said: 'Of course' and another who said 'Of course not' . . . Why in the hell should anyone say 'Of course'?. . .Did anyone see this process happening? No. Has anyone seen it happening now? No. The evidence of breeding is just a drop in the bucket. But there were thousands of books in which this was said to be *the* obvious solution. People were *certain* on grounds which were extremely thin."[4]

It is important to note that Wittgenstein is not commenting on whether the theory of evolution is actually true or false (although he may have objected to the way in which followers of Darwin transformed the theory from a principle of scientific explanation into a metaphysics of nature). He is interested in our tendency to see things in certain ways and the consequence this has for philosophical thinking in particular. As we shall see, the purpose of his own work was to undermine the tendency to think "*it must be like this*" by providing alternatives which we had not thought about. His method is to change the way we think by helping us understand the deeper reasons behind our adoption of certain theories. So against Hilbert's remark that "no-one shall drive us from the Heaven which Cantor has created for us", Wittgenstein replied "I would never dream of driving anyone from any Heaven. I would try to do something quite different; to show that it isn't Heaven. And then you'll leave of your own accord."[5]   Showing that something isn't *necessarily* the case is done by explaining "the surroundings of the expression [in such as way that we] see that the thing could have been expressed in an entirely different way. I can put it in a way in which it will lose its charm for a great number of people and certainly will lose its charm for me".[6]

The particular charm of the scientific world-view was its promise that everything could be explained. Wittgenstein's concern with it was not merely that he personally found the development of an industrial and mechanistic culture   distasteful   and   frightening,   although   these   are   significant

---

[4] Wittgenstein, L., *Lectures and Conversations on Aesthetics, Psychology and Religious Belief*, Oxford, Blackwell, 1966, p. 26

[5] Rhees, R., *Discussions*, p. 46

[6] Wittgenstein, L., *Lectures and Conversations*, p. 28

considerations. That he loathed hearing machinery in music and was convinced the new civilisation was a degenerate one was perhaps more a reflection of Wittgenstein's own cultural background, a fact which he readily admitted.[7] More objectively, Wittgenstein was worried about the spirit of the age; worried that it promised much more than it could hope to deliver and that humanity would be cheated by it. The sweeping away of the Central European dynasties had left a new world waiting to be built. The important thing was to bring the most up-to-date effective and scientific techniques available to this great work of construction.[8] The spirit of the age was progress but Wittgenstein did not think it was at all clear in which direction the progress was being made if indeed there was any. In the previous culture, progress had been a means to some greater end. Now, as far as Wittgenstein could see, progress had become an end in itself because civilisation had no direction. But that meant that there were ambiguities in how we should understand "progress". Rhees recalls Wittgenstein pointing out that the concept does not have an absolute meaning (there is no *progress-as-such*), hence the need to stop and examine what we mean in each particular case:

> When there is change in the conditions in which people live we may call it progress because it opens new opportunities. But in the course of this change, opportunities which were there before may be lost. In one way it was progress, in another it was decline. A historical change may be progress and also be ruin. There is no method of weighing one against the other to justify you in speaking of 'progress on the whole'.[9]

Wittgenstein's worry was not that people were being led to believe that progress was being made when it wasn't, but that no-one was really thinking about the kind of progress being made. It was assumed that all developments in technology were progress and that it was the kind of progress that was in the interests of humanity. Wittgenstein questioned this. It has been suggested that Wittgenstein's attitude towards progress belongs to his conservatism which manifests itself in his resistance to change, his loyalty towards all legitimate authorityand his rather romantic idea that the Russia of Tolstoy and Dostoyevsky might be a place of spiritual refuge for him.[10] His romanticism

---

[7] Wittgenstein, L., *Culture and Value*, p. 6

[8] Janik and Toulmin, *Wittgenstein's Vienna*, p. 246

[9] Rhees, R., [ed] *Ludwig Wittgenstein: Personal Recollections*, Oxford, Blackwell, 1981, p. 222

[10] See Englemann, P., *Letters from Ludwig Wittgenstein with a Memoir*, Oxford, Oxford University Press, 1967, p. 121

was somewhat tainted after he returned from a trip to Russia in 1935 although I think that his lifelong regard for the Russian writers, with their explorations into the human spirit and its capacity for freedom under suffering suggests that his interest in Russia was less political and more ethically idealistic. We might want to say that Wittgenstein was a conservative in some sense. It seems clear that this was not just because of his education, but also his ethics. Believing as Wittgenstein did so vehemently that the human spirit was the bearer of good and evil rather than any particular external events, his suspicion of material and scientific developments makes more sense. It comes out clearly in the following remarks:

> It isn't absurd e.g., to believe that the age of science and technology is the beginning of the end for humanity; that the idea of great progress is a delusion along with the idea that the truth will ultimately be known; that there is nothing good or desirable about scientific knowledge and that mankind, in seeking it, is falling into a trap. It is by no means obvious that this is not how things are.[11]

Wittgenstein's concern here shows the particular influence of Karl Kraus who had believed even more strongly than Wittgenstein in the connection between technological advances and the destruction of the human spirit. Kraus's stance against technology was so absolutist that he refused even to see it as an advance: "Progress is a standstill and has the air of being a movement." Bouveresse points out that this was in part because Kraus had come to equate advances in technology with the making of war weapons and the possibility for the first time of a new form of warfare which was inherently self-destructive, but we can also recognise that for Kraus, progress as an ethical category could only be applied to movements made by the human subject, hence his necessary rejection of the concept when applied to developments in the material world. It is impossible not to notice Wittgensteinian sentiments in these Krausian remarks however:

> How does [progress] reveal itself in daylight? In what form does it show itself when we imagine it as a more agile servant of the age? For we have bound ourselves to a representation of this kind; we would like to render account of progress, and we simply lack the perception of something of which we are convinced. We see, of everything that walks, runs and rolls but feet, hooves and wheels. The tracks fade away...

and again:

---

[11] Wittgenstein, L., *Culture and Value*, p. 56

The real end of the world is the destruction of the spirit. The other depends on the indifferent attempt that can be made to see whether after the destruction of the spirit, there can still be a world.[12]

Wittgenstein's own stance against the spirit of the time is found most particularly in his emphasis on the value of *standing still*. This comes out clearly in the following series of remarks:

Our civilisation is characterised by the word 'progress' . . . Typically it constructs. It is occupied with building an ever more complicated structure. And even clarity is sought only as a means to this end, not as an end in itself. For me on the contrary, clarity, perspicuity are valuable in themselves.[13]

And on the contrast between works of construction and works of clarity he continues: "one is constructive and picks up one stone after another, the other keeps on taking hold of the same thing", "one movement links thoughts with one another in a series, the other keeps aiming at the same spot", "where others go ahead, I stay in one place", and even more polemically against the age of building and construction Wittgenstein writes, "I destroy, I destroy, I destroy".[14] The reader familiar with the *Philosophical Investigations* will here be reminded of the rather striking remarks in §118:

where does our investigation get its importance from since it seems only to destroy everything interesting, that is, all that is great and important? (As it were the buildings, leaving behind only bits of stone and rubble.) What we are destroying is nothing but houses of cards . . .

The distinction Kraus made between the spirit of humanity and the mere existence of the world encapsulates a dichotomy which had developed in the nineteenth century between the human and the natural world which had

---

[12] Kraus, K., in Bourveresse, *Darkness of His Time*, pp. 32-6

[13] Wittgenstein, L., *Culture and Value*, p. 7

[14] Wittgenstein, L., *Culture and Value*, p. 7, p. 66, p. 21. See also the Forward to *Philosophical Remarks*: "This book is written for such men as are in sympathy with its spirit. This spirit is different from the one which informs the vast stream of European and American civilisation in which all of us stand. That spirit expresses itself in an onwards movements, in building larger and ever more complicated structures; the other in striving after clarity and perspicuity in no matter what structure. The first tries to grasp the world by way of its periphery – in its variety; the second at its centre – in its essence. And so the first adds one construction to another, moving on and up, as it were, from one stage to the next, while the other remains where it is and what it tries to grasp is always the same."

become most clearly represented in the separation of facts from values or ethics from science. In Wittgenstein's work, the dichotomy is manifested by him not only as a distinction between facts and values but in his keeping distinct the categories of logic and science (showing and saying or elucidation and explanation). Wittgenstein no doubt adhered to the distinction in part because of his intellectual background (a background which has been extensively traced by Janik and Toulmin, but his own work also required that the difference between the natural and the human was acknowledged precisely because he diagnosed the urge to philosophise as very much a human need which could not be treated by providing causal explanations of phenomena. Different kinds of questions required different types of answers and although this should have been obvious, the excitement surrounding new developments in the scope and success of science had encouraged the view that if a question was meaningful at all it was the property of scientific explanation. Indeed the developments in positivistic philosophies were an explicit attempt to make philosophy more like science so that progress in philosophy might at last be made. "People nowadays think that scientists exist to instruct them, poets, musicians, etc., to give them pleasure. The idea that these have something to teach them - that does not occur to them."[15]

Wittgenstein's anti-scientism was so strong that commentators have been tempted to think that he went so far as to reject scientific explanations altogether.[16] This is clearly a mistake. Wittgenstein did not think that there was anything wrong with science; engineering was, after all, his first degree choice and throughout his life he showed a lively interest in explaining and understanding phenomena scientifically. What he objected to was the scientific mentality which had become pervasive and he particularly found depressing the false promise that science could explain everything. Thus we find him at various times in his lectures and conversations telling his audience that he was "making propaganda" for a style of thinking, consciously trying to combat the

---

[15] Wittgenstein, L., *Culture and Value*, p. 36

[16] Bernard Williams for example, argues that it was Wittgenstein's practice to "stun" rather than assist further and more systematic explanation, see Williams, B., *Wittgenstein and Idealism* in *Moral Luck*, Cambridge, Cambridge University Press, 1974. Against this interpretation there is much evidence to the contrary, including the fact that when acting as a school teacher, Wittgenstein showed mastery of complicated scientific theory and was keen for his students also to acquire one. On the subject of Wittgenstein's interest in science see Kiesel's helpful discussion Kiesel, G., *Wittgenstein's Theory and Practice of Philosophy* in *British Journal for Philosophy of Science II*, 1960, pp. 238-52

scientific mentality because he was "disgusted" with they way it had captured the philosophical and the popular imagination. He says: "Jeans has written a book called *The Mysterious Universe* and I loathe it and call it misleading. Take the title. I might say the title *The Mysterious Universe* includes a kind of idol worship, the idol being science and the scientist."[17]

Underlying the scientific conception was the idea that every genuine question could be answered by science, against which Wittgenstein wanted to point out that not every instance of perplexity was an episode of factual ignorance. Some of the questions we ask demand explanations of a different sort. This is not because science is inadequate; it is because of the specific character of the questions asked. Modelling philosophy on science, as Bertrand Russell did, can, according to Wittgenstein, only lead philosophers further into confusion.[18] This is because on Wittgenstein's conception of philosophy, there is nothing to find out that is somehow hidden from view and as long as people continue to think that there is, they will remain puzzled by pseudo-questions.[19] One can perhaps now understand better what Wittgenstein might have meant when he said that one could achieve peace from philosophical questions by changing the mode of one's life. Living in the age of progress meant that one must be caught up in the drive for progress and the reckless pursuit of knowledge. Wittgenstein attempted to show not only that when philosophical knowledge was construed on the model of scientific knowledge this could only lead to further confusion. His work emphasises why this has to be so. If we are to satisfy the desire of which metaphysical thinking is the symptom, we must stand against the tide of the time; stand still and let perspicuity become an end rather than a means. Bringing philosophy peace can only be done when it is shown "once and for all that what first begins as the desire for a metaphysical theory is really something deeper, something which can only be satisfied by other than speculative concerns".[20] The concept of non-speculative or non-

---

[17] Wittgenstein, L., *Lectures and Conversations*, p. 27

[18] Russell, B., *On Scientific Method in Philosophy* in *Collected Papers Volume 8*, London, George Allen and Unwin, 1986, pp. 55-73

[19] In denying that in philosophy one makes discoveries, Wittgenstein is clearly using "discovery" as it is used in science. Certainly he would not want to deny that philosophy can bring understanding; that after all, is what he is after. But Wittgenstein suggests the different kinds of understanding need to be identified if we are to understand what philosophy can really achieve

[20] Drury, M., *Letters to a Student of Philosophy* in *Philosophical Investigations*, 1983, Vol. 6, No. 2, pp. 76-171

factual concerns proves to be central to Wittgenstein's enterprise. Indeed, we will come to see that Wittgenstein's work only makes sense if we make the crucial distinction between factual and non-factual knowledge. Wittgenstein's "grammatical reminders" or elucidations only get to answer philosophical questions because of the nature of the questions asked: "we may not advance any kind of theory. There must not be anything hypothetical in our considerations"[21] because metaphysical questions can only be satisfied by *other* than theoretical or hypothetical concerns:

> We must know what explanation means. There is a constant danger of wanting to use this word in logic in a sense that is derived from physics.[22]

Just how is the sense of explanation as used in philosophy different from that used in physics? It is essential to see not only *that* it is but also in what *sense* it is different.

Seeing "Connections" not Causes

It helps if we think of explanations in science as causal. This, I take it, is uncontroversial. But what kinds of explanations are given in philosophy? Not straightforwardly causal ones because the phenomenon to be explained is not quite "there" in the sense that it is in science. When we ask, for example, "what is gold?" we are asking for the constitution of the substance that we identify and call gold given to us via a chemical analysis. What we ask "what is truth?" or "what is knowledge?" our question doesn't "pick out" a substance in quite the same way and nor is it obvious where we go to find the answer. This is no accident but is an essential feature of philosophical questions, according to Wittgenstein. Because of the surface similarity between the two types of questions, we are tempted to obscure their differences and seek similar type of answers. This is what he claims leads philosophers away from gaining an answers to their questions:

> Philosophers constantly see the method of science before their eyes, and are irresistibly tempted to ask and answer questions in the way science does. This tendency is the real source of metaphysics, and leads the philosopher into complete darkness.[23]

---

[21] Wittgenstein, L., *Philosophical Investigations*, §109
[22] Wittgenstein, L., *Big Typescript*, p. 177
[23] Wittgenstein, L., *Blue and Brown Books*, p. 18

So how do philosophers answer questions like those given above? Wittgenstein's method is to make clear the grammar of the concept and this making clear consists of elucidating different features, thus "a perspicuous representation produces just that kind of understanding which consists in 'seeing connections'".[24]

The kind of understanding one acquires on gaining a clear view of language use is a different kind of understanding to that obtained when we have conducted an experiment and discovered a causal connection for example. Just how it is different will emerge as we proceed. Minimally, it is a different kind of knowledge simply because what it is knowledge of and the way in which it is acquired is different from scientific knowledge. Being unaware of the nature and significance of this difference had led Wittgenstein astray in the *Tractatus*:

> My notion in the *Tractatus* was wrong . . . because I too thought that logical anaylsis had to bring to light what was hidden (as chemical and physical analysis does).[25]

The influence of Spengler on Wittgenstein has already been mentioned in connection to cultural identity and the way this shapes the possibility of thought. But Spengler's influence is also evident both in the way Wittgenstein distinguishes between the two kinds of understanding and the methods we use to attain them. Spengler distinguishes between what he calls two kinds of morphology (two ways of conceiving or looking at the world). There is what he calls the morphology of the mechanical or the causal (the "Systematic") which is dealt with by means of an epistemological system of reasoned classification, and the morphology of the "Physiognomic" which is connected with all that bears the sign of direction, purpose and meaning (what Spengler calls "Destiny"). The Physiognomic morphology cannot be captured by the Systematic because it is connected to the character or meaning of phenomenon, and that is precisely what the Systematic must ignore. Spengler writes:

> the world-as-history in contrast to the morphology of the world-as-nature that hitherto has been almost the only theme of philosophy. And it reviews once again the forms and movements of the world in their depths and final significance, but this time according to an entirely different ordering which groups them, not in an ensemble picture inclusive of everything known, but in a picture of life, and presents them not as things-become, but as

---

[24] Wittgenstein L., *Philosophical Investigations*, §122. See also *Culture and Value*, p. 9. The philosopher "is very much like a draughtsman whose aim is to represent all the interrelations between things".

[25] Wittgenstein, L., *Philosophical Grammar*, p. 210

things becoming.[26]

> [The physiognomic] is intuitive and depictive through and through, written in a language which seeks to present objects and relations illustratively instead of offering an army of ranked concepts.[27]

Spengler's emphasis on the physiognomic can be made more clear by understanding that the underlying motivation for the production of *The Decline of the West* was his frustration with the inhuman treatment given to history. In asking "For *whom* is there history?"[28] Spengler is reclaiming the meaning of historical events and our relationship to them. History is *our* history; it is the history of *US.* So whereas the Systematic morphology renders historical facts, the Physiognomic communicates the living form, the meaning. His work, Spengler tells us, addresses itself "solely to readers who are capable of living themselves into the word-sounds and pictures as they read".[29] Importantly, Spengler's question "For whom is there history?" is mirrored in Wittgenstein's central post-Tractarian concern: "For whom is there meaning?" If he could get the metaphysician to understand that meanings belong to *us*, Wittgenstein would have brought peace to philosophy because the questions asked by philosophers only seem to make sense because the connection between signs and the livedness (their use) has been forgotten. Spengler's dictum that "truths are only truths in relation to a particular mankind"[30] matches Wittgenstein's remark that "every sign by itself seems dead. What gives it life? - In use it is alive."[31]

The distinction between knowledge of facts and understanding character or meaning is made perhaps more clearly here by Wittgenstein when he writes:

> People who are constantly asking 'why' are like tourists who stand in front of a building reading Baedeker and are so busy reading the history of its construction, etc., that they are prevented from *seeing* the building.[32]

In making the point that there is a difference between knowing historical or

---

[26] Spengler, O., *Decline of the West*, pp. 5-6
[27] Spengler, O., *Decline of the West*, p. xiv
[28] Spengler, O., *Decline of the West*, p. 8
[29] Spengler, O., *Decline of the West*, p. xiv
[30] Spengler, O., *Decline of the West*, p. 46
[31] Wittgenstein, L., *Philosophical Investigations*, §432
[32] Wittgenstein, L., *Culture and Value*, p. 19

architectural facts and comprehending or really seeing the building, Wittgenstein also suggests that concentrating solely on factual knowledge can destroy our ability to understand and comprehend meaningfulness. More significantly, if our question is about meaning, then seeking an empirical explanation will never produce a satisfactory answer to our question.

I am not suggesting here that Wittgenstein was a Spenglerian. They were obviously engaged in completely different projects. The latter tried to understand the development of history through the character of culture and through his technique of comparison, attempted to determine the archetypal forms taken by cultures through the passage of history and derive from them predictions about the development of culture in the future. Spengler thought that one could "discover the original form of all culture, which lies at the basis of all individual cultures, free of cloudiness and insignificances".[33] Wittgenstein certainly lists Spengler as an influential source but clearly did not accept the essentialism which characterised Spengler's position.[34] On the relationship between Spengler's view and his own, Wittgenstein writes: "Distortion in Spengler. The ideal doesn't lose any of its dignity if its presented as the principle determining the form of one's reflections."[35] In Wittgenstein we don't find Spenglarian doctrine, we find the central ideas applied as a method. Spengler's distinction between different kinds of knowledge and his particular method of comparing different epochs by drawing attention to physiognomic connections between them, can clearly be seen in Wittgenstein's central methodological concepts of language-games and family resemblances; the noticing of features in common between different concepts and their meaningful place within language-games.[36] I do not think it is accidental that Wittgenstein uses this method of comparison. According to Spengler, everything relevant to the physiognomic could be revealed through comparison: "the means for understanding the living form is the analogy".[37] Analogies and similes don't bring with them speculative knowledge but changed perceptions. They encourage us to *see* things in different ways: one no longer sees Heaven as Heaven (see above) although strictly speaking, the facts

---

[33] Spengler, O., *Decline of the West*, p. 140

[34] Wittgenstein, L., *Culture and Value*, p. 19

[35] Wittgenstein, L., *Culture and Value*, p. 27

[36] It has been suggested that Wittgenstein's concept of family resemblances has its origins in Spengler's notion of Ur-symbol; that which characterises each one of the great cultures. See G.H. von Wright, *Wittgenstein in Relation to His Times*, p. 116

[37] Spengler, O., *Decline of the West*, p. 4

haven't changed. The alteration of sensibility, culminating in a particular kind of self-consciousness and freedom, is the object proper of philosophical criticism.[38] Perception and sensibility belong to subjects; hence Wittgenstein's (and Spengler's) insistence that they were writing for those few individuals who would *find themselves* in their work. Analogies and similes *show* features; in themselves they *say* nothing. What they show depends on seeing, not on factual knowing.

Although there are clear parallels between their methods and the kind of understanding sought by both Wittgenstein and Spengler, there are also important differences. Spengler fatefully sought a generality and exactness which Wittgenstein claims can only seem possible by "ascribing the properties of the proto-type to the object we are viewing in its light . . . because we want to give the prototype's characteristics purchase on our way of representing things" and thus fell into the same kind of confusion that was indicative of metaphysics: "since we confuse prototype and object we find ourselves dogmatically conferring on the object properties which only the prototype necessarily possesses".[39] Also, Spengler's concept of the physiognomic was in effect, used pseudo-scientifically, despite his desired distinction between the scientific and the human. As I develop the concept for the purpose of accentuating important features of Wittgenstein's work, I deliberately reject Spengler's particular use which obscures the distinction between the scientific (or speculative) and the human (physiognomic).

Wittgenstein's criticism of Spengler was one we have seen he made often of different thinkers; of them wanting their method to be the method, of thinking their general laws were the laws according to which phenomena must conform.[40] Clearly however, Wittgenstein found very useful Spengler's method of comparison as a technique for elucidating and clarifying meaning. He also thought that the understanding one acquired this way was of an entirely different nature to a scientific explanation. Physiognomic connections draw attention to similarities, draw contrasts, notice particular features "as one might illustrate the internal relations of a circle to an ellipse by gradually transforming

---

[38] Edwards, J., *Ethics Without Philosophy: Wittgenstein and the Moral Life*, Gainsville, University of Florida Press, 1982, p. 153

[39] Wittgenstein, L., *Culture and Value*, p. 14

[40] Against the idea of one method being the only valid one, Wittgenstein says of his own: "We want to establish an order in our knowledge of the use of language: an order with a particular end in view; one out of many possible orders; not the order." (Wittgenstein, L., *Philosophical Investigations*, §132)

an ellipse into a circle, but not in order to assert that a given ellipse in fact, historically came from a circle".[41] They sharpen our eye for a connection that results in our understanding the meaning or significance of phenomena. The essential feature of a physiognomic explanation (and that which distinguishes it from a scientific explanation) is that we do not conduct an experiment to validate it. We either see the connection (hence are certain of it) or we fail to see it at all (Spengler). No experiment is relevant here. In claiming that philosophical puzzlement demands a physiognomic elucidation rather than a scientific explanation, Wittgenstein is claiming that it can be relieved not by amassing more factual or pseudo-factual knowledge but by seeing connections that we are currently unable to see. We bring something unknown into connection with something familiar and thus learn to see it in a new way, i.e. *as* something familiar.[42] Hence the relevant problems "are solved, not by giving new information but by arranging what we have always known".[43] Wittgenstein commonly calls "the arranging what we already know" an elucidation or clarification to distinguish it from an empirical explanation. Why the distinction between physiognomic (meaning) elucidations and scientific (theoretical) explanations was important for Wittgenstein's own project can be brought out by examining the analogy Wittgenstein perceived between his sort of explaining and the explanations of aesthetics and psycho-analysis. The analogy highlights Wittgenstein's understanding of the nature of philosophical perplexity and shows why he thought he could satisfy the philosophical quest for understanding without committing himself to a philosophical theory.

Parallels between Aesthetics, Psycho-Analysis and Philosophy

A substantial amount of Wittgenstein's work in the 1930s is devoted to exploring parallels between aesthetic, psychological and philosophical puzzlement. This exploration, in focussing specifically on the non-speculative nature of such puzzlement, assumes the distinction between scientific or causal explanations and explanations of a different kind. Wittgenstein notes that the most outstanding feature of explanations in psycho-analysis, aesthetics and

---

[41] Wittgenstein, L., *Remarks on Frazer*, p. 9e
[42] Redding, P., *Anthropology as Ritual: Wittgenstein's Reading of Frazer's Golden Bough*, in *Metaphilosophy*, 1987, Vol. 18, No. 3 and 4, p. 258
[43] Wittgenstein, L., *Philosophical Investigations*, §109

those which he claims for his own philosophical method is that the explanation is accepted, not because it matches some external data, but because it *makes a connection* which takes away the particular puzzlement. All explanations, scientific or otherwise, are, of course, designed to take away puzzlement. The difference between scientific and other kinds of explanations, however, is that for the latter, one is not explaining a phenomenon by hypothesising about data, but by *making something intelligible*. To emphasise the difference, Wittgenstein suggests that we don't treat intelligibility connections as causal explanations, or we do so only if we acknowledge that they are different to the causal explanations of science. He writes:

> You could say: 'An aesthetic explanation is not a causal explanation' [or that it is a causal explanation of this sort: that the person who agrees with you sees the cause at once].[44]

And in bringing out exactly how such explanations are grammatically different from scientific causal explanations, he writes:

> Freud wrote about jokes. You might call the explanation Freud gives a causal explanation. 'If it's not causal, how do you know it's correct?' You say: 'Yes that's right'. Freud transforms the joke into a different form which is recognised by us as an expression of the chain of ideas which led us from one end to another of the joke. *An entirely new account of a correct explanation. Not one agreeing with experience, but one accepted.* You have to give the explanation that is accepted. This is the whole point of the explanation.[45]

Aesthetic, psycho-analytic and philosophical explanations have common features because they address similar kinds of puzzlement with similar types of method. What leads Wittgenstein to suggest that it is a non-scientific form of puzzlement is that it can be satisfied by explanations which are not themselves scientific. Such explanations have the peculiar feature that one criterion for whether they are correct is that they are accepted. We don't (can't?) do tests to confirm the validity of the explanation. Its validity is just that it is accepted and it is accepted because it produces satisfaction; it brings peace to the puzzlement. To emphasise the fact that such explanations are of a different nature to those given in science, Wittgenstein prefers to call them elucidations or further descriptions. Moore recalls the following remark given during Wittgenstein's lectures in the early 1930s:

---

[44] Wittgenstein, L., *Lectures and Conversations*, p. 118
[45] Wittgenstein, L., *Lectures and Conversations*, p. 18

Reasons, he said, in Aesthetics, are of the nature of 'further descriptions,' e.g. you can make a person see what Brahms was driving at by showing him lots of different pieces of Brahms, or by comparing him with a contemporary author; and all that Aesthetics can do is to draw your attention to a thing, to 'place things side by side'.[46]

Although critical of what he perceived to be confusions in Freud's thinking, Wittgenstein found the analogy between Freud's work and his own fruitful. He called their common method the invention of new similes; new ways of looking at things[47] whose criterion of correctness is not whether they are empirically true, but whether they fulfil their purpose.[48] ("An entirely new account of 'correct explanation'"). The criterion is whether the patient or puzzled philosopher agrees and says "Yes, that is exactly how I meant it":

> The philosopher strives to find the liberating word, that is, the word that finally permits us to grasp what up until now has intangibly weighed down our consciousness . . . to express all thought processes so characteristically that the reader says 'Yes, that's exactly the way I meant it'. To make a tracing of the physiognomy . . . *Indeed we can only convict someone else of a mistake if he acknowledges that this really is the expression of his feeling . . . for only if he acknowledges it as such, is it the correct expression.* (Psychoanalysis).[49]

The (Wittgensteinian) philosopher tries to make intelligible the asking of philosophical questions rather like "when a dream is interpreted we might say

---

[46] Moore, G.E., *Lectures*, p. 106

[47] Wittgenstein, L., *Culture and Value*, pp. 19-20

[48]Freud of course would not have made such a concession. His understanding of his own work was that it was scientific and that his theory could be correct even when the patient failed to see this. Against the scientific nature of Freudian theory, Wittgenstein writes: "Freud did not in fact give any method of analysing dreams which was analogous to the rules which will tell you what are the causes of stomach-ache" (Moore, G.E., *Lectures*, p. 107). McGuiness also draws out the nature of Wittgenstein's criticisms when he writes of the concept of Freudian slips: "What good then does Freud's account of the origin of these slips do? It attempts to show why just these errors (and not all the others that would also be possible according to the principles) occurred. But we are not entitled to suppose that there has to be a reason why just these errors occurred, just as we cannot demand a cause for every coincidence . . . even if we conceive it as a causal explanation, the Freudian explanation of slips must also leave room for chance: it cannot hope to explain why just these Freudian slips and no others were made" (McGuiness, B., *Freud and Wittgenstein* in *Wittgenstein and his Times*, p. 35)

"Here starting from the supposed scientific character of the explanation given, we arrive instead at an insight into its mythological nature. Everything has an explanation, everything is significant: this is not the expression of a scientific attitude but of a primitive one" (McGuiness, B., *Freud and Wittgenstein*, p. 36).

[49] Wittgenstein, L., *Big Typescript*, p. 165, italics mine

that it is fitted into a context where it ceases to be puzzling".[50]

Perhaps the most controversial feature of Wittgenstein's work was not his diagnosis that philosophical questions are based on confusions about language, (after all, that idea was not new[51]) but his idea that what gives rise to our asking of philosophical questions is not reason over-reaching itself (Kant), but a primitive instinct. It is necessary here to explore what Wittgenstein means by this as it is central to his understanding of the nature of philosophy and his philosophical method. Again, Wittgenstein finds the analogy between philosophy, psycho-analysis and aesthetics helpful. The primitive nature of aesthetic puzzles is emphasised here:

> Perhaps the most important thing in connection with aesthetics is what may be called aesthetic reactions, e.g. discontent, disgust, discomfort . . . The important thing is [when] I say 'too high!', it is a reaction analogous to my taking my hand away from a hot plate . . . the reaction peculiar to this discomfort is saying 'too high' or whatever it is. [52]

A primitive reaction is one that is not the result of speculation. Here "too high" is taken to be primitive because it is very different to the reaction of someone looking at a door and saying "too high" and meaning, "I predict that if you lower the door, I will be satisfied".[53] Here we have a conjecture or prediction which can be tested and whose criterion of rightness is whether the test works. In most cases of aesthetic discomfort, Wittgenstein denies that they have the form of a prediction or conjecture; such responses are spontaneous. When this kind of aesthetic discomfort is expressed in questions like "what makes this beautiful?" and so on, the right answer is the one that relieves the discomfort (or puzzlement); the one therefore that satisfies. And because the discomfort is itself an expression of instinct, the "explanation" must speak to the instinct rather than the intellect. He explains:

> When I am furious about something, I sometimes beat the ground or a tree with my walking stick. But I certainly don't believe that the ground is to blame or that my beating can help anything. 'I am venting my anger'. Such actions may be called Instinct-Actions. - And an

---

[50] Wittgenstein, L., *Lectures and Conversations*, p. 45

[51] The idea that philosophical questions are based on confusions of language can be found in Plato and Kant of course, but more relevantly to Wittgenstein, in the nineteenth century with the work of Mauthner in particular (and his notion of "word superstitions", see Janik and Toulmin *Wittgenstein's Vienna*, Chapter Five)

[52] Wittgenstein, L., *Lectures and Conversations*, p. 14

[53] Wittgenstein, L., *Lectures and Conversations*, p. 14

historical explanation, say, that I or my ancestors previously believed that beating the ground does help is shadow-boxing, for it is a superfluous assumption that explains nothing . . . Once such a phenomenon is *brought into connection* with an instinct which I myself possess, this is precisely the explanation wished for: that is, the explanation which resolves this particular difficulty.[54]

The analogy with philosophy for Wittgenstein is clear. Philosophical discomfort is caused by deep feelings we have about our language; Wittgenstein identifies such feelings as "I simply don't know my way about", "something's wrong here", "the irritating character of grammatical unclarity . . . as if one had a hair on one's tongue; one feels it, but cannot grasp it and therefore cannot get rid of it".[55] Our attachment to particular forms of expression is likened to our attachment to our favourite clothes[56] and the difficulty of not using certain expressions as the difficulty in holding back tears or anger.[57] In the light of such remarks, it is no wonder Wittgenstein wrote that in giving up philosophy, "what has to be overcome is not a difficulty of the intellect, but of the will".[58] Because the discomfort is spontaneous and not speculative, it cannot be relieved by an explanation which is hypothetical. Such explanations give an external (systematic) rendering of the phenomenon, whereas one's initial reaction is internally connected to it and hence requires an explanation of a different sort.

The difficulty facing Wittgenstein is that there are many different ways in which we get caught up with language and so get lost in its labyrinth and it is thus impossible for him to give exact explanations of this.

When we say that by our method we try to counteract the misleading effect of certain analogies it is important that you should understand that the idea of an analogy being misleading is nothing sharply defined. No sharp boundary can be drawn round the cases which we should say that a man was misled by an analogy . . . it is, in most cases, impossible to show an exact point where an analogy begins to mislead us.[59]

Although they are commonly taken to be indicative of Wittgenstein's position on the nature of religious and magical beliefs, his remarks on Frazer

---

[54] Wittgenstein, L., *Philosophical Occasions*, p. 139, italics mine

[55] Wittgenstein, L., *Big Typescript*, p. 181, p. 173, p. 165

[56] Wittgenstein, L., *Blue and Brown Books*, p. 57

[57] Wittgesntein, L., *Big Typescript*, p. 161

[58] Wittgenstein, L., *Big Typescript*, p. 161

[59] Wittgenstein, L., *Blue and Brown Books*, p. 28

also contain much material that is relevant to our enquiry here. The interpretation of these remarks by Peter Winch[60] has obtained a degree of orthodoxy insofar as his work has been taken to be representative of Wittgenstein's own and yet in the light of the theme of this chapter, we may be unhappy with Winch's conclusion that the giving of causal or historical explanations for human practices (like ritual) is to be rejected. Although this is clearly an evident theme of Wittgenstein's remarks and certainly a theme which makes sense in the light of our exploration into Wittgenstein's notion of physiognomy, there is something unsatisfactory about Winch's wholesale rejection of causal explanations. It does not make clear the more subtle point of Wittgenstein's remarks which is to contrast the kind of explanations given by Frazer with the kind of questions he (and we) might be asking about the phenomena presented to us. Winchean orthodoxy has us admit that the essence of Wittgenstein's criticism of Frazer is that he gives rationalistic explanations of non-rational phenomenon. What we may not see, therefore, is the deeper point being made in these remarks. It connects with what Wittgenstein perceives to be Frazer's blindness to the kind of explanation he should be giving of the phenomenon given the way he himself has reacted to it.

In these remarks, Frazer's own desire to give explanations for the bizarre phenomena confronting him is treated by Wittgenstein as itself a kind of primitive need. In other words, Wittgenstein suggests that it is because Frazer was himself affected in a certain way by the phenomenon that he sought to explain it. And Wittgenstein points out, Frazer's response to the phenomenon was primitive rather than rational. His "why" questions therefore, reflect a physiognomic rather than scientific puzzlement. As Redding rightly suggests: "It is Frazer's feeling that these events are dreadful that prompts his implicit question 'why does this happen?' If the incidents had struck him as trivial or insignificant the question 'why does this happen?' would presumably have never been raised."[61]

Wittgenstein's critique of Frazer does not especially result in the rejection of scientific explanations for human activity. (Here Winch overstates his case.) It is better understood I think as the reiteration of Wittgenstein's point that we need to become more self-aware in understanding our questions and what we expect from them. The response demanded by the question should be

---

[60] Winch, P., *The Idea of a Social Science*, in Wilson, B. [ed], *Rationality*, Oxford, Blackwell, 1970, pp. 1-17

[61] Redding, P., *Anthrolopology as Ritual*, p. 263

"appropriate". What makes Frazer's explanations inappropriate is that he gives a systematic answer to a physiognomic puzzlement. Wittgenstein writes:

> When Frazer begins by telling the story of the King of the Wood at Nemi, he does this in a tone which shows that something strange and terrible is happening here. And that is the answer to the question 'why is this happening?' Because it is terrible. In other words, what strikes us in this course of events as terrible, impressive, horrible, tragic, &c., anything but trivial and insignificant, *that* is what gave birth to them.[62]

The criticism then is that "Frazer's response to his own question in which he ignores its tone and, responding merely ·to its syntactic form, offers an explanation, is, given what we can grasp about his needs from his tone, inappropriate or inadequate."[63]

Redding points out that it is not that Wittgenstein rules out the possibility of causal or historical explanations, but suggests that whether they should be given (are required) depends on what it is we want to know. Thus if Frazer's explanations are supposed to help us understand the rituals, they fail (are not what is appropriate) given the kind of understanding required. He explains them away by "shifting the focus from them to their causes".[64] If they work as explanations at all it is because they "appeal to an inclination in ourselves"; "the deep and sinister do not become apparent merely by our coming to know the history of the external action, rather it is we who ascribe them from an experience of our own."[65] Hence, "we only have to put together in the right way what we *know* without adding anything, and the satisfaction we are trying to get from the explanation comes of itself".[66]

It surely makes better sense of Wittgenstein's criticism of the giving of "explanations" in his remarks on Frazer, if we understand him to have in mind not historical or causal explanations per se, but explanations which are *inappropriate* (which in connection to Frazer just happen to be causal and historical). Thus, it is given Wittgenstein's description of Frazer's own activity and his real but unrecognised needs, that the construal of rituals in terms of expressive rather than effective actions is justified. Against Winch, "it would seem to contradict Wittgenstein's whole later philosophical orientation to

---

[62] Wittgenstein, L., *Remarks on Frazer*, p. 3e

[63] Redding, P., *Anthropology as Ritual*, p. 263

[64] Redding, P., *Anthropology as Ritual*, p. 265

[65] Wittgenstein, L., *Remarks on Frazer*, p. 6 and p. 16

[66] Wittgenstein, L., *Remarks on Frazer*, p. 2

suggest that there is something about the rituals themselves which always makes explanation (historically or causally construed) an inappropriate epistemic attitude to them".[67]

In Wittgenstein's Frazer, we find a model of Wittgenstein's confused philosopher. We find an individual who has misunderstood the tone of his own question and therefore given an entirely inappropriate answer to it, and thus will not find the satisfaction he was after in the initial asking. In Frazer, we find all the unclarity and 'injustices' of Wittgenstein's traditional philosopher. Frazer was not merely unable to recognise the kind of explanation he sought, but he failed to realise that his own critical account of superstition itself contained superstitions. For example, he failed to fully acknowledge the extent to which his own thinking was motivated by an underlying assumption that "everything has an explanation, everything is significant".[68] He clearly believed that data collection would fully confirm an interpretation rather than always presupposing one and that his "pseudo-scientific explanations of the ceremonies, and his general account of the movement of higher thought [were] themselves expressions of hope and faith in science".[69] We therefore find in Wittgenstein's remarks on Frazer, the themes central to the argument of this chapter; of the pursuit for perspicuity in order to avoid injustices and to gain a deep understanding. We can also see that when Wittgenstein distinguishes the two kinds of explanations, he does so as part of his desire to help the philosopher understand better the kind of questions they are asking which is in turn because "Wittgenstein is concerned as much with self-knowledge and self-deception as with knowledge and ignorance of some worldly phenomena".[70]

There is a felt disappointment and resignation for a philosopher when they realise that they can't see the other side of the limit; that there is no getting outside thought. Wittgenstein makes the same point in connection to dreams and what we are after when we seek to explain them:

> What is intriguing about a dream is not its causal connection with events in my life etc., but rather the impression it gives of being a fragment of a story - a very vivid fragment to be sure - the rest of which remains obscure . . . If someone now shows me that this story is not

---

[67] Redding, P., *Anthropology as Ritual*, p. 265

[68] McGuiness, B., *Freud and Wittgenstein*, p. 36

[69] Eldridge, R., *Hypotheses, Criterial Claims and Perspicuous Representations: Wittgenstein's Remarks on Frazer's Golden Bough*, in *Philosophical Investigations*, 1987, Vol. 10, No.3. p. 226, brackets mine

[70] Redding, P., *Anthropology as Ritual*, p. 266

the right one; that in reality it was based on quite a different story, so that I want to exclaim disappointedly 'Oh, that's how it was?' it really is as though I've been deprived of something.[71]

The emphasis in both cases is designed to show that what we desire from certain explanations (and this may not be obvious in the question), is a satisfaction of feeling rather than intellect. Feelings of deprivation, disappointment, frustration or satisfaction belong to physiognomic explanations rather than scientific ones. This is not because we never feel any of these things in relation to scientific explanations (we can certainly imagine being disappointed when an experiment fails), but because the kind of questions asked and answers sought are on a different level.

The resignation is not in having to give up the asking of philosophical questions but rather in coming to see what kind of answers that are possible for them. "The difficulty . . . is not that of finding the solution but rather that of recognising as the solution something that looks as if it were only a preliminary to it."[72]

We have seen how Trigg wanted to *speak* of a reality without using *language* to do so. Coming to see that this is unintelligible may bring with it a huge sense of disappointment because the desire or need for transcendence is real. But the resignation is not caused because there is some secret realm that you realise you will never get access to. "The great difficulty here is not to represent the matter as if there were something one *couldn't* do";[73] rather it is about the recognition of the nature of what one is seeking in philosophy and what constitutes an actual finding. Wittgenstein emphasises the point here:

> As I have often said, philosophy does not lead me to any renunciation, since I do not abstain from saying something, but rather abandon a certain combination of words as senseless. In another sense, however, philosophy requires a resignation, but *one of feeling and not of intellect*. And maybe this is what makes it so difficult for many. [74]

Although he saw a fruitful analogy between psycho-analysis and philosophy, Wittgenstein was also critical of Freud, effectively accusing Freud of encouraging a confusion between reasons and causes; of running together phenomena the explanation for which there is an objective procedure for

[71] Wittgenstein, L., *Lectures and Conversations*, p. 68

[72] Wittgenstein, L., *Zettel*, §314

[73] Wittgenstein, L., *Philosophical Investigations*, §374

[74] Wittgenstein, L., *Big Typescript*, p. 161

establishing its truth and phenomena for which no such procedure is either available or appropriate. Freud seems to overthrow the game of reasons by trying to demonstrate that an individual's actions are often determined by forces of which they are not consciously aware. He thought he'd made a scientific discovery about the true causes of human action, but Wittgenstein suggests, it is not clear that this is what he's done. It is not clear what the criterion is for the fact that a dream expresses a particular unconscious thought and in the absence of such a criterion, Freud is being dishonest (cheating the patient) by insisting that his interpretation is the right one: "Freud is constantly claiming to be scientific. But what he gives is speculation - something prior even to the formation of an hypothesis . . . ."[75] Freud does not "give any method of analysing dreams which was analogous to the rules which will tell you what are the causes of stomach ache" and therefore is cheating the patient if he insists that his interpretation is the correct one.[76] The giving of a cause scientifically requires that it can be established by experimentation, whereas reasons for an individual's actions are usually established by asking the agent of the action. In Freud, sometimes the analyst's account is treated as crucial; at other times, the patient's endorsement of the interpretation presented by the analyst and this is dishonest. Like Spengler and Frazer, Freud fails to make clear the principle that determines the form of his interpretation. He does not, for example, admit that he has not established the truth of his interpretative stance, nor that he does not even have a method for doing so (over and above the fact that for some patients he is able to relieve their anxiety). He implies that he has but this merely cheats the patient and results in dogma and hence injustice.

Frank Cioffi, who has done some excellent work on Wittgenstein, Frazer and Freud,[77] accuses Wittgenstein of "confusing the thesis that the analysis of an impression is not reducible to, or the equivalence of, a causal claim with the thesis that it does not imply a causal claim".[78] In other words, Cioffi thinks that Wittgenstein separates the Systematic and Physiognomic (causes and reasons) in an absolute manner - not allowing that reasons might have or be causes. But

[75] Wittgenstein, L., *Lectures and Conversations*, p. 44

[76] Moore, G.E., *Lectures*, p. 107

[77] See Cioffi, F., *Aesthetic Explanation and Aesthetic Perplexity*, in Shanker, S., [ed] *Ludwig Wittgenstein: Critical Assessments*, 1986, Volume 4, Beckenham, Croom Helm, pp. 334-359, Cioffi, F., *Wittgenstein on Freud's Abominable Mess*, in Griffiths, A.P. [ed], *Wittgenstein Centenary Essays*, Cambridge, Cambridge University Press, 1991, pp. 169-192

[78] Cioffi, F., *Aesthetic Explanation*, p. 356

I think Cioffi is wrong about this. Certainly Wittgenstein's stance against reductionism and essentialism entails that he stresses the legitimacy of different forms of explanation, but he isn't committed to denying that they have any connection at all. If the Redding reading of Wittgenstein's remarks on Frazer's *Golden Bough* is accepted over Winch's, then it is perfectly acceptable to think that a reason can have a cause and even (under certain circumstances) accept the stronger claim that reasons and causes might be equivalent. Everything depends on what one wants from the explanation. For example, in his notes on aesthetics, Wittgenstein explicitly considers the relationship between a causal explanation of an aesthetic impression and a physiognomic explanation, writing:

> Supposing it was found that all our judgements proceeded from our brain. We discovered particular kinds of mechanism in the brain, formulate general laws, etc. One could show that this sequence of notes produces this particular kind of reaction; makes a man smile and say 'Oh how wonderful'. Suppose this were done, it might enable us to predict what a particular person would like and dislike. We could calculate these things. *The question is whether this is the sort of explanation we should like to have when we are puzzled about aesthetic impressions.* e.g. there is a puzzle – 'Why do these bars give me such a peculiar impression?' Obviously it isn't this, e.g. a calculation, an account of reactions etc., we want – apart from the obvious impossibility of the thing.[79]

Clearly it is not the case that Wittgenstein confuses the thesis of reductionism with the thesis that certain explanations have no causal implications. Rather he wants to emphasise that the non-causal explanation is not necessarily inferior to the causal. What Wittgenstein objects to is one method elbowing others out. We can see the return of the theme of injustice (reductionism and essentialism):

> If you are led by psycho-analysis to say that really you thought so and so, or that really your motive was so-and-so, this is not a matter of discovery but of persuasion. In a different way you could have been persuaded of something different . . . Those sentences have the form of persuasion in particular which say 'This is really only this'. (This means there are certain differences you have been persuaded to neglect).[80]

There is nothing wrong with persuasion. It is after all what Wittgenstein is engaged in. What is wrong is the insistence on one's own interpretation without being upfront about what is presupposed by it:

---

[79] Wittgenstein, L., *Lectures and Conversations*, p. 20
[80] Wittgenstein, L., *Lectures and Conversations*, p. 27

Freud does something which seems to me immensely wrong. He gives what he calls an interpretation of dreams. In his book, he describes one dream which he calls a 'beautiful dream'. A patient, after saying that she had a beautiful dream, described a dream in which she descended from a height, say flowers and shrubs, broke the branch off a tree, etc. Freud shows what he calls the 'meaning' of the dream. The coarsest sexual stuff, bawdy of the worst kind . . . Freud called this dream 'beautiful' putting beautiful in inverted commas. But wasn't the dream beautiful? I would say to the patient: Do these associations make the dream not beautiful. Why shouldn't it be? I would say Freud had cheated the patient. [81]

We don't, claims Wittgenstein, put "perfume" in inverted commas just because it comes from acids which have intolerable smells. We could, but what would make it right to do so? The causal explanation has no inherent right over the description of the smell as beautiful. Sometimes the latter is exactly what is required.[82]

An even more vivid example was given by Wittgenstein in the same lecture in an attempt to show up the misleading nature of reductionist explanations:

If we boil Redpath (who was a student present at the lecture) at 200°C, all that is left when the water vapour is gone is some ashes etc. 'This is all Redpath really is.' Saying this might have a certain charm, but would be misleading to say the least.[83]

Compare: Redpath is really just some ashes.
            Redpath is more than just some ashes.

Both *could* be correct. Wittgenstein is careful, therefore, not to fall into what he perceives to be the same confusions (and injustices) found in the work of Freud, Frazer, and Spengler. He does not attempt to give a scientific explanation of why we ask philosophical questions:

---

[81] Wittgenstein, L., *Lectures and Conversations*, p. 23-4

[82] Although he does not commit himself to much here, we might get some insight to the relationship between the two from the following remarks: "Suppose Taylor and I are walking along the river and Taylor stretches out his hand and pushes me in the river. When I ask why he did this he says: 'I was pointing out something to you', whereas the psycho-analyst says that Taylor subconsciously hated me . . . Both explanations may be correct. When would we say that Taylor's explanation was correct? When he had never shown any unfriendly feelings, when a church steeple and I were in his field of vision and Taylor was known to be truthful. But under the same circumstances, the psycho-analysts explanation may also be correct. Here there are two motives - conscious and unconscious. The games played with the two motives are utterly different. The explanations could in a sense be contradictory and yet both be correct" (Wittgenstein, L., *Lectures and Conversations*, p. 23).

[83] Wittgenstein, L., *Lectures and Conversations*, p. 24

It was true to say that our considerations could not be scientific ones. It was not of any possible interest to us to find our empirically 'that contrary to preconceived ideas, it is possible to think such-and-such' – whatever that may mean.[84]

Wittgenstein also insists that his own work is devoid of the fatal essentialism found in Freud's; "Freud would ask: 'What made you hallucinate that situation at all?' One might answer that there need not have been anything that made me hallucinate it."[85] (What made you ask that philosophical question? One might answer that there need not have been anything that made me ask it). If his role is akin to that of an analyst, Wittgenstein, unlike Freud, is not going to insist that his explanation is correct no matter what the "patient" says because this would be an instance of dogmatism and injustice:

> The analyst is supposed to be stronger, able to combat and overcome the delusion of the instance. But there is no way of showing that the whole result of analysis may not be 'delusion'. It is something which people are inclined to accept and which makes it easier for them to go certain ways: it makes certain ways of behaving and thinking natural for them. They have given up one way of thinking and adopted another. Can we say we have laid bare the essential nature of mind? 'Concept-formation'. Couldn't the whole thing have been differently treated?[86]

Wittgenstein's own philosophical technique, of arranging linguistic facts in such a way that philosophical questions are answered, is itself answerable to that particular end. Thus unlike Spengler, Wittgenstein makes clear "the object from which [his] way of viewing things is derived" so that the discussion will not be distorted. He must also avoid claiming that his arrangements and comparisons are themselves somehow metaphysically valid:

> We think our view will not have the generality we want it to have if it is really true only of one case. The prototype ought to be clearly presented for what it is so that it characterises the whole discussion and determines its form. This makes it the focal point so that its general validity will depend on the fact that it determines the form of discussion rather than on the claim that everything which is true only of it holds too for all the things that are being discussed.[87]

Wittgenstein's remarks about philosophical problems are grammatically

---

[84] Wittgenstein, L., *Philosophical Investigations*, §109

[85] Wittgenstein, L., *Lectures and Conversations*, p. 49

[86] Wittgenstein, L., *Lectures and Conversations* pp. 44-45

[87] Wittgenstein, L., *Culture and Value*, p. 14

akin to the giving of reasons, not causes. A reason fulfils its function, not by reporting something that occurred but by making an action intelligible as the action of a conscious individual. Causal or empirical explanations could not fulfil the role performed by what I have here been calling physiognomic explanations or so Wittgenstein thought. He could not achieve peace for philosophy by providing an empirical explanation of what causes us to ask philosophical questions (whatever that might be). Nor could he answer philosophical questions by providing empirical or meta-empirical (metaphysical) theories. What he had discovered was a method for dissolving philosophical perplexity, akin to the method used in psycho-therapy for quieting anxiety of a different sort. It is successful when "the other person acknowledges. . .the analogy I am proposing to him as the source of his thought".[88]

What Perspicuity Achieves

I suggested at the outset that the concept of perspicuity was central to Wittgenstein's philosophical purpose and method. It is one of the most original and difficult ideas in Wittgenstein's work. Having examined what Wittgenstein meant by it and having seen why it was so important to him, we are now in a position to understand why, according to Wittgenstein, perspicuous seeing of our world through language is the only form of philosophical objectivity that is attainable.

It is easier to see that Wittgenstein was seeking a special kind of philosophical understanding in the *Tractatus* than it is to realise that his later work is also pursuing such an understanding. His rather unfortunate and often misunderstood appeal to philosophy as an illness and his own philosophical method as therapy has led many to dismiss his later work outright. It is certainly not easy, on a quick reading of his work, to reconcile the two seemingly very different aspects of his work, identified here by Kenny:

> Wittgenstein seems at first sight to have two rather different views of philosophy. On the one hand, he often compares philosophy to a medical technique, to a therapy, a method of healing. On the other hand, he seems to see philosophy as the giving overall understanding, a clear view of the world.[89]

---

[88] Wittgenstein, L., *Big Typescript*, p. 165

[89] Kenny, A., *Wittgenstein on the Nature of Philosophy*, in McGuiness, B. [ed], *Wittgenstein*

What I have tried to show in this chapter is that rather than think of these two themes as independent of each other, we need to see they are intimately related. What Kenny calls a problem is not really a problem at all. To gain perspicuity is to be healed. If you like, perspicuity is both the goal and the method. But it is only possible for Wittgenstein to connect the two themes in this way because of his diagnosis of philosophical questions. It is a miscasting of the nature of philosophical questions that leads Kenny into difficulties. He understands Wittgenstein the doctor as attempting to make philosophical questions more palatable to our intellect, rather like "a dietitian who has to cater to an invalid with a weak stomach".[90] But on my reading, Wittgenstein is doing the exact opposite. When he writes that "philosophical questions, when you boil them down to what they really amount to, change their aspect entirely. What evaporates is what the intellect cannot take", Wittgenstein is not suggesting that the philosopher boils down problems to make them more palatable to our intellect. On Kenny's interpretation we would not be able to make sense of Wittgenstein's vivid metaphor which emphasises the intellectual emptiness of philosophical questions; that they can be dissolved as completely as lumps of sugar in water.[91] Appealing to his connection between kinds of questions and their solutions, Wittgenstein concludes that philosophical questions can be completely dissolved, not by proposing new theories or acquiring new knowledge, but by seeing clearly what is already before us. It is not the case, however, that we gain nothing by asking them. On the contrary, we gain a special kind of understanding which is acquired through coming to see what is before us in a new way. We wrongly expect an explanation, "whereas the solution of the difficulty is a description, if we give it the right place in our considerations".[92]

Kenny rightly points out that there is something strange about Wittgenstein's insistence that the most important discovery is that which makes it possible for us to stop doing philosophy. "It would be absurd to say, for instance, that the most important musical discovery is the one which enables you to stop making music when you want."[93] One is led to ask "Why do philosophy at all?" Kenny again:

---

and his Times, Oxford, Blackwell, 1982, p. 2

[90] Kenny, A., *Wittgenstein on Philosophy*, p. 2

[91] Wittgenstein, L., *Big Typescript*, p. 183

[92] Wittgenstein, L., *Zettel*, §314

[93] Kenny, A., *Wittgenstein on Philosophy*, p. 10

Is there not a simpler way of getting rid of these worries, namely never look at a book of philosophy? . . . If philosophy is only good against philosophers, why do philosophy at all?[94]

Kenny develops an interesting answer to the question, namely that philosophy is important because there is a philosopher in us all. Asking philosophical questions is an unavoidable human condition because "philosophy is not laid down in sentences but in a language".[95]

The idea that philosophy lies in our language is central to Wittgenstein's account of philosophical confusion. Kenny concludes that on a Wittgensteinian understanding, the task of philosophy is not to enlighten the intellect, but to strengthen our resistance to certain temptations: "you are better off if you have done philosophy. . .not because you know more, but because you have gone through the discipline which enables you to resist certain temptations."[96] I think Kenny is right to make this point, but I also think that Wittgenstein was motivated by more than the desire to provide a series of "spiritual exercises" for philosophers.[97] There is clear hope for real philosophical enlightenment. Perspicuity and peace were, as we have seen, Wittgenstein's declared goals. I suggest we add a third to that list. Wittgenstein wanted to bring philosophers out of the dark musty passage-ways of the labyrinth of grammatical confusion to the open spaces of ordinary language where "the light will be better, the air will be fresher and we shall be freer".[98] It is not accidental that Fania Pascal concludes her personal memoir with a section on "Wittgenstein's Freedom". Pascal suggests that "the awe in which he was held by those who knew him was due to this freedom of his, and to the means he used to become free and assure his freedom. He simply gave up . . . everything inessential and trivial . . . He became the freest of men".[99]

This freedom is made possible when we have learnt how to negotiate the traps of language and gain philosophical perspicuity. We cannot do this by attaining something like the Tractarian vision of the world sub specie

---

[94] Kenny, A., *Wittgenstein on Philosophy*, p. 12

[95] Wittgenstein, L., *Big Typescript*, p. 189

[96] Kenny, A., *Wittgenstein on Philosophy*, p. 14

[97] This is what Fergus Kerr calls them. See Kerr, F., *Theology after Wittgenstein*, Oxford, Blackwell, 1986

[98] Wisdom, J., "Foreword" in Lazerowitz, M., *The Structure of Metaphysics*, London, Routledge & Kegan Paul, 1955, p. xii

[99] Pascal, F., *Wittgenstein: A Personal Memoir* in Rhees, R. [ed], *Personal Recollections*, Oxford, Blackwell, 1981, p. 60

aeternitatis or by insisting on an objective reality as Trigg does and then believing that we have somehow brought it into being. We gain perspicuity by commanding a clear view of language and thought. The possibility of such a view may be available but that does not mean that everyone will want to attain it. Wittgenstein was well aware that our desire for transcendence and the kind of transcendence that we can actually attain are in some tension with one another. This tension is never more clearly expressed than in Trigg's desire to break free of language and speak of reality. Giving up one's preferred paper draft description of reality for a proper understanding may be too hard to do. As Wittgenstein comments in his Cambridge lectures: "there is a conflict between the aim of a person who wants to catch his thumb and the fact that he would not be satisfied had he done it."[100] And more seriously perhaps he writes: "Working in philosophy - like work in architecture in many respects - is really more a working on oneself. On one's own interpretation. On one's way of seeing things. (And what one expects of them.)"[101]

---

[100] Wittgenstein, L., *Lectures: Cambridge 1932-35* [ed] Ambrose, A., Oxford, Blackwell, 1982, p. 166
[101] Wittgenstein, L., *Culture and Value*, p. 16

Chapter Three

Grammar

"In logic there is no such thing as a hidden connection. You can't get behind the rules because there isn't any behind."[1]

In his critical analysis of metaphysics, Wittgenstein frequently appealed to what he called the "grammar" of an expression, claiming that what the metaphysician does wrong is to confuse rules of language (grammar) for truths about reality.[2] In Chapter One, we saw that Wittgenstein's goal in philosophy was to show the limits of language in order to prevent the illegitimate (and ultimately meaningless) transgression of these limits. Wittgenstein distinguishes rules of language from descriptions about reality. It is only when we have a meaningful language that we can make true or false claims about reality. Grammatical rules are what give us meaningful language; they make possible descriptions of reality. Our concern in this chapter is with this apparent distinction between rules of grammar and truths about reality.[3] Orthodox interpretations of Wittgenstein pursue this dichotomy between grammatical propositions and truths about the world (Hacker, Malcolm, Rhees, Winch, Albritton), and the Neo-Wittgensteinian accounts of religious belief that we will be considering also employ it in their analysis of religious language. D.Z. Phillips makes the distinction explicit when he tells us, for example, that "doctrinal statements . . . give us rules for the use of the word 'God' and that the claim 'God is love' may mislead us into thinking that it is a descriptive statement rather than a rule for the use of the word 'God'".[4]

The Neo-Wittgensteinian critique of the way in which philosophy of religion is traditionally done mirrors Wittgenstein's critique of philosophy

---

[1] Wittgenstein, L., *Philosophical Grammar*, p. 244

[2] Wittgenstein, L., *Blue and Brown Books*, p. 49

[3] Where "truths about reality" are to be glossed as "true descriptions of how things are"

[4] Phillips, D.Z., *Faith after Foundationalism*, London, Routledge, 1988, p. 218

generally, in that they desire to show that anyone who construes a rule of language as a statement about the world is guilty of a metaphysical confusion. Traditionally philosophers of religion (and philosophically influenced theologians) have been guilty of such confusions, claims Phillips. They *have* treated rules as truths and this is the kind of bad philosophy Wittgenstein came to put a stop to.[5] According to Phillips and fellow Neo-Wittgensteinians, philosophers are inclined to construe religious language as truth-apt or descriptive because they treat it on the model of empirical language - language which tells us how things are in the world. To treat it like this is to misunderstand its *grammar* and this effects an imposition of an alien criterion of meaningfulness and justification; one to which religious language cannot conform and which makes it look epistemically inferior to the language of science. Religious philosophers then think that they have to provide a defence for the meaningfulness of their language which shows how it can meet the standards we require from empirical statements and this, claim the Neo-Wittgensteinians, moves us further and further away from recognising and appreciating the unique grammar (and hence the meaning) of religious language.[6] In keeping with their Wittgensteinian heritage, the Neo-Wittgensteinians claim that we do not have to impose a criterion of meaning on language in order to understand it. We only have to look and see the use to which it is put and the place it has in the lives of those who use it and we will come to appreciate the meaning that the language has. They claim to be doing just that in their investigations into religious language. In the next chapter I shall examine the Neo-Wittgensteinian claim that religious language does not purport to tell us how things are but rather provides us with religious perspectives and ways of expressing religious attitudes. Their position involves two central assumptions: 1) that religious language is used primarily to *express* religious attitudes and feelings, (the implications of this claim will be examined in a later chapter on Expressivism); and 2) that religious language is not descriptive but gives us rules for the use of religious concepts. This position is motivated by a particular understanding of what Wittgenstein meant by grammar and the distinction he employed between grammatical and non-grammatical propositions.

Clearly the two assumptions are related. The Neo-Wittgensteinians are motivated to deny the descriptive nature of religious language in part because

---

[5] Phillips, D.Z. *Faith after Foundationalism*, p. 36
[6] Phillips, D.Z., *Religion Without Explanation*, Oxford, Blackwell, 1976, p. 26, p. 41

they want to treat it as expressive. The use they make of the concept of grammar warrants an investigation in its own right because it rests on a different distinction; not between descriptions and expressions, but between rules of language and truths about the world.

It is not my intention in this chapter to show that Wittgenstein makes no distinction between rules of language and truths about the world. Rather I want to argue that when properly understood, it is like one of his Tractarian propositions which can be thrown away when one has learnt the lessons it was designed to teach. In other words, I shall argue that the distinction between rules of language and descriptions of reality is not the kind of distinction that can be used to do the work asked of it by the Neo-Wittgensteinian philosophers. Whereas Wittgenstein uses the distinction to undermine the legitimacy of transcendent metaphysics, the Neo-Wittgensteinian philosophers of religion apply the distinction in order to undermine the legitimacy of the ordinary religious believer's claim that when they believe that God exists, they are believing that there is something, in reality, that exists. In other words, an ordinary religious believer takes their belief in God to be a belief about reality that may or may not be true. The Neo-Wittgensteinian philosophers argue that such a claim is illegitimate in Wittgenstein's sense of metaphysically illegitimate (of going beyond the limits of language). When an ordinary religious believer claims that they believe that there is a being who exists in reality and who would exist whether or not human beings had developed the concept of such a being they are, according to the Neo-Wittgensteinian philosophers, attempting to get to a reality outside language in the same way the metaphysical philosopher tries to get outside reality. I will argue that the Neo-Wittgensteinian position rests on a mistaken interpretation of Wittgenstein's philosophy and that the claims they make about the meaning of ordinary religious beliefs are themselves illegitimate.

In order to build up a compelling argument we must first be clear on what Wittgenstein meant by grammar and how he distinguished rules of language from truths about the world. Only then will we be in a position to apply Wittgenstein's philosophical insights to the nature of religious language. When we do so, we will see what has gone wrong with the Neo-Wittgensteinian account of religious belief. In this chapter, I shall first sketch how the concept of grammar developed in Wittgenstein's work. We will examine how Wittgenstein's thoughts on the constituents of meaning changed and how the idea of language-games and rules emerged. This section will be primarily exegetical. We will then examine two different ways of understanding the relationship of grammar to reality, effectively contrasting Wittgenstein's position with the Logical Positivists' more robust theorising on semantical relations. I will show that despite obvious points of similarity, there are important differences, most notably in how we might apply the distinction between grammar and propositions about reality to ordinary uses of language. In the following chapter we will apply these insights to religious language and belief and it will be shown that the Neo-Wittgensteinian philosophers adopt and apply the Positivistic account of grammar and not one that is genuinely Wittgensteinian. This results in them offering the interpretation of religious language that is unacceptable to believers themselves.

Wittgenstein on Grammar - Exegetical

P.M.S. Hacker gives us a good general guide to what Wittgenstein meant by grammar when he tells us that "grammar" is used by Wittgenstein to mean the study and description of the rules of language (primarily semantic) and also to mean the network of rules themselves.[7] We have seen that Wittgenstein construed his own philosophical activity as the study and description of the rules of language, engaged in for the purpose of providing clarifications of actual language use which he claimed philosophers are blind to when they propose their theories and explanations. What it is that Wittgenstein investigates are the rules of language themselves and these are part of what he called grammar. We do not need a strict definition of the concept in order to understand what Wittgenstein wanted to do with it. It is clear that Wittgenstein himself did not think of grammar as something determinate for which we could give necessary and sufficient conditions. The concept was one that he found useful, as he makes clear when he writes: "Nonsense always arises from forming symbols analogous to certain uses, but 'makes sense' is vague and will have different senses in different cases, but it is useful, just as 'game' is useful. Just as 'sense' is useful, so is 'grammar', 'grammatical rule' and 'syntax'".[8]

Given Wittgenstein's own remarks here, it is clear that the way to understand what he meant by grammar is to see what he uses the concept to do. As his thoughts on this are neither static nor singular, we can usefully begin by tracing the genesis and development of the concept in his work.

---

[7] Hacker, P.M.S., *Insight and Illusion*, Oxford, Oxford University Press, 1975, p. 151
[8] Moore, G.E., *Lectures*, p. 67

The Development of the Concept of Grammar

Although the Positivists treated the *Tractatus* as a positivistic manifesto, it is not clear how close Wittgenstein's concerns in that document were to those of the Positivists. Certainly there has been much speculation without any clear answers. This is in part because the *Tractatus* is a notoriously difficult document, and in part (and relatedly) because Wittgenstein himself was non-committal about explaining his ideas. One thing is certain and that is Wittgenstein was adamant about the extent and success of its scope. As late as 1932, more than a decade after its publication, Wittgenstein responded to Carnap's attempted development of the Tractarian philosophy and logic. He wrote to Schlick voicing his concerns that Carnap's work added nothing new: "You know very well yourself that Carnap is not taking any step beyond me when he stands for the formal and against 'the material mode' of speech. And I cannot imagine that Carnap should have misunderstood so completely the last few propositions of the *Tractatus* - and hence the basic ideas of the entire book."[9]

Wittgenstein's reference to the final propositions of the *Tractatus* and Carnap's apparent blindness to the "basic ideas of the book" is interesting. Although we will be developing an account of Wittgenstein's relationship to the Positivists on grammar we can see that Wittgenstein distinguished himself from Carnap at least on the basic ideas which concern the limits of language. The Positivists were motivated by epistemological concerns as they attempted to justify and explain the language of science, whereas Wittgenstein's interests were clearly broader than this. Of immediate interest are the formal aspects of Wittgenstein's work, particularly those that display his commitment to a distinction between empirical and logical propositions (or what can be said and what must be shown). It is a distinction which pervades the *Tractatus*, as Wittgenstein emphasised to Russell to whom he wrote saying "the main point is the theory of what can be expressed by propositions . . . and what can not be expressed by propositions, but only shown; which I believe is the cardinal problem of philosophy".[10]

Wittgenstein's early concern with what marks the general difference between sense and nonsense resulted in the picture theory. We have already

---

[9] Wittgenstein, L., "Letter to Schlick 8 August 1932", published in German, quoted and translated by Hintikka , M and J., *Investigating Wittgenstein*, Oxford, Blackwell, 1986, p. 11
[10] Wittgenstein, L., *Letters to Russell, Keynes and Moore*, Oxford, Blackwell, 1974, p. 71

seen that this was an a priori explanation which accounted for the possibility of meaning by matching the form of language with the form of the world. To understand a statement involves knowing its form and therefore the form of what it represents. In whatever way one characterises the nature of the Tractarian form of the world, what is most important for our purposes is to acknowledge that the argument was motivated by a feeling Wittgenstein had that there *must* be something, external and determinate, which grounded and guaranteed meaningfulness. Wittgenstein's commitment to the determinacy of meaning comes out in his early notebooks and the *Tractatus* in his appeal to a fixed form of the world; he didn't reason from the world to meaning, but had the unexamined conviction (he later called it a superstition) that for a statement to mean anything it had to mean something exact and therefore there had to be something to guarantee its exactness. Although an ordinary sentence may be vague, what is meant by that sentence (the proposition) cannot be vague, or so it seemed to Wittgenstein: "A proposition must determine reality in one way or the other: yes or no."[11] For Wittgenstein "there [could] be no in between".[12] When he later spoke about the character of his Tractarian assumptions concerning the requirement of exactness, Wittgenstein wrote: "The sense of a sentence - one would like to say - may, of course, leave this or that open, but the sentence must nevertheless have a definite sense. An indefinite sense - that would really not be a sense at all."[13]

Although Wittgenstein's prejudices about meaning seem strange today, it is important to grasp just how real they were for him as the development of his concept of grammar is integral to the loosening of these superstitions. The idea that meaning (logic) must be determinate and distinct from anything contingent, vague or inexact continued as a theme in Wittgenstein's later work. What changed was that he came to reject his view that "what the names in language stand for must be indestructible; for it must be possible to describe the situation in which everything destructible is destroyed. And this description will contain words; and what corresponds to these cannot then be destroyed, for otherwise the words would have no meaning".[14] As the superstition was given up, so Wittgenstein's understanding of meaning changed. The concept of "grammar" emerged as the non-superstitious replacement for the fixed form

---

[11] Wittgenstein, L., *Tractatus*, 4.023

[12] Malcolm, N., *Wittgenstein: Nothing is Hidden*, Oxford, Blackwell, 1986

[13] Wittgenstein, L., *Philosophical Investigations*, §99

[14] Wittgenstein, L., *Philosophical Investigations*, §55

of the world as that which is responsible for meaning. It was not a simple transition however. Wittgenstein puzzled about meaning in the late 1920s and throughout the 1930s. As we trace the nature of the transition, we will see that Wittgenstein retained his commitment to two Tractarian assumptions: that logical propositions were of a completely different nature to empirical ones and relatedly, that logical investigations can only yield logical results, not empirical ones. Because our concern in this chapter is how we are to construe the relationship between logic and reality, it might help to have these assumptions made more explicit before we proceed.

Perhaps their fullest statement is made by Wittgenstein in the following remarks:

> Our fundamental principle is that whenever a question can be decided by logic at all, it must be possible to decide it without more ado.
> (And if we get into a position where we have to look at the world for an answer to such a problem, that shows that we are on a completely wrong track).
>
> The 'experience' that we need in order to understand logic is not that there is such-and-such a situation, but that something *is*: that however is *not* an experience.
> Logic is *prior* to every experience - that something *is so*.
> It is prior to the question 'How?', not prior to the question 'What?' [15]

The first remark emphasises the fact that in logic we cannot discover anything about the world (in other words, philosophy is not science; a constant theme in Wittgenstein's remarks). In the second set of remarks, we find Wittgenstein separating our experiences of the world from experiences associated with logic (or meaning). He thus sets up a distinction between experiential and logical propositions which naturally seems to imply a distinction between propositions which tell us how things are (empirical truths) and propositions which define; propositions which in Wittgenstein's terminology, give us the "What" or the "That" something is.

Realising that in the *Tractatus* he had been seduced by the feeling that there *must* be something to which meaning is responsible, Wittgenstein did not leave his preoccupation with the boundary between sense and nonsense alone, but was forced to reconsider the grounds for its possibility. Abandoning the "metaphysical must" resulted in Wittgenstein abandoning his a priori assumptions about meaning and engaging in an a posteriori enquiry into the actual use of language. This is where the idea of grammar began to develop.

---

[15] Wittgenstein, L., *Tractatus*, 5.551-2

The Autonomy of Language

In abandoning the central assumption of the *Tractatus*, Wittgenstein was essentially abandoning the idea that the ways we speak (or think) are made possible (or determined) by the way things are. This idea had demanded that there be something external to the language we use to speak about the world which was fixed and determinate and in which that language was grounded. Wittgenstein gave up the idea that there must be something external to language which guarantees and justifies our use of it more easily than he gave up his commitment to determinacy. Although he quickly rejected the idea that the relationship between language and reality (their common form) must be the key to meaning, his thoughts at the time show him searching for something determinate that would take its place. His a posteriori investigation into the actual use of language showed him first and foremost that language belongs to human life and engaging in speech and thought is something that we do. The question of what guaranteed that at any one time, we were talking sense rather than nonsense therefore had to be investigated in the context of language as a human activity.

In the spirit of his a posteriori investigation, Wittgenstein observed that the most obvious answer to the question as to how we know we are talking sense is that other people will understand us if we are, and they won't understand us if we aren't. The distinction between sense and nonsense must therefore have something to do with other people and what they take to be meaningful or not. This of course results in our having to recognise that, minimally, meaning has little to do with a fixed form of the world (a notion Wittgenstein had come to see as quite superfluous), and everything to do with what people do: with a shared and public criterion of meaning. The denial that there is something external which language has to match up to in order to be meaningful is what has come to be known as the autonomy of language thesis.[16]

We can emphasise the nature of Wittgenstein's autonomy thesis by contrasting it with Russell's theory of acquaintance. For Russell, we understand sentences because we understand their constituent phrases and we understand them because we stand in a direct relation to their meaning. Acquaintance was the ultimate explanatory factor in Russellian semantics and because it was an acquaintance with something external to language,

---

[16] It is important to note that Wittgenstein's claim about the autonomy of language has nothing to do with what makes our descriptions of reality *true*

meaning/language was anything but autonomous.

On recognising how important the human context of an expression was for the determination of its meaningfulness, Wittgenstein now saw that the interesting question is how an expression gets to be part of a common usage and how we come to learn the usage. What must be in place in order for us to master language? It is on this issue that most of Wittgenstein's later philosophical concerns are focussed. Wittgenstein still clearly thought that being clear on the distinction between propositions which say how things are and propositions which show how things are was the cardinal problem for philosophy. Although his own understanding of the nature of propositions in general had changed, he was still preoccupied with the limits of sense because that is where philosophical confusions were most likely to arise.

Language-Games, Rules and Meaning

The first step in Wittgenstein's conversion was to recognise that meaningfulness does not require a metaphysical underpinning. The second step was to see the connection between meaning and human behaviour. The philosophical views Wittgenstein was most concerned to undermine therefore were those that he had himself worked with and advanced in a not insignificant way. We can characterise the view under critique here as (loosely) the view that the primary function of words is to name simple objects and the development of this to the view that words only have meanings if they have their correspondent "metaphysical objects". These are the simples, the constituent features of reality that our words name. The meaning of a name, because it corresponds to something determinate, is invariant in all its applications whatever the context of its occurrence. It always stands for the same object. This is the way in which the essence of language mirrors the essence of the world. Understanding, or knowing the meaning of a word, consists in the mental association of a word with an object. It is a form of mental pointing to an object. Wittgenstein emphasises the nature of the view (and how he was misled into it) when he writes in *Philosophical Grammar*:

> The concept of meaning I adopted in my philosophical discussions originates in a primitive philosophy of language. The German word for 'meaning' (Bedeutung) is derived from the German word for 'pointing' (Deuten).[17]

---

[17] Wittgenstein, L., *Philosophical Grammar*, p. 56

The view that all words are names and that knowing what a word means requires that one knows what it stands for entails that the teaching and learning of language is a matter of establishing correct correlates between words and things. The fundamental form of teaching is therefore by ostensive definition. You know what words mean when you know what they stand for and you understand a sentence by knowing the meaning of its parts.

Wittgenstein's rejection of this view is categorical. Not only does it not do justice to how we in fact learn language; it completely mischaracterises the nature of language that for the most part, has nothing to do with naming objects. It is also entirely inadequate as an explanation of meaning because, if language did consist only in correlations between words and objects, then understanding as we know it would be impossible. This latter observation is particularly important because it denies ostension as a necessary constituent of meaning. In denying the primacy of ostension, Wittgenstein is denying the centrality of an individual's experience as a meaning-constituent and moving closer towards a concept of meaning that cannot be explained by appealing to experiential content (one can begin to anticipate the private language argument). We can see how Wittgenstein's thoughts on meaning developed via his emphasis on language as an activity that is learnt by receiving a specific training. The concept of a grammatical rule therefore connects naturally with the idea of being trained - with learning what one must do and say in order to be able to participate meaningfully in human life.

Training and Augustine's Infant

As is well known, Wittgenstein opens the *Investigations* with an extract from Augustine's *Confessions*. It tells us how Augustine himself perceives the process by which he learnt language as an infant. It is a perfect representation of the philosophical picture Wittgenstein wanted to criticise. It "gives us a particular picture of the essence of human language".[18] Augustine writes:

> When they (my elders) named some object, and accordingly moved towards something, I saw this and I grasped what the thing was called by the sound they uttered when they meant to point it out. Their intention was shown in their bodily movements, as it were the natural language of all peoples: the expression of the fact, the play of the eyes, the movement of other parts of the body, and the tone of voice in which expresses our state of mind in seeking, having, rejecting, or avoiding something. Thus, as I heard words repeatedly used

---

[18] Wittgenstein, L., *Philosophical Investigations*, §1

in their proper places in various sentences, I gradually learnt to understand the objects signified; and after I had trained my mouth to form these signs, I used them to express my own desires.

For Augustine's account to make sense we need to make various assumptions. First, that the child already has a language of thought - an internal vocabulary that is completely private. The child reasons with this inner-language in order to master the public language of the adults. The child has a knowledge of concepts like "naming", "intention", "correctness" ("I heard words used repeatedly in their proper places"), "object", "signification" and "desire". Wittgenstein's criticism of all that is assumed in Augustine's account of language acquisition is that it seems to assume that the infant has a private understanding of public concepts prior to his being trained in the language. As we saw, the infant operates with concepts like "naming", "desiring", "intending" but these have their meaning only within the public sphere and cannot have been anticipated in a purely private one. Because he is now a competent language user, Augustine recollects his infancy by imposing on it the picture which now seems natural. To undermine this gripping picture, Wittgenstein gives us another one in its place - the language-game of the builders.

The language-game of the builders is designed to undermine that apparent naturalness of the picture that understanding what a word means comes about through learning what it stands for, "what object it signifies". Unfortunately the naturalness of the picture obscures from us the fact that naming objects is only a very small part of what we use our language to do and that naming itself will not determine meaning. This language-game also emphasises that speaking is part of an activity - that learning language is preparation for action.

Wittgenstein had been preoccupied with the idea of language as an activity. The idea comes to fruition in the *Investigations*, but in his middle period, we also find the emphasis firmly on language as part of a broader activity. For example, in *Philosophical Grammar*, he writes:

When someone learns a musical notation, he is supplied with a kind of grammar. This is to say; this note corresponds to this key on the piano, this sign sharpens the note, this sign flattens the note etc . . . One can view this instruction as part of the preparation that *makes the pupil into a playing machine*.[19]

---

[19] Wittgenstein, L., *Philosophical Grammar*, p. 191

In the language-game of the builders, there are only words and objects, although importantly no "naming" takes place. The training of someone in this language "can be said to establish an association between the word and the thing" but notice that the connection is not one between word and object but between order and action. To understand what "Slab" means in this language, one not only has to know what stone is being referred to, but also has to understand that an order is being given. Thus if the builders were to have a dictionary, the entry next to "slab" would read something like this:

> slab: a sound to be produced by a person [builder] when he wants another person [assistant] to bring one slab from a pile of stones; such an utterance is the hearers reason for bringing the slab to the builder.[20]

Of course if we are to take the example literally and say that these people have no other language then the idea of a dictionary will not make sense. But this does not matter, for the importance of the example lies in its emphasis on meaning being a matter of training, not a matter of naming. In this language-game there is no such thing as asking something's name.[21] What makes the sound "slab" mean what it does it not that it refers to some object but that it occurs within a wider context (in this case, of the building operation). Learning which stone to bring when "slab" is called would involve some sort of ostensive training; the pointing to the appropriate stone. But to think that the word gets its meaning from this pointing is to forget that the pointing and naming connection needs to be set up in the first place. Writes Wittgenstein:

> Naming is not so far a move in the language-game - any more than putting a piece in its place on the board is a move in chess. We may say: nothing has so far been done, when a thing has been named. It has not even got a name except in the language-game.[22]

The view under critique assumes that everything has been done when something has been named as if naming determined meaning all by itself. Ostensive training, the pointing at an object, will not determine meaning however. Much else needs to be going on besides. The pointing will not even determine what is being pointed at without some further context. If someone

---

[20] An example I have adapted from Max Black. See *Wittgenstein and Language-Games* in Shanker, S. [ed], *Ludwig Wittgenstein: Critical Assessments*, 1986, Vol. 2, Beckenham, Croom Helm, pp. 74-88

[21] Wittgenstein, L., *Philosophical Investigations*, §27

[22] Wittgenstein, L., *Philosophical Investigations*, §49

points at two nuts in order to give a definition of the number two, it is perfectly possible to imagine that "two" is the name given to this particular group of nuts and they "might equally as well take the name of a person, of which I give an ostensive definition, as that of a colour, of a race, or even of a point on the compass. That is to say: an ostensive definition can be variously interpreted in *every* case".[23] And against those who are tempted to think that ostensive definitions set up a connection between language and reality in a way that other definitions do not, Wittgenstein writes:

> The ostensive definition of signs is not an application of language, but part of the grammar ... How does an ostensive definition work? Is it put to work every time the word is used, or is it like a vaccination which changes us once and for all? A definition as a part of the calculus cannot act at a distance. It acts only by being applied.[24]

In his critique of Russell's theory of acquaintance and indeed any theory of meaning that attempts to explain the connection between words and the world as a kind of magical operation in which a word hooks onto the world, Wittgenstein tries to show that the connection made done by us. The world does not come already labelled:

> 'The connection between words and things is set up by the teaching of language'. What kind of connection is this? A mechanical, electrical, psychological connection is something which may or may not function. *Mechanism* and *Calculus.* The correlation between objects and names is simply the one set up by a chart, by ostensive gestures and simultaneous uttering of the name, etc. It is part of the symbolism. Giving an object a name is essentially the same kind of thing as hanging a label on it. It gives the wrong idea if you say that the connection between name and object is a psychological one.[25]

But if ostensive training does not guarantee meaning, what does? What stops the infinite regress of possible interpretations if not some bedrock experience?

Training and the Giving of Examples

Faced with the possibility of an infinite regress of interpretations, we might be tempted to assume that what stops the regress is that we reach a point where

---

[23] Wittgenstein, L., *Philosophical Investigations*, §28

[24] Wittgenstein, L., *Philosophical Grammar*, p. 88 and p. 80

[25] Wittgenstein, L., *Philosophical Grammar*, p. 56

interpretations have to cease. Here it would be natural to appeal to metaphysical facts or to immediate experience as the ultimate resting place for meaning. But the problem of an infinite regress of interpretations only arises according to Wittgenstein, if we misrepresent the process by which we learn a language. Initial learning needs to be contrasted with interpreting: "there is a way of grasping a rule which is not an interpretation, but which is exhibited in what we call 'following a rule' and 'going against it' from case to case."[26] In his extensive discussion on following a rule, Wittgenstein makes the point that interpretations are only possible when meaning is already in place. Thus, in the first instance, it makes no sense to speak of interpreting an instruction or a rule. By "interpreting" he suggests we mean "the substitution of one expression of a rule for another".[27] Acting in accordance with the rule is therefore not an interpretation.

So what is it to understand the meaning of an expression? In *Philosophical Grammar* Wittgenstein writes: "Meaning, in our sense, is embodied in the explanation of meaning . . . the understanding here spoken of is a correlate of explanation."[28] In order to cure us of the temptation to postulate ontological determinants of meaning, Wittgenstein gets us to look at what goes on when in actual practice someone asks: "What do you mean by x?" This question asks for an *explanation* of x, and the answer given will be part of the grammar of the word "x". The answer will show what is meant by "x". It will determine or fix a use for the word in one of our language-games (or applications of use). This fixing of a position is what Wittgenstein calls the giving of rules for the use of the word. We learn that with regard to the word "x", we can say some things and not others. If we use "x" in a way that has no specified place in the game, or break the rules of application, we will be saying something meaningless. If we want to specify a new use for the word, we have to explain the new position or explain a new game (set up a new set of rules for the application of the word). The explaining is also what Wittgenstein calls the giving of rules for the use of the word. When we train a child we do not give a list of all the rules for the use of the word in question. The child acquires an understanding of these rules gradually by learning how to use the word, (uttering it on occasions and being met by either smiles or frowns), by seeing how others use it and so on. The relevance of rules for meaning is that when

---

[26] Wittgenstein, L., *Philosophical Investigations*, §201

[27] Wittgenstein, L., *Philosophical Investigations*, §201

[28] Wittgenstein, L., *Philosophical Grammar*, p. 60

someone uses a word in a way others don't understand, they will ask for an explanation, or show that the word "cannot" be used that way. What undermines the appeal to an ontological determinant is that in giving an explanation, we must still use language. We can't in fact, get outside it, nor do we need to. Wittgenstein writes:

> When we explain the meaning of a sentence, we translate it into a language less prone to misunderstanding.
>
> Yes, but how can these explanations satisfy us? - Well, your very questions were framed in this language; they had to be expressed in this language, if there was anything to ask. Your questions refer to words; so I have to talk about words.[29]

The idea that explanations of meaning don't take us outside language at all is vital to Wittgenstein's concept of grammatical explanations and the way in which they are distinct from empirical explanations. Meaning does not lie *behind* the signs we use:

> If I give anyone an order I feel it to be quite enough to give him the signs. And I would never say: this is only wrds, and I have got to get behind the words. Equally, when I have asked someone something and he gives me an answer (i.e. a sign), I am content . . . and I don't raise the objection: 'but that's a mere answer'.[30]

Although Wittgenstein toyed with the idea that meaningfulness required strict rules (one of the most predominant themes in his transitional notes), he soon gave even that prejudice away. The context of activity - the language-game actually has semantic priority because as Wittgenstein recognised, although rules played an important part in learning how to use an expression, one could not say that its meaning is just the list of rules for its use. For a start, the list would be indefinite. You could never get a complete list. It is also obvious that someone could be perfectly adept at playing a language-game (participating in it meaningfully) without being able to recite the rules at all:

> Is it only by being told the rules that the game is learnt and not also simply by watching it while it is being played . . . There's certainly such a thing as learning the game without explicit rules.[31]

---

[29] Wittgenstein, L., *Philosophical Investigations*, §120

[30] Wittgenstein, L., *Philosophical Investigations*, §503

[31] Wittgenstein, L., *Philosophical Grammar*, p. 62

Being able to play the game (engage meaningfully with others) is what it is to understand language. There is not a further thing, "understanding the meaning of the word" or "experiencing the meaning of the word" which is essential to meaning. To know what a word means is to know how to use it and to be able to give an explanation for it when asked:

'What does it mean to understand the word "perhaps"'? - Do I understand the word 'perhaps'? - And how do I judge whether I do? Well, something like this: I know how it's used, I can explain its use to somebody, say by describing it in made up cases. I can describe the occasions of its use, its position in sentences, the intonation it has in speech. - Of course this only means that I understand the word "perhaps" comes to the same as: 'I know how it is used.'[32]

And against the idea that understanding must therefore entail the grasping of explicit rules, Wittgenstein writes:

'He grasps the rule intuitively' . . . But why the rule? Why not how he is to continue?[33]

So we might summarise by making two points about rules. First, they are not sufficient to guarantee meaning because the rules themselves have to be understood. Secondly, we don't necessarily need rules because we might know how to proceed without them.

Wittgenstein's preoccupation with rules becomes more natural when we realise that rules only become relevant when they are transgressed. In ordinary practice, when we object to an expression "you can't say that" or "you can't do that", or even "I don't understand what you mean", we are implicitly appealing to the rules of usage to point out that the particular application of a word doesn't belong, or if it does, *how* it does must be further explained. The explanation consists in showing how it can be applied: in giving further rules for its use.

We have seen the two major steps in the development of Wittgenstein's thinking about meaning. Having moved away from his own paper draft of "the world", he looked to actual human behaviour and practices. Doing this showed him that something else was required if meaning was to be possible: we must share not only practices but also a nature or what Wittgenstein famously called a form of life.

---

[32] Wittgenstein, L., *Philosophical Grammar*, pp. 64-5
[33] Wittgenstein, L., *Zettel*, §303

Forms of Life and the Possibility of Meaning

By the time he wrote the material for the *Philosophical Investigations*, Wittgenstein had completely abandoned the idea that in order for an expression to be meaningful there must be something strict that determines its meaning. We have seen that he toyed for a while with the idea that it was only by using an expression in accordance with strict rules that its meaning could be guaranteed, but the demand for strict rules was soon recognised to be a legacy from his earlier days; a remnant of that metaphysical must. A strong theme in his later work is the sense of surprise at how we are able to communicate at all given how little we can formally identify as necessary in the learning and understanding of language. Like ostensive definitions, even rules avail themselves to interpretation:

'But how can a rule show me what I have to do at this point? Whatever I do is on some interpretation, in accord with the rule' - No, that should not be said, but rather: any interpretation hangs in the air along with what it interprets, and cannot give it any support. Interpretations by themselves do not determine meaning.[34]

In notes written as preparation for the material that would eventually end up in the *Investigations*, we find Wittgenstein developing the idea that understanding what an expression means involves not much more than receiving a certain training in how to use it. The possibility of meaning therefore depends on our ability to understand the training we receive - that we are capable of receiving a certain training. Without the presence of the latter capacity, Wittgenstein contends that the learning of language as we currently do it, would be impossible. Wittgenstein brings out just how much must be assumed if language is to be possible when he writes:

If I explain the meaning of a word 'A' to someone by pointing to something and saying 'This is A', then this expression may be meant in two ways. Either it is itself a proposition already, in which case it can only be understood once the meaning of 'A' is known, i.e. I must now leave it to chance whether he takes it as I meant it or not. Or the sentence is a definition. Suppose I have said to someone 'A is ill' but he doesn't know who I mean by 'A' and I now point at a man, saying 'This is A'. Here the expression is a definition, but the kind that can only be understood if he has already gathered what kind of object it is through his understanding of the grammar of the proposition 'A is ill'. But this means that any kind of explanation of a language presupposes a language already. *And in a certain*

---

[34] Wittgenstein, L., *Philosophical Investigations*, §198

sense, the use of language is something that cannot be taught, i.e. I cannot use language to teach it in the way in which language could be used to teach someone to play the piano. - And that of course is just another way of saying: I cannot use language to get outside language.[35]

Accounting for the possibility of meaning, therefore, must include not only that one undergoes a certain training, but that one possesses the natural capacities which make the mastery of a technique possible and that we share the same capacities. These are the grounds Wittgenstein identified as that on which meaning depends. Wittgenstein came to call them "natural facts" or "forms of life". So one of the answers to his question as to what makes meaning possible, as yielded by an a posteriori rather than an a priori enquiry, is that we share natural capacities, ways of going on. Certain facts of nature ground the possibility of meaning and understanding, as Wittgenstein brings out in numerous places in his text.[36]

Wittgenstein distinguishes various ways in which forms of life and natural capacities may effect the possibility of meaning and understanding. Creatures with entirely different capacities would be incapable of learning certain procedures. He writes for example of a cat's incapacity to be taught to retrieve,[37] of a dog's inability to understand time[38] and of whether we would be able to understand a talking lion.[39] These examples are designed to emphasise just how much of what we do is part of our natural history ("commanding, questioning, recounting, chatting . . . walking, eating, drinking, playing",[40] which is in turn designed to emphasise how language is tied to such practices and must be understood as such if we are not to distort it in our philosophical theorising.

It follows that if shared ways of going on are necessary for meaning and understanding, there will always be the possibility of human beings who share basic capacities but who do not "go on in the same way" in particular cases. They are thus teachable to the point where what is natural to the rest of us is natural to them, but beyond this point, they have to either go against what they find natural in order to follow the procedure, or they refuse to do so and

---

[35] Wittgenstein, L., *Philosophical Grammar*, p. 54, italics mine

[36] See for example Wittgenstein. L., *Philosophical Investigations*, §24, §241, p. 174, p. 226, p. 230; Wittgenstein, L., *Zettel*, §350, §352, §355

[37] Wittgenstein, L., *Zettel*, §186

[38] Wittgenstein, L., *Philosophical Investigations*, p. 174

[39] Wittgenstein, L., *Philosophical Investigations*, p. 223

[40] Wittgenstein, L., *Philosophical Investigations*, §25

therefore will not be able to join in with our practices. The moral of this imagined case is to bring out just how important our natural ways of going on are for the possibility of sharing language. Wittgenstein writes:

> If we teach a human being such-and-such a technique by means of examples, - that he then proceeds like this and not like that in a particular case, or that in this case he gets stuck, and thus that this and not that is the 'natural' continuation for him, this of itself is an extremely important fact of nature.[41]

One of the facts of nature that are important to meaning is that we share a natural propensity to understand each other and to be able to learn. If we did not, the learning of certain concepts, and of sharing language, would become difficult if not impossible. People lacking our natural capacities would be incapable of learning: "There may be mental defectives who cannot be taught the concept 'tomorrow' or the concept 'I', nor to tell time. Such would not learn the use of the word 'tomorrow' etc."[42] Apart from stressing the point about natural capacities, we can also note here the emphasis Wittgenstein places on language as an activity. Rather than saying that there is something the defectives don't know (what "tomorrow" means for example), Wittgenstein prefers to say that there is something they cannot "do", thus emphasising the nature of language as an activity. One can't separate learning and using language from knowing what it means. The meaning of the concept of tomorrow cannot be separated from what the word "tomorrow" means.

Wittgenstein also recognised the possibility that a person could learn language by rote: by being taught by drill as to what to do and when to do it and yet we may not be happy to say that they have mastered a language. There is something more to understanding than merely being drilled in the techniques of using signs. "I might say of a little child 'he can use the word, he knows how it is applied'. But I only see what that means if I ask 'what is the criterion for this knowledge?' In this case it isn't the ability to state rules."[43] Meaning cannot just be a matter of sharing forms of life and being able to master a technique. We could imagine a case where both conditions were satisfied and still the person could not really be said to understand the signs they were using. Wittgenstein asks: "Can [we] speak of a grammar in the case where a language is taught to a person by a mere drill? It is clear that if I were to use the word

---

[41] Wittgenstein, L., *Zettel*, §355
[42] Wittgenstein, L., *Remarks on Colour*, Oxford, Blackwell, 1977, §118
[43] Wittgenstein, L., *Philosophical Grammar*, p. 62

'grammar' here I can do so only in a 'degenerate' sense."[44] The case of Ireneo Funes perhaps illustrates the point Wittgenstein has in mind here.[45] Funes (a Uruguayan positivist) had an extraordinary memory but no real understanding of what was contained in it. He could not understand sentences he had not seen before and although he could answer questions when asked, it was obvious he was only answering from memory and that he had no real understanding of what he was saying. Funes' understanding was clearly a "degenerate" one in Wittgenstein's sense. If Funes were the norm, the kind of communication we enjoy at present, which is of course so natural to us, would not be possible.

Wittgenstein is prepared to make a further and most striking claim. If Funes were the norm (or if human beings were just trained animals), Wittgenstein claims that not only would human communication be impossible, there would be no such thing as philosophy either. "A trained child or animal is not acquainted with any problems of philosophy."[46] The dependence of philosophy on signs is brought out by Wittgenstein in the following remarks:

> Is word language a necessary condition for the existence of philosophy? It would be more proper to ask: is there anything like philosophy outside the region of our word-languages? For philosophy isn't anything except philosophical problems, the particular individual worries that we call 'philosophical problems'.[47]

Wittgenstein's a posteriori conditions for the possibility of meaning are that a) we share ways of going on, or as he sometimes puts it, we all behave in the same way, and b) we possess capacities that enable us to be trained and to master language; capacities of the kind Funes was lacking. Exactly what these capacities are is not Wittgenstein's concern. That is, he tells us, a question for scientific psychology.[48] In ruling out the possibility of philosophical (and by that he seems to mean a priori/non-experimental) explanations, he is not ruling out the possibility of scientific ones. Towards the end of the *Investigations* he writes: "'If the formation of concepts can be explained by facts of nature, should we not be interested, not in grammar, but rather in that in nature which is the basis of grammar'? - Our interest certainly includes the correspondence

---

[44] Wittgenstein, L., *Philosophical Grammar*, p. 191

[45] See Coffa, J.A., *The Semantic Tradition from Kant to Carnap*, Cambridge, Cambridge University Press, 1991, p. 178

[46] Wittgenstein, L., *Philosophical Grammar*, p. 138

[47] Wittgenstein, L., *Philosophical Grammar*, p. 138

[48] Wittgenstein, L., *Philosophical Investigations*, p. 230

between concepts and very general facts of nature . . . But our interest does not fall back on these possible causes of the formation of concepts; we are not doing natural science; nor yet natural history."[49]

The conditions offered by Wittgenstein as necessary for the possibility of meaning are not necessary for the possibility of meaning per se. He is not claiming that if they weren't fulfilled, meaning would be impossible. They are the necessary conditions for meaning as we know it. If things were different, and we didn't share ways of going on etc., then we would end up with a different set of phenomena to investigate and we cannot tell a priori what the outcome of that enquiry would be. Wittgenstein's conditions here are contingent on the ways in which we actually do go on. They are not offered as Kantian transcendental conditions of what *must* be the case if we are to go on.

Language as both Arbitrary and Necessary

The recognition that the meaningfulness of language is not determined by anything external to human nature and our ways of going on saw Wittgenstein reject his earlier view that somehow the concepts we use have necessity built into them because they mirror the form of the world. Whereas he had previously seen certain concepts as necessary, he now preferred to call them arbitrary. Acknowledging the autonomous nature of language brings with it the recognition that the necessity we feel about it, a feeling that had motivated Wittgenstein in the *Tractatus*, cannot be accounted for by metaphysical speculation. The necessity we feel about our concepts turns out to consist in nothing more than the fact that we use them and don't use others. (We could put the point by saying that their necessity lies simply in the fact that we use them.) He writes in *Philosophical Grammar*:

> 'I couldn't think that something is red if red didn't exist'. What that proposition really means is that the image of something red, or the existence of a red sample *is part of our language*. But of course one can't say that our language *has to* contain such a sample; if it didn't contain it, it would just be another, a different language. But one can say, and emphasise, that it does contain it.[50]

The realisation that we could use different concepts, or that creatures with different natures and different interests might use others should quieten the

---

[49] Wittgenstein, L., *Philosophical Investigations*, p. 230
[50] Wittgenstein, L., *Philosophical Grammar*, p. 143

metaphysicians insistence that there must be a set of concepts that are absolutely the right ones. In calling our concepts arbitrary, Wittgenstein did not mean to imply that the ways in which we speak are trivial or a matter of whim or even that they are a matter of choice. 'Arbitrary' here is meant to signify both that we cannot show our concepts to be necessary and that our concepts are somehow inexplicable. We cannot justify them *philosophically* nor can we show them to be unjustified. It therefore makes no sense to speak of them as justified or not. As he puts it, the ways in which we think just have to be accepted, they are there like our life.

In emphasising the arbitrary nature of our concepts, Wittgenstein is emphasising just that they cannot be justified:

> One is tempted to justify the rules of grammar by sentences like 'But there really are four primary colours'. And saying that the rules of grammar are arbitrary is directed against the possibility of this justification, which is constructed on the model of justifying a sentence by pointing to what verifies it.[51]

Imagining the use of other concepts is a way of realising the contingent nature of those we do use:

> A tribe has two concepts akin to our 'pain'. One is applied where there is visible damage and is linked with tending, pity, etc. The other is used for stomach-ache for example, and is tied up with mockery of anyone who complains. 'But then do they really not notice the similarity?' - Do we have a single concept everywhere where there is a similarity? The question is: Is the similarity important to them? And need it be so? And why should their concept 'pain' not split ours up?[52]

The claim that our concepts are the right ones (the metaphysical must) cannot be justified. It cannot even be rendered intelligible if by "right" we mean that they match a reality that is independent of them It is not only confused to attempt a justification by appealing to the world that we somehow see or think we can imagine independently of our concepts. Equally confused is the attempt to explain necessity in terms of the mind. Kant's explanation of the conditions of intelligibility was just as speculative as those he sought to criticise. Kant's position was obviously closer in detail to Wittgenstein's own than it was to that of the dogmatists. His argument is not unlike the one Wittgenstein advances for the impossibility of justifying grammar. He was

---

[51] Wittgenstein, L., *Zettel*, §331
[52] Wittgenstein, L., *Zettel*, §380

aware of the incoherence of placing conditions of intelligibility outside the thinking mind, but in his own attempt to show how a priori knowledge of nature is possible, he too had to tell a metaphysical story that could not have a happy ending. For Kant, "those things we think about will, of necessity, be characterised by those features which are necessary to our thinking about them - not because the independent nature of real things can be deduced from the nature of thought (as the dogmatist supposes) - but because the real things at issue are precisely the things we think about".[53]

Kant's transcendental conditions of subjectivity are the rules of the understanding which must be presupposed if knowledge is to be possible. Any intelligible judgement we make accords with the conditions of intelligibility and these are conditions in our thinking, not conditions of nature. The analogy with Wittgenstein's own thoughts on necessity are clear here but we can see that because Wittgenstein does not give us a philosophical explanation of necessity (but merely a descriptive account of how in fact necessity is operative), he does not fall into the equally unsupportable dogmatism of Kant's position. Kant tells us what the necessities are for: that without them thinking would be impossible and so on, but he cannot elucidate what it means to say that we have them or give content to the claim that they are a priori in us. As Schwyzer puts it, for Kant, "the necessities seem to hang in mid-air, or rather, in the mind, as unresolved as Principles of the Understanding".[54] For someone who set out to give an account of such necessities, we may ask whether the solution is not more disquieting than the riddle. Kant's appeal to mystery is never more explicit than when formulating his transcendental doctrine of judgement and referring to the schemata of pure concepts, he writes:

> This schematism of our understanding, in its application to appearances and their mere form, is an art concealed in the depths of the human soul, whose real modes of activity, nature is hardly likely ever to allow us to discover, and to have open to our gaze.[55]

More significantly, Kant's all important notion of the nature of the understanding is left unexamined, and necessarily so because on Kant's own view, there are some things about which nothing can be said without falling

---

[53] Schwyzer, H., *Thought and Reality: The Metaphysics of Kant and Wittgenstein*, in Shanker, S. [ed], *Ludwig Wittgenstein: Critical Assessments*, Beckenham, Croom Helm, 1986, Vol. 2, p. 154

[54] Schwyzer, H., *Thought and Reality*, p. 157

[55] Kant, I., *Critique of Pure Reason*, London, Macmillan, 1933, p. 183

into idle speculation, but such things must be taken on faith because the rules of intelligibility demand it.

The difference between the Kantian and the Wittgensteinian project can perhaps most clearly be stated thus: whereas Kant wanted to give us the transcendental conditions for subjectivity in his attempt to "explain" necessity, Wittgenstein wanted to show why such conditions cannot be given. Wittgenstein is able to give sense to the idea that necessity lies in the nature of our thinking because he equates the nature of our thinking with "how we intelligibly speak". Necessity becomes a grammatical affair for Wittgenstein: concepts are neither grounded in mind nor matter but are operative in contexts of behaviour and practice and beyond that, there is nothing more to be said. Their necessity is just their place in our practice. Kant had tried to show that the concepts themselves were necessary - that without them thinking would be impossible. For Wittgenstein, such a claim says no more than we cannot imagine not using the concepts we do but this in no way justifies or makes intelligible the claim that they are necessary in themselves. Their necessity is just that they are the concepts we use. Wittgenstein can thus maintain that they are both arbitrary and in some sense necessary.

Necessity must be properly understood, not as something that is transcendental or what Wittgenstein sometimes calls "superhard". The temptation that Kant falls into is to think that there is something predetermined about the way we think or the concepts we use:

> The rule 'add 2' may be misunderstood or disobeyed or mistakes may be made in its application, but yet is seems that *in itself*, as just *this rule*, it necessarily determines in a precise and unbendable way a unique series of terms. We do not normally think of our conception of a simple rule like this as 'transcendental', yet as a form of ideal predetermination settling atemporally and in a 'superhard' fashion the order of the series, that is what it is. Wittgenstein believed that such an attittude toward rules was visible 'everywhere in our lives'. Not only in the technique of calculating but in 'innuerable related practices'. His critique of the concept of a rule is aimed at showing that the form of a rule is essentially multiple and that it is always possible to deviate from the established application of a rule while continuing to adhere to its form. In Wittgenstein's later work there is no inviolable boundary of form to meaning.[56]

To guarantee order instead of chaos (form instead of formlessness) which is essentially what motivates the criticism made of Wittgenstein by Trigg in Chapter One (and was an instinct Wittgenstein understood well because the

---

[56] Staten, H., *Wittgenstein and Derrida*, p. 14

whole of the Tractarian system was predicated on it), we think we have to have the superhard concept. In practice, however, we find that we are not in chaos even though there is nothing to guarantee absolute exactness or order:

> Consider also the following proposition: 'The rules of a game may well allow a certain freedom, but all the same they must be quire definite rules.' That is as if one were to say 'You may indeed leave a person inclosed by four walls a certain liberty of movement, but the walls must be perfectly rigid' – and that is not true. 'Well the walls may be elastic all right, but in that case they have a perfectly determinate degree of elasticity.' – But what does that say? It seems to say that it must be possible to state the elasticity, but that again, is not true.[57]

In keeping with his descriptive stance, Wittgenstein wants to deny that his position entails that there is a necessary connection between our nature and the concepts we use such that it would follow that that if we had a different nature we would have different concepts. To say that would be to advance a hypothesis and "there must be nothing hypothetical in our considerations".[58] His considerations are designed to show those of us who think that our concepts are absolutely the right ones (because "reality" determines them to be so) that in fact, our concepts are contingent and indeterminate. What makes us think that they are absolutely the right ones is that *we* can't imagine using different ones. We feel somehow that our concepts are necessary. Wittgenstein's imagined cases are designed to show how easily things could have been different. He does not want us to deny the necessity we feel but to understand it properly. Understanding it entails seeing that the necessity has its foundation not in the world but in features of our language and us. Wittgenstein writes:

> I am not saying: if such-and-such facts of nature were different people would have different concepts (in the sense of a hypothesis). But: if anyone believes that certain concepts are absolutely the correct ones, and that having different ones would mean not realising something we realise - then let him imagine certain very general facts of nature to be different from what we are used to, and the formation of concepts different from the usual ones will become intelligible to him.[59]

Coffa puts the point this way: "Wittgenstein's conventionalism gives us a

---

[57] Wittgenstein, L., *Zettel*, §441

[58] Wittgenstein, L., *Philosophical Investigations*, §109

[59] Wittgenstein, L., *Philosophical Investigations*, p. 230

doctrine of necessity, for it tells us what people call necessary is indeed necessary when one looks at it, as it were, from the inside; but in order to understand it fully, one must also look at it from the outside - and what one sees then is that it is really conventional."[60]

We need to be a little careful with the notions of "inside", "outside" and "conventional" here. If "outside" is to be understood in Wittgenstein's sense of gaining a perspicuous view, then there is no harm done. What Wittgenstein doesn't mean is that our language, when looked at from some ideal absolute standpoint, turns out to be merely conventional. The internal/external distinction appealed to here by Coffa operates at all times for Wittgenstein from within a purely descriptive stance. This is what conventionalist readings of Wittgenstein get wrong. We can usefully bring out where the error lies in looking at Dummett's conventionalist Wittgenstein.

Agreement in Conventions and Agreement in Behaviour

On Dummett's reading, Wittgenstein is a full-blooded conventionalist who makes logic (the distinction between sense and nonsense) to be a matter of choice - something which we can alter at will and which we are free to construct as we please. It is easy to see how Dummett (and others) could have come to think like this. Once logic has been cut off from any ontological grounding, there is nothing to stipulate its form except, perhaps, human agreement. We can slide very easily into an "anything goes" mentality. Relativist readings of Wittgenstein also take this route. The picture presented is made most explicit with reference to mathematics and here Dummett brings out what he considers to be the essence of Wittgenstein's view. When faced with a mathematical proof:

> at each step we are free to choose to accept or reject the proof; there is nothing in our formulation of the axioms and of the rules of inference, and nothing in our minds when we accepted these before the proof was given, which of itself shows whether we shall accept the proof or not; and hence there is nothing which forces us to accept the proof. If we accept the proof, we confer necessity on the theorem proved; we 'put it in the archives' and will count nothing as telling against it. In doing this, we are making a new decision, and not merely making explicit a decision we had already made implicitly.[61]

---

[60] Coffa, J.A., *Semantic Tradition*, p. 268
[61] Dummett, M., *Wittgenstein's Philosophy of Mathematics*, in *Philosophical Review*, 1959, No. 68, p. 330

As a standard description of what amounts to conventionalist procedure, Dummett is not saying anything controversial here. What marks the conventionalist thesis is the emphasis they place on "choosing" (and Dummett's paragraph brings this out nicely with related verbs like "accepting", "rejecting" and "conferring"). Dummett rightly points out that for the conventionalist, necessity is imposed by us upon our language and this results in "our recognition of logical necessity [becoming] a particular case of our knowledge of our intentions".[62] To use Dummett's metaphor, to know our intentions here is to know what it is that we have put in the archives to be preserved.

The emphasis Dummett (and all orthodox conventionalists) places on "choosing" is what should make us suspicious here. For Dummett, the necessity conferred on a statement is that "we have expressly decided to treat [it] as unassailable".[63] The result of this is that anyone can simply "lay down that the assertion of a statement of a given form is to be regarded as always justified, without regard to the use that has already been given to the words contained in the statement".[64] Not surprisingly, Dummett finds these consequences "hard to swallow" and "mistaken". It is hard to see how anyone could make sense of that view and Dummett is right to point out that if it were true, communication and understanding would be more of a problem than they are.[65] The problem with Dummett's reading can be traced back to a misunderstanding concerning the nature of the agreement that Wittgenstein thought was essential to logic and the necessity contained therein.

Cutting logic off from any metaphysical grounding does not result in there being nothing to constrain it at all. It certainly doesn't mean that we are free to choose it at will. Wittgenstein makes this explicit when he writes:

> So is the calculus something we adopt arbitrarily? No more so than the fear of fire, or the fear of the raging man coming at us .[66]

We have no more choice about the rules we adopt or the games we play than we have a choice about whether to be afraid of fire or of an angry person. If we had chosen our rules we should be able to cite reasons for the choices we

---

[62] Dummett, M., *Philosophy of Mathematics*, p. 328
[63] Dummett, M., *Philosophy of Mathematics*, p. 329
[64] Dummett, M., *Philosophy of Mathematics*, p. 329
[65] Dummett, M., *Philosophy of Mathematics*, p. 339
[66] Wittgenstein, L., *Philosophical Grammar*, p. 110

have made. But Wittgenstein has already given us an argument to show that any justification (the giving of a reason) for our rules is incoherent. The model on which orthodox conventionalism works, namely that of choosing our rules, cannot therefore be applied in relation to Wittgenstein's own so-called conventionalism. We have seen that by "conventions" Wittgenstein means shared ways of behaving. Humans:

> agree in the language they use. That is, not agreement in opinions but in forms of life . . . there is no opinion at all; it is not a question of opinion. They (the truths of logic) are determined by a consensus of action; a consensus of doing the same thing, reacting in the same way. There is a consensus but it is not one of opinion. We all act in the same way, count the same way.[67]

This "acting" is what Wittgenstein calls "primitive". And by primitive, he means that it is not the result of thought but is prelinguistic.[68] Our language-games are based on such behaviour - they are the proto-types for our ways of thinking. It is the foundation of our language and our logic and any philosophical investigation into such foundations must stop at our primitive forms of behaviour.

What then is Meaning?

We should have been struck by what we have seen so far, that Wittgenstein's later views on meaning provide nothing in the form of exactness or determinacy. His remarks about rules, and games, forms of life and behaviour are designed to drive home the point that meaning is not safe, settled, pure, determined or rigid. Even the boundary between language and non-language is unclear and unsettled. Wittgenstein's claim is so striking that Saul Kripke, for example, has attributed to Wittgenstein a "new form of scepticism", namely "that there can be no such thing as meaning anything by any word".[69] How close Kripke's interpretation of Wittgenstein is to what Wittgenstein himself thought about meaning need not concern us here.[70] More interesting is Kripke's

---

[67] Wittgesntein, L., *Philosophical Investigations*, §241 and *Remarks on Foundations of Mathematics*, p. 332

[68] Wittgenstein, L., *Zettel*, §541

[69] Kripke, S., *Wittgenstein on Rules and Private Language*, Cambridge, Mass, Harvard University Press, 1982, p. 60 and p. 55

[70] Norman Malcolm is highly critical of Kripke's interpretative stance in Malcolm, N., *Nothing is Hidden;* especially Chapter Nine. Malcolm doesn't seem to have acknowledged Kripke's

idea that according to Wittgenstein, there are no facts about meaning. Obviously this is not the claim that there are no empirical facts required for meaning; we have seen that Wittgenstein concedes a list of such facts (our nature, our interests, our ways of behaving etc.). Kripke is making the more pertinent point that on Wittgenstein's view, there is nothing meaning *is* beyond what one gets when one asks for an explanation of the meaning. Wittgenstein's autonomy of language thesis therefore entails a necessary denial of the intelligibility of semantic realism; the view that symbols mean what they do because they correspond to or mirror the world. It also entails the unintelligibility of semantic idealism, the alternative to realism that holds that the world is the mirror of meaning. Both views conflate ontology with semantics, they just reverse the priority awarded to each.

Wittgenstein himself goes some way to answering the question about meaning when he writes:

> What is the meaning of a word? Let us ask this question by first asking, what is the explanation of a word . . . asking first 'what's an explanation of meaning?' has two advantages. You in a sense bring the question 'what is meaning?' down to earth. For surely, to understand the meaning of 'meaning' you ought also to understand the meaning of 'explanation of meaning'. Roughly: 'let's ask what the explanation of meaning is, for whatever that explains will be the meaning' Studying the grammar of the expression 'explanation of meaning' will teach you something about the grammar of the word 'meaning' and will cure you of the temptation to look about you for some object which you might call 'the meaning'.[71]

The most we can say is that the meaning is what you get when you ask for the explanation of meaning. ("It sounds incoherent, chaotic; but it was in just such scenes as this that we learned to speak."[72]) It is dangerous I think, to treat these remarks as a definition of meaning. Doing so attributes to Wittgenstein what we might call a *positive* meaning thesis. Such a thesis would develop in the direction of providing a philosophical account of meaning rather than acknowledging that Wittgenstein's interest in the role behaviour and our nature plays in the determination of meaning is designed to make problematic any such positive philosophical account. So although it looks rather uncontroversial

---

own admission however, that his "interpretation" is not really an interpretation at all but rather "the argument as it struck me, as it presented a problem for me" (Kripke, *Wittgenstein on Rules*, viii).

[71] Wittgenstein, L., *Blue and Brown Books*, p. 1

[72] Staten, H., *Wittgenstein and Derrida*, p. 86

to say that for Wittgenstein, "the meanings of words are determined by the form of life within which the language-game is played",[73] there are two ways to render the content of such a claim. The first way is to see here a theoretical explanation of meaning, against which other explanations compete (such as Russell's theory of acquaintance). The second way acknowledges an uncontroversial observation of what does in fact go on when we learn the meanings of words which is designed to show up either the surplufluity or the impossibility of philosophical theories about meaning (whilst leaving completely open the possibility of scientific theories that can explain the acquisition of certain languages or concepts on the structure and function of the brain and so on).[74]

In the next section, I will explore the relationship between grammatical propositions and truth. It will revolve around a discussion of how we might make intelligible the separation of explanations of meaning from truths about the world. I will argue that although a separation of rules and truths can be defended on Wittgenstein's view, we need to be careful with how we characterise the nature of the distinction. In pointing out the dangers of saying too much here, I will compare Wittgenstein's semantic commitments with those of Carnap. The comparison is designed to show how easy it is for philosophical assumptions to enter into an account of the distinction; assumptions which do not belong to a genuinely Wittgensteinian stance. In the next chapter I will show how just these illegitimate assumptions enter into the Neo-Wittgensteinian position on the nature of religious language. In arguing that religious language is grammatical, the Neo-Wittgenstein's help themselves to the denial that it can therefore be descriptive or fact-stating. The way they understand the distinction between grammatical and non-grammatical truths will show itself to have more affinity with Carnap than with Wittgenstein.

Grammar, Rules and Reality

Perhaps the most controversial aspect of Wittgenstein's remarks on meaning lies in how we are to understand the consequences they might have for our

---

[73] Barrett, C., *Wittgenstein on Ethics and Religious Belief*, Oxford, Blackwell, 1991, p. 155

[74] The success of Wittgenstein's stance against philosophical explanations depends on accepting the contrast he draws between empirical and non-empirical explanations. The former somehow explain subject matter from the outside, whereas philosophical explanations of meaning must always presuppose a meaningful language which is the very thing they are trying to explain

understanding of the relationship language has to reality. Wittgenstein's rejection of the world (or its form) in favour of natural capacities and interests coupled with specific training as that which is ultimately responsible for meaning, has invited the conclusion that according to Wittgenstein, meaning is in no sense responsible to the world. Michael Dummett's Wittgenstein is perhaps the most extreme advocate of such a view, but even the more orthodox commentators like Hacker can't help but see the denial of ontological grounds for language being replaced by the alternative theory that reality is somehow grounded in our language. It is certainly tempting just to reverse a realist reading of the *Tractatus*, turning the supposed semantic realism into some form of linguistic idealism or semantic conventionalism. Hacker appears to be advocating something like this when he tells us that in Wittgenstein's later thought, "the atomistic picture of reality is rejected . . . the notion of pictorial form is greatly relaxed, becoming radically conventionalist . . . the theory of the structure of language as the mirror of the structure of reality is turned on its head".[75]

Or as he puts it elsewhere, "we are continually tempted to take our grammar as a projection of reality, instead of taking our conception of the structure of reality to be a projection of grammar".[76]

We can see that Hacker's remarks lend themselves towards a potentially dangerous misunderstanding. Speaking of the structure of reality as the *projection* of grammar makes it look as if we do something with grammar (project it). The intuition behind Hacker's remark is correct however. Because meaning should be construed as being constituted by grammar not by the world, reality itself appears to become parasitic on grammar. All this really means of course is that whenever we are speaking meaningfully about anything, we must be using language to do so. To say that no distinction can be enforced between meaning and reality is simply to say whatever can be meaningfully spoken of "is" something. This is not ontology of course. Serious confusions arise if we think that it is. Wittgenstein's use of "reality" or "the world" is always to be construed semantically, not ontologically. He willingly concedes that we can speak meaningfully about things that do not in fact exist. Because his preoccupation was with semantics and logic, it is easy to think that his remarks encompass ontology; that he is attempting to show *what there is* and to rule out metaphysical speculations about what exists. For the Positivists,

---

[75] Hacker, P.M.S., *Insight and Illusion*, p. 146
[76] Hacker, P.M.S., *Insight and Illusion*, p. 160

a conflation between the two was very much a danger. (Indeed one could argue that it was part of their philosophical intentions.) I want to argue that it was not a danger Wittgenstein succumbed to, and will do so by contrasting their respective positions on the relationship of meaning to reality in the context of their respective philosophical projects. It is important to get clear on the differences between Wittgenstein's account of grammar and the Positivitic account because I will be appealing to the difference when I examine the Neo-Wittgensteinian construal of the nature of religious language in the next chapter.

The Positivists on Grammar and Reality

Empirically minded philosophers have always faced two central problems: to show how representations in the mind relate to an external world and to show how general concepts acquire meaning. The positivists as good empiricists were also plagued by these problems and the concept of "grammar" emerged as one of the ways in which they tried to overcome them. Contrasting Wittgenstein's notion of grammar with the Positivists will not only help elucidate the differences, but will stand us in good stead when we come to examine the Neo-Wittgensteinian use of the concept. It will be shown that despite their denials, they adhere to something that looks suspiciously like the positivists' notion which as we shall see, depends on various substantive philosophical assumptions that Wittgenstein himself did not hold and indeed, thought were unintelligible.

The Positivist declaration that every meaningful proposition must rest on experience raises the question of what exactly does the ultimate verifying. If a propositions' meaning consists in what verifies it there must either be verifiers that are not themselves propositions or propositions whose meaning lies in themselves. The idea of formal systems provided a way beyond the impasse of strict empiricism: of how to bring together the experiential foundation of knowledge and the apparent structures assumed by it.

Schlick's early attempt to work out how raw experience can provide the necessary foundation for knowledge that is structured failed, but it did set the agenda for his colleagues by making explicit where the particular difficulties lay.[77] Schlick's account went roughly like this: by "experience" he meant the

---

[77] See especially Schlick, M., *General Theory of Knowledge*, New York, Springer Verlag, 1974, trans. Blumberg, A.M.

experience of a mind, "my" experiences (although it is only by analysis that it they are revealed to be mine and mine only). The verifiability of experience therefore means verifiability by mental states which I alone can experience. The difficulties here are clear: if meaning and verification are identical, then only I can know what a proposition means and it makes no sense to say of anybody else "he knows what that proposition means". This is clearly an unacceptable conclusion and Schlick tried to overcome it by appealing to the view that knowledge is always structured, so although when we experience "red" we are enjoying a private experience, there are structural relations between our experiences and the experiences of others. On the structural view, red takes its place in a system of relationships, for example, on a colour chart. Formally, the word "red" does not name an experience but marks a feature of logical space. Its meaning is now given by the rules which govern the structural relations; the rules which describe how the colour chart is to be employed. In this way, physics (general laws) manages to separate itself from psychology (individual experiences).

Schlick of course still needed to give an account of the relationship between logical form (the colour chart) and empirical content (our experience of colour). He insisted that what is primary is the experience because this guarantees us knowledge of the world. Real knowledge can only be gained through our experience of the world. Schlick was never able to provide a coherent account of how experiential content could fill theory because of his commitment to the privacy (subjectivity) of experience. His fellow positivists were tempted to treat his conclusions as metaphysical because the relations between structure and content remained ineffable.

Carnap's work was an attempt to make good where Schlick had failed. His early theories held onto the idea that scientific knowledge is ultimately constituted out of private experiences but this was later abandoned when it became clear that no coherent explanation of how this relationship between form and content could be given. Neurath's solution, the doctrine that verification is a relation between sentences rather than between sentences and experiences gave Carnap a clue to the way out of Schlick's and his own dilemma (although he certainly did not accept Neurath's extreme form of semantic ascent). What Carnap liked about Neurath's account was the suggestion that we stop treating the foundations of science as incorrigible, nonverbalisable encounters with experience (an idea which for him was hopelessly metaphysical), and instead translate all statements into what he called "protocol" sentences. These are records of experience expressed in their relations to space and time. Such sentences were not incorrigible but neither were any of the propositions of science. All sentences are offered to a system of sentences and either rejected (if it stood in contradiction to the system) or the system could be altered to accommodate it. We are free to do either, as there is no priority for one or the other given by any experience itself. Here we clearly have the beginnings of Quinean holism.

Carnap retained his former view that what lay at the foundation of science was experience but saw a way to make this intelligible using the idea of protocol sentences (although against Neurath, he maintained that they were still records of direct experience). Carnap maintained that all science rests on protocol statements - records of direct experience - but this experience cannot be private and ineffable because that would make science impossible. Instead of separating structure from content in the style of Schlick, Carnap held that both must be expressible in a single language. Anything that could not be so expressed (metaphysics, morality, aesthetics and religion) was simply an expression of feelings. Any philosophical propositions which remain are either descriptions of the language scientists employ or recommendations for its modification. So when philosophers talk about kinds of entities like relations, qualities, numbers, meanings and so on, they are merely talking about the different forms of language used by science (or else making meaningless metaphysical statements).

Each formal language brings with it a particular theoretical world and the reality of the entities spoken of within the system cannot intelligibly be questioned from outside its formal framework. Writes Carnap:

> If someone wishes to speak in his language about a new kind of entity, he has to introduce a system of new ways of speaking, subject to new rules; we shall call this procedure the construction of a linguistic framework for the new entities in question . . . to accept the thing-world means nothing more than to accept a certain form of language . . . but the thesis of the reality of the thing-world cannot be among these statements, because it cannot be formulated in the thing-language or it seems in any other theoretical language.[78]

It is important to notice that for the positivists, this construction of linguistic frameworks was a way of introducing new concepts to account for empirical data in a variety of compatible rather than contradictory ways. And because meaning was enclosed within systems, there could be no genuine disputes between systems. A system was adopted or rejected on pragmatic grounds. It

---

[78] Carnap, R., *Meaning and Necessity*, Chicago, University of Chicago Press, 1967, pp. 206-8

made no sense to ask whether any of the systems were true or whether any of the entities spoken of really existed, as to do so was to slip into metaphysics.

One outcome of Carnap's approach was that ontology became system dependent which, in effect, made it meaning dependent. For Carnap the reality of anything was nothing other than the possibility of being placed in a certain system. There were two ways in which one could meaningfully speak of reality; using "real" to refer to those things we can discover empirically and those things whose "reality" depends on the stipulations of convention. As the final court of appeal for Carnap was the systems of science, it would be fair to say that the notion "is real" whatever its subject, could be ·construed not as a property but as a relation to a framework.

Carnap and Schlick both accepted that an expression could be meaningful in one of two ways. Either because its referent was given by experience or because we have defined its terms and therefore, its meaning was based purely on chosen conventions. We can mark the difference between them using Schlick's dichotomy between explicit and implicit definitions.

> Explicit definitions: based on ostension and defined by experience (the meaning of 'green' can be defined only by pointing to the foliage of a tree etc.).

> Implicit Definitions: the archetype were geometric concepts 'whose whole being is to be bearers of the relations laid down by the system [of axioms]. This presents no special difficulty since concepts are not real things at all.'[79]

In Carnap's terms, both implicit and explicit definitions were legitimate, but the former only if they could be justified within an explanatorily adequate system. The way in which implicitly defined concepts are part of the world is just via their usefulness to a scientific theory.

Carnap on Meaning and Ontology

Because of their anti-metaphysical bias, the Positivists were suspicious of ontological questions. Carnap was no exception. He did however, help to clarify traditional "metaphysical" debates in which he saw two distinct issues that were not always clearly separated. In *The Logical Structure of the World*, Carnap explains that we must distinguish between questions of reality and questions of essence. A (meaningful) question of reality has the form "Is X

---

[79] Schlick, M., translated and quoted in Coffa, A., *Semantic Tradition*, p. 176

real?" or "Does X exist?" and a question of essence has the form "What is X?" The answer to a question of reality is given via an examination of what is licensed by the system and hence has an internal and external interpretation. The important thing about such questions was that if they were meaningful, they could be answered. One is instructed by science, and the answer will be system relative.

An answer to the question of essence was more complicated and the area Carnap focussed most of his attention on. In keeping with his empiricist heritage, Carnap also argued that questions of existence and essence have a good and a bad interpretation. Answers to the good questions can be given by science. If we ask for example, about the existence and nature of dogs, we turn to science which instructs us to answer "Yes. Of course they exist. They are four legged, furry, canines etc."

Questions about existence and essence also have a bad interpretation, or what for the empiricist Carnap was a non-scientific interpretation. In asking them, we are asking whether there *really* are dogs or whether dogs really are just clusters of sensations, and seemingly require an answer from an extra-scientific perspective. These kinds of questions Carnap thought senseless. For Carnap, if we take science as a guide to what there is and what it is, we cannot go wrong. Not only can we not go wrong, but we cannot even conceptualise what "going wrong" might mean. Carnap's suspicion of philosophical interpretations led him to refuse legitimacy to questions most of us would naturally consider coherent. For example, even if we accept that science is the measure of all things, there are still legitimate questions about what exactly science tells us when it tells us what there is. Here the realist/idealist debate takes its place, as the realist interprets what science tells us within an ontological framework of the sort Carnap denies intelligibility.

From the realists' standpoint, it seems that what is at issue is a conception of the link between language and the world. Some words refer to things and thereby allow us to make claims about them. What Carnap grants the realist is the existence of the entities spoken of, but glosses what we can intelligibly mean by their existence as consisting in nothing more than the fact that we speak meaningfully about them. In dialogue with Carnap, the realist will be confounded by the realistic sounding nature of Carnap's talk; he will concede that numbers are real, that electrons are real, indeed, anything that belongs to (or can be reduced to) scientific theory is real, and really is real. The realist will suspect that Carnap doesn't mean what they mean by real. The realist means existentially or ontologically (not semantically) real, thus requiring the intelligibility of a gap between language and the world; a gap which as we have seen, will not be conceded by Carnap.

Despite his concession to the "realist" way of talking (providing the appropriate interpretation of it), Carnap clearly can't account for something that is central to the realist; the possibility of being mistaken.[80] The hall-mark of realism is, as Putnam has pointed out, not that one believes that the relevant claims are true, but that they might be false. This is the test that Carnap's constructivism fails for it leaves us without the ability to distinguish between what scientific theory says is the case and what is in fact the case.[81] According to Carnap, there is no difference between what science says is the case (i.e. the theoretic commitments and empirically verified truths) and what is "in fact" the case because the notion of what is "in fact" the case, when applied outside the scientific parameter is incoherent.[82] Changes in scientific frameworks are not, therefore, changes in what we believe is in fact the case, but simply changes in our construction of the world - changes in what we mean by *the world*. Given that we ordinarily do think of scientific frameworks that have been rejected as false, it is clear that Carnap is placing an interpretation on what the rejection comes to which goes against our ordinary understanding of it. As we know, Wittgenstein's work does not suffer this consequence. He was famously a defender of ordinary language and its usage.

Carnap's interpretative stance is the hall-mark of a substantive philosophical (or perhaps one should say scientific) bias. One of the main consequences of Carnap's conventionalism was his inability to accommodate the ordinary sense in which we understand non-factual (or what we might call "grammatical") disagreements. Carnap insisted that all such disputes arose from differences in the construction of conventions. There was nothing at stake between disputants except perhaps theoretic efficiency. Indeed, Carnap effectively organised things so that all disputants could see that there was nothing at stake and live

---

[80] The intelligibility of the possibility of being mistaken or of when it would make sense to say that a mistake is possible should not be taken for granted. A discussion of such intelligibility will follow in the next chapter

[81] I am not here referring to trivial empirical truths which science could clearly be wrong about, but rather the idea that the whole body of scientific theory; its theoretic frameworks, might conceivably be false. The distinction is between local and global mistakes (see Antony, L., *Can Verificationists make mistakes?*, in *American Philosophical Quarterly*, 1987, Vol. 24, No.3, pp. 225-236)

[82] I am not suggesting here that Carnap denied that straight-forward empirical propositions could not be false, merely that for Carnap it made no sense to think about framework propositions being true or false

peaceably with their chosen system without accusing others of having adopted the wrong one. The fact is, however, that the disputants themselves were unhappy with Carnap's interpretation of their disputes. The position is illustrated here by Coffa:

> There is a widespread image associated with Carnap's attitude towards 'ultimate' philosophical questions . . . that depicts it as a version of utopian socialism in the field of epistemology. We think of Carnap as contemplating the messy mathematicians and philosophers as they build what seems to him a Tower of Babel; he stares at them in astonishment, shrugs his shoulders, and shaking his head walks away from the noise to a remote and quiet place where he builds a variety of linguistic phalansteries intended to conform to the variety of Babelonian tastes. When he invites everyone to move into the structure of their choice, no one comes. Carnap shakes his head once more and hopes for a more reasonable future, although he promptly says to himself that what 'reasonable' means is a matter of conventions and proposals and one shouldn't quarrel about that either. If asked whether any of the Babelonians are saying something false or something meaningless, Carnap will smile tolerantly and say 'Who am I to judge?' . . . Let each do as he chooses and let us all live in peace.[83]

In treating linguistic frameworks as entirely constitutive of meaning, Carnap was forced to sever any link between constitution and extra-semantic elements. His semantic conventionalism was both a requirement and a consequence of his philosophical stance. One could not say that his view on the nature of framework (grammatical) disagreements reflected how these disagreements were perceived by the disputants themselves however. The Babelonians would not move into Carnap's custom-built structures.

It is not unusual to find commentators attributing to Wittgenstein something like Carnap's view on the nature of disagreement. Such commentators pick up on Wittgenstein's concept of meaning as constituted by rules and argue that it must follow from this that disagreements between users of different concepts (rules) cannot have a truth at stake because like Carnap's constructive frameworks, disputants mean different things by their terms and hence do not contradict each other. That there are difficulties in making sense of this hard and fast distinction comes out particularly when we examine ordinary disputes. Rarely in an argument over what goodness is, for example, do we find the argument dissolved by the disputants agreeing that there is nothing really at stake between them; agreeing that they just mean something different by "goodness" and that is all there is to be said on the matter. It is the nature of the

---

[83] Coffa, A., *Semantic Tradition*, p. 315

dispute that each party feels that there is something at stake: that they are right about goodness. It is not just a matter of definition.

Whenever we characterise what appears to be a genuine dispute as linguistic, we are not describing the dispute but placing an interpretation on it. Carnap was upfront and unrepentant about his interpretative stance and the motivations behind it. It is more difficult for a Wittgensteinian to adopt the same kind of stance (or arrive at the same conclusions) because of the philosophical presuppositions implied by it and the difficulties in avoiding the revisionary consequences it has for ordinary discourse. In the next section I will show why I think it is wrong to attribute to Wittgenstein a Carnapian incommensurability despite evidence to the contrary.

Wittgenstein on the Connection between Language and Reality

The reason it is tempting to attribute to Wittgenstein a semantic conventionalism akin to Carnap's is because he too appears committed to a conventional rather than a realist semantics. We have already seen how Wittgenstein's position differs to the conventionalism attributed to him by Dummett but we have not explored the consequences of his conventionalism for ontology. We must also remember that the Positivists were trying to provide epistemological guarantees for science (every abstract concept could be "anchored down" logically and epistemologically to a protocol sentence whose terms are defined by ostension – our experience – private or otherwise). Wittgenstein's concerns are not epistemological at all. He is interested in the logical limits of meaning which do in fact limit the possibilities of knowledge but Wittgenstein's motives for understanding the limits were philosophical not scientific.

What have we learnt so far about Wittgenstein's thoughts on the nature of grammar? We know that he treated as "grammatical" anything to do with the meaning of a word, statement or gesture. We could say that for Wittgenstein, anything that has meaning must have a grammar because the grammar is what is given when one asks for an explanation of the meaning. We have also seen how Wittgenstein's thoughts on meaning-constituents underwent a dramatic change; from appealing to the form of the world in the *Tractatus*, to an appeal to forms of life and shared language-games as the basic semantic categories. It is now time to develop a more exact understanding of how Wittgenstein understood the relationship between grammar and reality.

Grammar as the Connection between Word and World

Although Wittgenstein had assumed a direct connection between word and world (meaning and object) in the *Tractatus*, the giving up of *the world* necessitated a revision of his semantic story. After toying with the idea that ostension operates as the basic semantic category, we have seen that Wittgenstein recognised that even ostension can be misunderstood or interpreted in different ways and so could not clinch meaning and could not in itself, set up a connection between word and world. When he finally decided that grammar was responsible for meaning, Wittgenstein was happy to declare that "the harmony between thought and reality is to be found in the grammar of the language".[84]

Carnap's position was that anything spoken of meaningfully was real within the system in which it belonged. We saw that for Carnap, this really meant that he chose to define "real" as a relation rather than a property. As a positivist, Carnap glossed "meaningfulness" in terms of what belonged to a scientific system which was explanatorily adequate. But if we include all language-games (and not just those belonging to science), we can see something of Carnap's semantic position in Wittgenstein's remark here. In claiming that the harmony between thought and reality lies in grammar, is Wittgenstein to be understood as claiming with Carnap, that what is real is whatever is meaningful? And if he is saying that, is he also saying that there is no other sense in which we may ask whether the object spoken of is real?

I do not think that Wittgenstein is committed to anything like Carnap's view. Certainly Wittgenstein shared with Carnap the desire to rule out as unintelligible a metaphysical sense of real. But Carnap not only ruled out the metaphysical sense. He insisted that there was only one way in which we could intelligibly ask whether an object spoken of was real: whether science (or particular scientific frameworks) instructed us to do so. Certain reality claims are true just because they belong to science. If we allow Wittgenstein his multitude of language-games (not just science), on a constructivist semantics, we would also expect to find him defining "real" as that which is given by the grammar of the game and disallowing any other sense of "real" as metaphysical. So it would follow that whatever has meaning (in whichever language-game) is real and we could not make intelligible any question asking whether it is in fact real. Notice how easily one can be led to conflate semantics

---

[84] Wittgenstein, L., *Philosophical Grammar*, p. 162

and ontology. Construing "meaningful" as "real" makes problematic any sense in which we can meaningfully ask whether something exists (is real). What happens if within the framework or language-game the question does arise as to whether X is real? It looks as though asking the ontological question (about the existence of X) is simply to ask whether "X" has meaning, and Carnap glosses that question further by insisting that to ask whether "X" has meaning is just to ask whether one wants to adopt the framework to which "X" belongs. A conventionalist (or constructivist) semantics, because it rules out the intelligibility of some reality to which the meaning of X can be held responsible, also rules out as genuine any dispute which implies such a reality. Was this Wittgenstein's view?

Wittgenstein on the Accountability of Grammar to Reality

Because both Wittgenstein and Carnap share anti-metaphysical assumptions and some form of conventionalism, it is more difficult to identify what it is exactly they differ on. The most obvious difference is in their view on the nature of language/logic. The Hintikkas[85] have provided a dichotomy that is useful to us here. They suggest that we can identify two very different conceptions of language; what they call "language as the universal medium", the view which they attribute to Frege and Wittgenstein; and "language as calculus".[86] The latter view holds that we can raise meta-theoretic questions about logic whereas the former holds that it is impossible to theorise about language because we can only use language to talk about something if we can rely on a given interpretation, an existing network of meaning relations. Any attempt to talk about such relations must therefore presuppose them. Those who treat language as the universal medium invariably commit themselves to the ineffability of semantics. Convincingly, the Hintikkas argue that Frege, Wittgenstein and even Quine are committed to such a view; that effectively they are semanticists without semantics.[87]

On the Hintikka model, Carnap is a believer in language as calculus, shown explicitly in his willingness to theorise about semantical relations. Defending Wittgenstein against a Carnapian-constructivist conception of reality therefore can be done by showing that Wittgenstein really did hold that semantical

---

[85] Hintikka., M and J., *Investigating Wittgenstein*, Oxford, Blackwell, 1986

[86] Hintikka, M. and J., *Investigating Wittgenstein*, p. 1

[87] Hintikka, M. and J., *Investigating Wittgenstein*, p. 2

relations are ineffable. Part of what follows from doing so, is that one cannot theorise about the relationship between meaning and reality. Nor can one insist on a conception of real as the only legitimate one. In both instances, to do so requires a robust semantics and thus some theoretical stance which abuses the commitment to ineffability.

That Wittgenstein held the view that language is a universal medium and that this for Wittgenstein meant that semantics is ineffable, is I think, uncontroversial. The following remarks are indicative of his view. Certainly we are all familiar with it as a central theme of the *Tractatus*, indicated specifically in remarks such as:

A picture cannot, however, depict its pictorial form; it displays it.[88]

A picture cannot, however, place itself outside its representational form.[89]

In the 1930s, the same sentiment was being expressed:

'But language can expand'. Certainly but if this word 'expand' has a sense here, then I know *already* what I mean by it. I must be able to specify how I imagine such an expansion. And what I can't think, I can't now express or even hint at. And in *this* case the word 'now' means 'in this calculus' or 'if the words are used according to these grammatical rules' ... No sign leads us beyond itself and no argument either.[90]

He writes elsewhere: "the limit of language shows itself in the impossibility of describing the fact that corresponds to a sentence . . . without repeating that very sentence".[91]

Wittgenstein's constant emphasis in the *Investigations* on the impossibility of an ideal language which can somehow explain ordinary language is just a version of the same argument:

In giving explanations I already have to use language full blown (not some sort of preparatory, provisional one); this by itself shows that I can adduce only exterior facts about language.[92]

---

[88] Wittgenstein, L., *Tractatus*, 2.172
[89] Wittgenstein, L., *Tractatus*, 2.174
[90] Wittgenstein, L., *Philosophical Grammar*, p. 114
[91] Wittgenstein, L., *Culture and Value*, p. 10
[92] Wittgenstein, L., *Philosophical Investigations*, §120

So: "How do I know that this colour is red? It would be an answer to say: 'I have learnt English.'"[93]

It would *not* be an answer to say "because it is red" or "because I am experiencing redness". "Experience decides whether a proposition is true or false, but not its sense."[94]

Anyone who holds the view of language as the universal medium believes that there is something suspicious about all attempts to explain or justify meaning because any explanation or justification, to be genuine, must be able to get outside the language it is trying to explain. The whole idea of getting outside language is rejected because any meaningful justification or explanation requires the very language it purports to have gotten outside. Wittgenstein insists that "you can't get behind the rules (meaning) because there isn't any behind".[95] Even ostensive definition, which seems to break free of language and connect with reality "does not get us away from symbolism... All we can do in an ostensive definition is to replace one set of symbols by another".[96]

In treating meaning as accountable to something (reality), we would have to think that the rules could be correct or incorrect. In denying that meaning is accountable to reality, Wittgenstein is denying that we can make sense of that notion of correct in relation to rules. His argument depends on drawing a distinction between the sense in which we ordinarily justify a statement and the sense in which we might try to justify a grammatical rule. Wittgenstein insists that the ordinary sense is not available in the grammatical case:

> An explanation of a sign can replace the sign itself. This gives an important insight into the nature of the explanation of signs, and brings out a contrast between the idea of this sort of explanation and that of causal explanation.[97]

Notice here that the contrast is explicitly drawn between empirical/causal explanations and explanations of meaning on the grounds that when we provide the latter, we must still be operating within meaning. We cannot look at language from the outside as it were, in the way that we can for other objects

[93] Wittgenstein, L., *Philosophical Investigations*, §381

[94] Wittgenstein, L., *Philosophical Remarks*, p. 65

[95] Wittgenstein, L., *Philosophical Grammar*, p. 244, brackets mine

[96] Wittgenstein, L., *Wittgenstein's Lectures: Cambridge 1930-32*, Lee, D. [ed], Oxford, Blackwell, 1980, p. 23

[97] Wittgenstein, L., *Philosophical Remarks*, p. 99

which can be identified, examined, discussed and theorised about. Using language to talk about language however, presupposes that a network of meaning relations are already operative and thus that one cannot significantly talk about what those meaning relations are without assuming them. So it is not that the idea of explanations is completely unintelligible when applied to meaning (semantic relations) but that one must be aware that they are not like empirical or causal explanations in which the explanandum can be separated conceptually from the explanans. We might recognise here the theme of the previous chapter where physiognomic explanations were separated from empirical ones for precisely the same reason. Physiognomic explanations are concerned with meaningfulness and hence it is entirely to be expected that Wittgenstein's work on grammar and the impossibility of its justification should fall within the compass of the physiognomic. So too we might expect Wittgenstein to prefer to talk of elucidations rather than explanations when our subject matter is grammar.

To genuinely justify a grammatical rule we would have to do one of two things: either provide an argument to show why just this rule is the right rule for the purpose (this is one way in which we use the concept of justification), or we would have to provide an argument to show how a grammatical proposition captures a feature of reality (another way in which we use the concept of justification). Wittgenstein contends that the first is not so much a justification but a reiteration ("we replace one sign with another"); and the second is impossible, indeed unintelligible. Any such argument (if it were to be meaningful) would have to use the grammar of the proposition it was attempting to justify. Hence it would not be a justification at all but would collapse into a reiteration or elucidation.[98] For example, the argument that would justify the rule that "there are four primary colours" would have to say something like "'There are four primary colours' is justified as a rule because there are in fact four primary colours." The worry for Wittgenstein, is that in justifying a rule we are simply repeating what we *must* say, in this case about primary colours. The rule qua rule tells us that it is meaningless (not part of the game) to state its opposite: it is meaningless to say that there are not four primary colours. But if the statement "there are in fact four primary colours" is going to be a genuine assertion and so act as a legitimate justification for the rule, it must be possible to state its opposite. And the conclusion from this is

---

[98] This is of course why Wittgenstein insists that the *Tractatus* contains nothing but elucidations and why philosophical explanations are impossible

that it is incoherent to justify rules because the justification will undermine itself. To successfully justify a rule would be to show that it could be violated which is the very thing we are supposed to be denying in treating it as a rule.

The difficulty in appealing to reality in order to justify grammatical rules is more than suggested here when Wittgenstein writes:

> Yet can't it after all be said that in some sense or other the grammar of colour words characterises the world as it actually is? One would like to say 'May I not really look in vain for a fifth primary colour? Doesn't one put the primary colours together because there is a similarity among them, or at least put colours together, contrasting them with shapes or notes, because there is a similarity among them?' Or, when I set this up as the right way of dividing up the world, have I a pre-conceived idea in my head as a paradigm? Of which in that case I can only say: 'Yes, that is the kind of way we look at things' or 'We just do want to form this picture'. For if I say 'there is a particular similarity among the primary colours' - whence do I derive the idea of this similarity? . . . 'Then might one also take red, green and circular together?' - Why not?![99]

We have already examined the relationship between Wittgenstein's comment that "what looks as if it had to exist is part of the language"[100] and Kant's "we can know a priori of things only what we ourselves have put into them".[101] What Wittgenstein and Kant both agree on is that "all attempts to derive these . . . concepts . . . from experience, as so to ascribe them a merely empirical origin, are entirely vain and useless".[102] We have also seen that Kant distinguished the different kinds of propositions a priori and drew theoretical conclusions about mind and meaning from them. If with Wittgenstein, we rule out the intelligibility[103] of all such conclusions (on the grounds that semantics is ineffable), what more can we say about the relationship of grammar to reality? If we treat some propositions as grammatical, are we committed to denying that they tell us how things are? And if we are committed to that, aren't we also committed to something like a Carnapian characterisation of disputes between users of different rules?

---

[99] Wittgenstein, L., *Zettel*, §331

[100] Wittgenstein, L., *Philosophical Investigations*, §50

[101] Kant, I., *Critique*, p. xviii

[102] Kant, I., *Critique*, p. 139

[103] And here "unintelligible" connects with Wittgenstein's use of meaningless as idleness. Such explanations do not (cannot) perform the explanatory function required of them if that function is modelled on the explanations of science

Wittgenstein and Ontology

We have seen that for the Positivists, the idea of grammatical or framework propositions was introduced to mark a distinction between expressions whose meaning is given by experience and expessions the meaning of which are stipulated by convention. They needed this distinction to justify their empiricism and to show how experience could give us knowledge of the world. Wittgenstein's interest in grammar was, as we have seen, particularly related to how meaning is possible and how the distinction between sense and nonsense operates in our practices. There is no question that in his work a distinction between grammatical and non-grammatical propositions is operative. There are important differences in what this distinction is being called upon to do however.

1. For Carnap, the distinction is used to identify propositions whose meaning was stipulated by convention and those whose meaning was given by experience. Because for Wittgenstein, there is no such thing as a proposition whose meaning is given by experience, the distinction cannot capture for him what it does for Carnap. On his model of language-games and grammar as that which is taught in preparation for playing the game, we must think of grammatical propositions, not as those whose meaning is stipulated by convention (all meaning is in some sense conventional for Wittgenstein), but as those which must be accepted if one is to play the game.[104]

2. It follows from 1 that in identifying what counts as a grammatical proposition, we do not look for a proposition for which no experience is

---

[104] Wittgenstein is sensitive to the fact that what counts as essential to the game is indefinite and is entirely dependent on the context:

> Let us say that the meaning of a piece is its role in the game. Now let it be decided by lot which of the players gets white before any game of chess begins. To this end one player holds a king in each closed fist while the other chooses one of the two hands at random. Will it be counted as part of the role of the king in chess that it is used to draw lots in this way?
>
> So I am inclined to distinguish between the essential and the inessential in a game too. The game, one would like to say, has not only rules but also a *point*. (Wittgenstein, L., *Philosophical Investigations*, §§563/4)

relevant to its content, but look for the propositions which count as rules of the game. On Wittgenstein's account therefore, grammatical propositions are best identified by examining the context of use: whether the proposition is being used to say that things are thus and so, or whether it is being used to explain a meaning ("this is called 'x'"). The same proposition can operate both as a rule and a description as Wittgenstein makes explicit when he writes:

> Don't I have to admit that sentences are often used on the borderline between logic and the empirical, so that their meaning [use] shifts back and forth and they are now expressions of norms, now treated as expressions of experience? For it is not the 'thought' (an accompanying mental phenomenon) but its use (something that surrounds it) that distinguishes the logical proposition from the empirical one.[105]

It is important to recognise that Wittgenstein does not enforce a substantive distinction between grammatical and non-grammatical propositions of the Carnapian kind. He does not insist that it belongs to the nature of the proposition that it defines rather than describes. This is important because it rules out the more positive thesis that rules of grammar *cannot* be truths. Certainly when functioning as rules, it is either inappropriate to think of them being true or false, or we must think of their truth as unassailable (this is the sense in which they are necessary). But to acknowledge this is just to recognise an uncontroversial feature of grammar. To function as grammatical rules these propositions must be removed from the possibility of doubt and hence remove themselves from questions of truth and falsity. Clearly, if someone were to doubt whether in chess the pawn can move forward, it would be impossible for them to play chess. Accepting the rule is a condition for playing the game.

Because the distinction between grammar and non-grammar is itself a grammatical one for Wittgenstein, (a descriptive observation of games and their rules), it is impossible to rule that grammatical propositions cannot have ontological entailments. To do so would require access to a substantive distinction between types of proposition. But such a distinction would require a theoretical semantics and that is precisely what Wittgenstein denies that we have access to. The distinction between a positive (Carnap) and negative (Wittgenstein) semantics shows especially on what one can say about ontology. Carnap ensures the limits of language by insisting that in adopting a framework we are simply adopting a way of speaking. The framework propositions do not

---

[105] Wittgenstein, L., *On Certainty*, Oxford, Blackwell, 1977, §19

themselves commit us to any truths about reality. To say this is to say something substantive about framework propositions which is natural given Carnap's need to distinguish between such propositions and empirical truths, assuring the former a sense despite their lack of empirical content:

> whenever we speak meaningfully of concepts, we are always dealing with concepts designated by means of signs or which could at least in principle be so designated; and so in the end we are always talking of these signs and their laws of application.[106]

Without commitment to a distinction between meaning construed experientially and meaning construed conventionally, Wittgenstein cannot make the same contrast. Indeed because of the grammatical (as opposed to theoretical) nature of Wittgenstein's distinction, investigating meaning and asking about objects can come to the same thing: not because meaning is ever an "object" but because the distinction between rule and empirical proposition is fluid enough in actual practice to eradicate a hard and fast distinction as Debra Aidun illustrates:

> 'Having a length' is an essential characteristic of those things we call 'rods' but it is a fact of grammar that nothing we call a 'rod' can sensibly be said to lack a length. This accounts for Wittgenstein's cryptic remarks to the effect that 'Grammar tells what kind of object anything is' (PI 373) and 'Essence is expressed by grammar' (PI 371) Because talking about objects and talking about words comes to the same in such cases, the grammatical rule about the use of the word 'rod' can be captured in an expression which is not ostensibly about words: 'Every rod has a length.'[107]

And Wittgenstein makes the reverse point that what belongs to the nature of an object can be captured by examining how words are used: "One ought to ask, not what images are or what happens when one imagines anything, but how the word 'imagination' is used. But that does not mean that I want to talk only about words. For the question as to the nature of the imagination is as much about the word 'imagination' as my question is."[108]

So when Wittgenstein makes remarks such as "3+3=6 is a rule as to the way we are going to talk . . . it is preparation for a description, just as fixing a unit

---

[106] Carnap, R., *Logical Structure*, p. 4

[107] Aidun, D., *Wittgenstein on Grammatical Propositions*, in Shanker, S. [ed], *Ludwig Wittgenstein: Critical Assessments*, Volume 4, Beckenham, Croom Helm, 1986, p. 145

[108] Wittgenstein, L., *Philosophical Investigations*, §370

of length is preparation for measuring",[109] he is not suggesting (a la Carnap) that grammatical propositions are simply about words or ways of speaking. In denying this I am not suggesting that Wittgenstein somehow thinks grammar is about *more* than words (and actions). Both positions are confused on Wittgenstein's account. Both draw conclusions about grammar which on the view of ineffability, are rendered illegal. We noted earlier that Dummett's conventionalist Wittgenstein would have been guilty of such conclusions and it was on precisely those grounds that I criticised Dummet's characterisation. Wittgenstein's negative position (designed to show why theorising about language is confused) can therefore be contrasted with a more positive position like Carnap's. Such a view does not merely emphasise the place that rules have in our language-games. It theorises about the nature of these rules.

Even propositions that don't look like rules may in fact function as rules because to doubt them is to make the playing of the game impossible.

> There seem to be propositions that have the character of experiential propositions, but whose truth is for me unassailable. That is to say, if I assume that they are false, I must mistrust all my judgements.[110]

In summary, we can conclude that for Wittgenstein, the criterion for whether or not a proposition belongs to grammar is whether it makes sense to question it when one is playing (or learning to play) the game in which it belongs as a rule. And the criterion for whether it makes sense to question it is also given by context, not content. This is very different to the positivists' distinction between propositions that can be compared to experience and those which are analytic or true in virtue of their meaning. There will be overlaps of course. Sometimes what makes a proposition "uncertain" is just that we have not established its truth. But the important difference between the positivists and Wittgenstein on the nature of grammar was that Wittgenstein had no difficulty in accepting that the same proposition can function both as an assertoric statement and as a rule of meaning and this was because he didn't define grammatical as those propositions whose meaning could be given independent of all experience.

---

[109] Moore, G.E., *Lectures*, p. 72
[110] Wittgenstein, L., *Remarks on Colour*, p. 63

Chapter Four

Religious Language as Grammar

"The claim 'God is love' may mislead us into thinking that it is a descriptive statement rather than a rule for the use of the word 'God'."[1]

"The question of the existence of God is the question whether I can find a use for the word 'God' in my talk."[2]

I claimed earlier that the Neo-Wittgensteinian critique of traditional philosophy of religion mirrors Wittgenstein's critique of philosophy generally in that they aim to show that whenever a rule of grammar is treated as a truth about reality, one has slipped into a confused metaphysics. We saw in the previous chapter that for Wittgenstein, the confusion lies in appealing to reality in order to justify meaning claims. Because rules of grammar are construed as meaning-constituents, the distinction emphasises what for Wittgenstein is a trivial truth; that it makes no sense to think that we can coherently explain or justify meaning by appealing to a reality independent of it because to do so implies the possibility of getting outside meaning and that idea is incoherent. Outside meaning there is not further meaning, but no meaning at all. The idea of explanation in connection to meaning is therefore suspect (I "explain" nothing if I say "this is (means) 'red' because this is red"). We also saw that the criterion for whether a proposition was to be counted as a rule or a statement was not the positivistic one of whether experience could be appealed to in order to verify or falsify it, but the use to which the proposition was being put. Grammatical propositions turn out to be those propositions that are deeply embedded in the game. That is how they acquire their status as rules. Doubting them brings the intelligibility of the entire game into question. Therein lies their necessity.

---

[1] Phillips, D.Z., *Faith after Foundationalism*, p. 218
[2] Moore, G., *Believing in God*, Edinburgh, T&T Clark, 1988, p. 39

The Neo-Wittgensteinian philosophers of religion make substantial use of the distinction between rules of grammar and truths about the world (or what they gloss as "descriptions"). They frequently deny that a statement can be treated as a description just because it is a rule. Phillips' remark that "the claim 'God is love' may mislead us into thinking that it is a descriptive statement rather than a rule for the use of the word 'God'", is indicative of their general position. An important part of their project is to show why it is confused to treat religious language as if it refers to or describes some reality "outside itself".[3] The Neo-Wittgensteinians appeal to the grammatical status of religious language to defend their claim that it does not (*cannot*) refer to reality, and it is this appeal which will be the critical focus of this chapter.

We have, in the previous chapters, examined the reasons why Wittgenstein claimed that meaning could not be held accountable to (or be understood as referring to) an independent reality. It is a philosophical confusion to think that grammatical rules can be held to be true or false just in case they match or fail to match reality. Wittgenstein's entire polemic against speculative metaphysics depends on recognising this seemingly innocuous but philosophically far-reaching claim. As we have seen, Wittgenstein attempts to show that for any reality you appeal to, if you are appealing to it meaningfully, then you must be appealing to it through meanngful language (concepts or ideas). But then reality itself can't justify this meaning because you do not have the right sort of gap between meaning and reality that is needed to produce a genuine justification. You can't get behind your signs in order to glimpse or even conceptualise a reality that doesn't in some sense depend on you thinking with them.

When the Neo-Wittgensteinian philosophers of religion criticise philosophers for attempting to justify language about God by appealing to the existence of God they are rightly applying Wittgenstein's central philosophical insight. When they claim that language about God is not intended to be referential, they are claiming something much stronger. As a philosopher persuaded by Wittgenstein's insights about the limit of meaning, I may accept that it makes no sense to justify the language I use to talk about pain by appealing to the nature of pain – as if the meaning of the word "pain" could be explained by the sensation I feel when I am in pain. The required gap between my concept of pain and the sensation I feel isn't available to me because I cannot help but think of the sensation in terms of the concept. That is,

---

[3] Keightly, A., *Wittgenstein, Grammar and God*, London, Epworth Press, 1976, p. 97

presumably, how I am able to identify it *as pain* in the first place. Accepting this central insight in no way leads to the conclusion that the language of pain is not referential. That would be to deny that when we talk about pains we are intending to talk about something that exists in reality. Now someone may want to argue that when we talk about pains, we are not talking about something that exists in reality but to do so would require a much stronger claim than Wittgenstein's claim about the limit of language. So too with the religious case. I may accept that the *meaning* of religious language cannot be explained or justified by appealing to a divine being which the language purports to be about because I am trapped within the meaning through which I think this divine being's purported existence. As we saw in chapter one, to think I am doing anything more than this is to be deceived by the imagination. This does not mean, however, that my language can't refer to a divine being.

When the Neo-Wittgensteinian philosophers claim that language about God is not about anything "outside itself", we can now see how there are two different ways to understand the claim. The first is uncontroversial. We can accept it as meaning that I can't think what the language refers to independently of the language I am thinking with. So, for any divine being that I imagine, I am depending on some concept of a divine being. If I am not doing that then I am either thinking of something other than a divine being or I am thinking nothing at all. We may concede happily enough that we do not want our language about God to be about anything "outside itself" just because because it would then either be about something else entirely or about nothing at all. We surely want our language for God to be about God and not about something else entirely!

The second and more controversial interpretation of the Neo-Wittgensteinian claim that language about God is not about anything "outside itself" is the more difficult intepretation to understand. The discussion that follows in this chapter is an attempt to both understand and critically engage with it.

The crucial point lies in how we understand language as referring to or being about something "outside itself". In the previous chapter, I drew a distinction between semantics and ontology. I acknowledge that this distinction is, in itself, a controversial one but I will take the liberty of using it all the same. If we loosely define meaning as semantic and existence as ontological then we can draw a rough and ready distinction between the meaning and the reference of words. Some words will have meaning but no intended reference and some will have both meaning and intended reference. Indeed, the truth of a proposition will depend on it having not merely a meaning but a reference to something and it is this reference that confers on it the possibility of being true or false. The philosophical point made by Wittgenstein is that semantics is prior to reference. To speak truly or to form true beliefs, we need a meaningful language (or concepts) in which we do so.

When the Neo-Wittgensteinian philosophers of religion apply Wittgenstein's philosophical insights to religious language they come to the rather striking conclusion that religious language has no intended ontological (or referential) status.[4] In what follows I shall examine how they come to this conclusion and argue that they are mistaken in drawing conclusion. Non-Wittgensteinian philosophers of religion have, of course, objected to the conclusion and the way they voice their objection is instructive. The kind of objection is typified by the comments given here by Ronald Hepburn when he writes: "Within traditional Christian theology, the question about divine existence cannot be deflected into the question 'Does God play an intelligible role in the language-game?'"[5] and by John Hick who voices the same sentiment when he writes that "the unacceptable feature of the position is that by treating religious language as autonomous, it deprives religious statements of 'ontological' or 'metaphysical' significance".[6]

Hick's reference to the metaphysical significance of religious language might raise the alarm for philosophers who accept Wittgenstein's criticism of speculative metaphysics. Indeed, I have tried to show that it is good philosophy to accept Wittgenstein's critique. So what follows for the so-called metaphysical significance of religious language? Can one accept Wittgenstein's critique of metaphysics and leave what is perceived to be the "metaphysical" aspect of religious language untouched? I believe that we can but only when we clearly separate philosophical metaphysics from the metaphysics of religious belief and so following Hick, I will use the term "ontological" rather than "metaphysical" when discussing that aspect of religious language that we

---

[4] I say that it has no "intended" rather than no referential status because if religious language was referential then we could know also that it was true. If the proposition "there is a God" had a referent for "God" then its truth would be assured. In the discussion that follows, I focus on the question of whether religious language could be referential, not whether it actually is. The Neo-Wittgensteinian philosophers deny that it could be about an actual exisiting being and it is this claim that I want to criticise

[5] Hepburn, R., *From World to God* in *Mind*, 1963, Vol. LXXII, p. 41

[6] Hick, J., *Sceptics and Believers*, in Hick [ed], *Faith and the Philosophers*, London, Macmillan, 1964, pp. 239-40

might take to refer or intend to refer to an independent reality. When Phillips writes that "talk of God's existence or reality cannot be considered as talk about the existence of an object"[7] this is what I take to be a denial that God *could be* ontologically real and not merely semantically real (i.e. that "God" is meaningful).

What then does it mean to characterise religious language as grammar and is the Neo-Wittgensteinian characterisation in keeping with what we have seen as Wittgenstein's casting of the distinction between grammatical and non-grammatical propositions? We can answer these questions by examining the criticisms D.Z. Phillips makes of Alvin Plantinga's particular epistemology of religion. Both Plantinga and Phillips are interested in the non-hypothetical nature of religious belief. For Phillips, its non-hypothetical nature is evidence of its grammatical status, which in turn is evidence that it can't be ontologically significant. The debate between Plantinga and Phillips usefully brings out both what Phillips means when he characterises religious language as grammar and where the problems lie in his account.

Some Preliminary Remarks

It needs to be said at the outset that Plantinga is ultimately interested in religious epistemology. He is not examining the ontological or semantic implications of religious belief, but, rather, attempting to show that it is rational to believe in God. The point of common ground between Plantinga and Phillips is not obvious. There is a connection, however, and it is forged by Plantinga's criticism of the traditional foundationalist model of epistemic justification.

Alvin Plantinga approaches religious epistemology from his commitment to the Calvinistic Reformed view of the nature of religious belief. Reformers maintain the immediacy of religious belief, arguing that it distorts the nature of belief to treat it as if it rests on argumentation or the acquisition of evidence. The religious idea of faith is that it is unconditional, not "unstable and wavering". On the traditional foundationalist criterion of rationality however, religious beliefs have been treated as beliefs that do stand in need of evidence or argument if they are to be justified. The Reformers approach is not to question the foundationalist criterion of rationality, but to question the place they award religious belief within their critierion.

---

[7] Phillips, D.Z., *Religion without Explanation*, p. 174

On the foundationalist view of rationality, propositions are of two sorts. There are those which stand in need of evidence and those which provide the required evidence. Those that don't stand in need of evidence are said to be foundational or basic to our noetic structure. The Reformers argue that belief in God should be considered as among those propositions that are basic to our noetic structure, rather than those which stand in need of evidence. "The capacity to comprehend God's existence is as much a part of our noetic equipment as the capacity to apprehend perceptual truths, truths about the past and truths about other minds."[8] Beliefs in other minds, perceptual truths and so on have, of course, traditionally been thought of as foundational and Plantinga's point is that belief in God should be also.

Plantinga's argument against the classical foundationalist concentrates on the criterion they provide for judging whether or not a belief is foundational to a noetic structure. He points out that the standard criterion: a proposition p is properly basic for a person S if and only if p is either self-evident to S, or incorrigible for S or evident to the senses for S, is a criterion that foundationalists themselves do not meet. The criterion of basicality should itself be basic or supported by evidence. In the absence of it meeting any of these conditions, the reformers argue that the criterion itself does not have the authority to rule that belief in God is not properly basic. How do we know that it is not "entirely right, rational, reasonable and proper to believe in God without any evidence or argument at all"?[9] In the absence of a legitimate criterion, the believer can trust that their beliefs are rational and therefore true.

Plantinga is not unaware that the absence of a criterion of basicality not only gives the religious believer "permission" to place their beliefs in the foundations of their noetic structure. It seemingly gives everyone permission to do so. Plantinga writes:

> If belief in God is properly basic, why can't just any belief be properly basic? What about the belief that the Great Pumpkin returns every Halloween? Could I take that as basic?[10]

Clearly there are problems if we are to give permission for any belief to be placed in the foundations of a noetic structure. What is important about basic beliefs is their connection to truth. If any belief can be counted as basic, any

---

[8] Plantinga, A., *Reason and Belief in God*, in Plantinga, A., and Wolterstorff, N. [ed], *Faith And Rationality*, Notre Dame, University of Notre Dame Press, 1983, p. 90

[9] Plantinga, A., *Reason and Belief*, p. 17

[10] Plantinga, A., *Reason and Belief*, p. 74

belief can be counted as rational and the connection between rationality and truth becomes obsolete - which completely undermines the Reformed endeavour altogether. Aware of these problems, Plantinga suggests that although we don't have a criterion that excludes belief in the Great Pumpkin as properly basic, we can fairly reject it. We can reject it for the same reason that someone who doesn't accept the positivistic strict criterion for meaning could still reject as nonsense "Twas brillig: and the slithy toves did gyve and gymble in the wabe". Just as no criterion is necessary in the second case, none is necessary in the first.[11]

Plantinga suggests that we can arrive at a criterion for basicality inductively. We can look and see what seems to count as basic in particular instances. "We must assemble examples of beliefs and conditions such that the former are obviously properly basic in the latter, and examples of beliefs and conditions such that the former are not properly basic in the latter."[12] Criterion for basicality should thus emerge from the relevant set of examples and "the Christian community is responsible for its set of examples".[13] The atheists will also assemble their set of examples to show why the belief that there is no God is properly basic. Both will be making claims to rationality (and therefore truth) but claims Plantinga: "if our criteria conflict, then at least one of them is mistaken, even if we cannot agree as to which it is."[14]

The central assumptions of Plantinga's position are as follows:

1. There is a legitimate distinction between basic and non-basic beliefs.
2. Basic beliefs are true beliefs.[15]
3. We cannot be certain which beliefs are basic beliefs.
4. We must allow that beliefs that we think are basic may not be basic because they may not turn out to be true.

---

[11] Plantinga, A., *Is Belief in God Rational?*, in Delaney [ed], *Rationality and Religious Belief*, Notre Dame, University of Notre Dame Press, 1979, p. 26

[12] Plantinga, A., *Is Belief in God Properly Basic?*, In *Nous*, 1981, Vol. 5, p. 50

[13] Plantinga, A., *Nous*, p. 50

[14] Plantinga, A., *Reason and Belief*, p. 76

[15] In what follows I am going to assume a connection between basicality and truth. I realise that the account Plantinga gives of basicality, and his epistemological model generally (in which the emphasis is on warrant rather than truth), does not require a necessary connection between basicality and truth. However, it helps bring out the issues between Phillips and Plantinga if the connection is so understood. As the connection is assumed by Plantinga between self-evidence and truth, my discussion will focus almost exclusively on basic beliefs characterised as self-evident

5. If two claims to basicality are made which contradict each other, then only one of them can be legitimate, even if we cannot judge which one it is.

D.Z. Phillips provides a strong criticism of these assumptions in *Faith after Foundationalism*. His particular target is Plantinga's appeal to a philosophical criterion of rationality that might judge between noetic structures and declare one rational and the other irrational. According to Plantinga, the religious believer and the atheist may both claim that it is self-evident to them that God exists (or does not exist) but only one of them has a valid claim, even if we never find out which one it is. The claim would be validated by some external criterion of what it is to be rational and to have the "correct" noetic structure.

Phillips' suspicions are aroused by Plantinga's appeal to a "correct" noetic structure. Examining the nature of his criticisms helps us to understand the assumptions of Phillips' own view; assumptions which I shall argue, turn out to be unacceptable from within a Wittgensteinian philosophical position.

Self-Evidence and Logic

Phillips provides such an extensive study of Plantinga's position because he is worried that Plantinga's criticism of foundationalism might be confused with Wittgenstein's criticisms of foundationalism in *On Certainty*.[16] What makes Plantinga's position look like Wittgenstein's (to the "philosophical unwary") is that they both reject foundationalism and they both acknowledge that God is believed in without God's existence being seen as a presupposition for which prior evidence must be sought. Wittgensteinian's agree with Plantinga that "when we turn to Scripture, it is patently obvious that belief in God is not a matter of believers entertaining a hypothesis. It is not a matter of embracing the best available explanation given the evidence at hand".[17] Phillips is concerned however, with the way Plantinga understands what it is for a proposition to be basic and here the deep differences between Plantinga and Wittgenstein come out. Although Plantinga pays lip service to the non-hypothetical nature of religious belief, Phillips worries that by the end of his account, it is very unclear as to whether religious believers are right to be certain about their beliefs. In the absence of a philosophical guarantee of rationality, believers just

---

[16] Phillips, D.Z., *Faith after Foundationalism*, p. 38
[17] Phillips, D.Z., *Faith after Foundationalism*, p. 9

have to trust that they are justified and accept that they could be wrong.

> Plantinga denies that there is something called reason, external to our practice, which can show that the practice could not be mistaken. Therefore, he must allow the possibility that he could be wrong, while acting with certainty in practice.[18]

Phillips thinks that there is something confused in the Plantinga proviso that although we can act with certainty, we still have to accept that we could be wrong. He believes that this notion of "being wrong" is completely superfluous and a legacy from the foundationalist commitment to a metaphysical conception of rationality. In certain contexts, the possibility of being mistaken is entirely absent and in such contexts therefore, the proviso that one could be mistaken makes no sense. Phillips argues that for any genuinely basic belief, the possibility of being mistaken is ruled out. That is what makes a belief qualify as basic in the first place. If religious beliefs are basic therefore, the possibility of them being mistaken is unintelligible. Plantinga's proviso is empty.

The dispute between Plantinga and Phillips is obviously centred around the notion of "basicality". Against Plantinga, Phillips 1) denies that basicality is something we can be uncertain about, 2) denies that basic propositions are those propositions which are known unconditionally to be true and 3) denies that conflicts between claims to basicality should be construed as having a truth at stake. Examining the way Phillips treats basicality is crucial for our comparison between his position and that held by Wittgenstein.

The Nature of Basicality

Phillips' main criticism of Plantinga's account of basicality is that he makes it a psychological affair.[19] In characterising it in terms of the responses of an individual he is psychologising and relativising it. Phillips claims that self-evidence is a logical property of a proposition, given to it by its place in our practices, not bestowed by the arbitrary psychological reactions of individuals. Using the example of mathematics as illustrative of all epistemic practices, Phillips maintains that being able to give the correct answer to a mathematical problem has nothing to do with what you happened to experience while you were working it out. Whether or not you had any experiences at all is irrelevant

---

[18] Phillips, D.Z., *Faith after Foundationalism*, p. 48
[19] Phillips, D.Z., *Faith after Foundationalism*, p. 26

to the question of whether the answer you give is the correct answer. That is determined by what is counted as the correct answer in the game you are playing, which is ultimately a public and shared affair. Logic has nothing to do with psychology, although the psychology may be interesting and relevant to a different enquiry. According to Phillips, Plantinga makes logic a psychological affair by connecting self-evidence to the experience of an individual:

> Plantinga makes the reaction of the individual all-important and self-evidence a mere function of it. He puts the emphasis on the individual's psychology instead of on the practice.[20]

It is important to notice the nature of Phillips criticism here. In emphasising the public nature of self-evidence (which he calls "logic") and denying "experience" as a genuine criterion for what counts as basic, Phillips is making Wittgenstein's point that it is not the experience of an individual that sets up the criterion for what can and cannot be counted as a move in the game; our rules and public practices are the criterion for that. In fact I think that Phillips mischaracterises the role "experience" plays in Plantinga's account. Phillips argues that the experience of an individual cannot be relevant to the getting of the correct answer, but here he has clearly jumped from what is self-evident to what is the correct answer. This is not an obvious equivalence. One can get the correct answer in arithmetic without finding the answer self-evident. No-one would suggest that whether an individual finds the answer self-evident is the criterion for whether it is the correct answer. To do that would take us to Wittgenstein's private language quandary (whatever we thought was right would be right and thus undermine the intelligibility of any distinction between being right and being wrong) and would also do violence to the variety of ways in which "certainty" is related to truth. We will be exploring the relationship between certainty and truth in a later section. Returning to Phillips' critique of Plantinga, we find him accusing Plantinga of muddling the separate issues of whether a proposition is self-evident to a particular person and whether the proposition is self-evident per se. "The question of whether something appears to be self-evident to a person is different from the question of whether a person can see what is self-evident. Plantinga's relativism and psychologism lead him to conflate these questions."[21]

---

[20] Phillips, D.Z., *Faith after Foundationalism*, p. 27

[21] Phillips, D.Z. *Faith after Foundationalism*, p. 27

Phillips is here clearly applying the Wittgensteinian distinction between logic and experience and accusing Plantinga of running together the logical and experiential status of a proposition; a distinction that we have seen Wittgenstein keen to enforce and which is made explicit when he writes: "The system of language is not in the category of experience. The experiences characteristic of using the system are not the system. (Compare the meaning of the word 'or' and the or-feeling)."[22]

Plantinga's position depends on the connection the foundationalist perceives between self-evidence and truth. He claims that because a proposition can only be genuinely self-evident when it is true, we could all be wrong about which propositions are self-evident because we can never have a guarantee of their truth. Phillips counters this with the claim that self-evidence isn't something we can intelligibly be wrong about. This is because it is not the property of psychology but of logic. "The self evidence of 2+1=3 does not emanate from the epistemological and phenomenological properties of the propositions considered in relation to the reactions of an isolated individual. The proposition enjoys its status in arithmetic. It is within the practice that the proposition has its application and its sense."[23]

We saw that Phillips criticised Plantinga for making self-evidence a psychological rather than a logical affair. I suggested that self-evidence can be a psychological affair. A young child for example, would not find 2+1=3 self evident, although in Phillips' sense, it would still be a proposition of logic (or a foundational proposition in mathematics). Clearly, therefore, self-evidence and logic can be distinguished. So Phillips' criticisms of Plantinga's psychologism and relativism are relevant only if we are speaking of logic (meaning) and not to self-evidence construed psychologically. Importantly, Phillips' criticisms of Plantinga are focussed on self-evidence construed logically. Here matters are not up to individual psychology. Basicality is a feature of a public practice; basic propositions understood this way would then be better classified as the rules of grammar, the rules of the game. "Basicality is not a matter of what cannot be otherwise, but a matter of what cannot be otherwise in the ways we think."[24]

There are perhaps tensions in Plantinga's account between self-evidence construed psychologically and self-evidence construed logically and Phillips'

[22] Wittgenstein, L., *Philosophical Grammar*, p. 170

[23] Phillips, D.Z., *Faith after Foundationalism*, p. 28

[24] Phillips, D.Z., *Faith after Foundationalism*, p. 36

material is a helpful contribution to clarifying where the tensions lie. Wittgenstein separates them thus: "With the word 'certain' we express complete conviction, the total absence of doubt, and thereby we seek to convince other people. That is subjective certainty. But when is something objectively certain? When a mistake is not possible. But what kind of possibility is that? Must not a mistake be logically excluded?"[25]

Phillips is right I think, to insist that whether self-evidence is construed psychologically or logically, (subjectively or objectively), in neither case does it make sense to speak of being wrong about the certainty. If an individual finds 2+1=3 self-evident, this is a feature of their psychology which they cannot be mistaken about, and whether 2+1=3 is a rule of mathematics is a feature of our practice and is not something we can be wrong about either.[26]

Plantinga of course, does not think that we could be wrong about whether 2+1=3 is a rule of mathematics (in anything but the trivial sense of getting the answer wrong). He thinks we could be wrong about whether 2+1=3, i.e. the mathematical rule could be false. Hence, if we were to come across beings who added 2+1 and didn't get 3, but got some other answer, there would be a truth at stake between us.[27] One of us would be doing arithmetic right and the other doing it wrong. So the issue between Phillips and Plantinga is not primarily over self-evidence, but how our self-evident propositions are related to truth. Because of Plantinga's commitment to the foundationalist connection between self-evidence and truth, he must allow that a proposition we think is self-evident is in fact not: "A proposition is self-evident after all, only if its true, and it certainly seems possible that we should believe a proposition is self-evident when in fact it is not."[28]

In other words, we must always be prepared to capitulate on self-evidence because self-evidence is only guaranteed by truth and such guarantees are hard come by - hence the proviso that in the absence of knowing, we must trust that our epistemic practices are correct. Phillips' criticism of this proviso takes us to the heart of his own understanding of grammar and its relationship to truth.

Accepting with Phillips that basic propositions are those which are

---

[25] Wittgenstein, L., *On Certainty*, §194

[26] There are of course boring ways in which we could be wrong about this; someone might not understand what it is for something to be a rule of mathematics or be wrong about particular examples of when something is a rule. When one is not making a mistake in either of those senses however, I am denying that there is any other sense we can make intelligible.

[27] Plantinga, A., *Reason and Belief*, p. 76

[28] Plantinga, A., *Reason and Belief*, p. 76

embedded in our practices, that they are those propositions which stand fast for us (of which 2+1=3 is one), we are now faced with the question of how these propositions stand in relation to truth. Does accepting with Phillips (and against Plantinga) that we cannot be mistaken about basicality, rule out the possibility that our basic propositions might be false? If we construe basic propositions as rules of grammar, then what we are really asking is whether our rules of grammar can turn out to be false. We shall see that Phillips answer it very clearly "No, they cannot". His argument, as we shall see, betrays his philosophical commitment to a Carnapian rather than a Wittgensteinian account of grammar.

We might lay out the assumptions of Phillips' argument against Plantinga in the following way:

1. There is a legitimate distinction between grammatical and non-grammatical propositions.
2. Grammatical propositions are necessarily true within the language-game in which they operate as grammatical propositions (which is to say that they cannot be false).
3. We can be certain which propositions are grammatical.
4. It makes no sense to think that grammatical propositions may not turn out to be grammatical because they may turn out not to be true (because grammatical propositions cannot be false; see no.2 above).
5. If two claims to grammar contradict each other, then it is not the case that this is an ordinary dispute that has a truth at stake; rather, each will be necessarily true within the language-game in which is operates as grammatical.

Basicality and Truth

We saw earlier that Wittgenstein was happy to separate meaning claims from claims about the world on contextual grounds. A proposition was awarded a grammatical status if it was being used to teach or explain meaning. Its grammatical status was secured by the fact that it functioned as a rule in a game. There was nothing in the *content* of the proposition that decided its grammatical status because unlike Carnap, Wittgenstein did not allow that some propositions acquire meanings from experience and others from conventional definition. Wittgenstein ruled out questions about the truth or rightness of a grammatical proposition by showing that they made no sense when applied to grammar. We saw Wittgenstein's argument against the possibility of showing a rule of grammar to be justified; one would have to get *outside* the meaning it constituted to show that it was correct, and the idea of getting outside meaning in that way can be given no content. Because we have no method for testing or justifying a grammatical proposition, it makes no sense on Wittgenstein's account to speak of grammar as true or false, correct or incorrect. These concepts cannot be meaningfully apply to grammar as grammar. We also saw that this did not commit Wittgenstein to the stronger semantic view that grammatical propositions have a purely stipulated content and hence cannot be separated from how things are in the world like they did for Carnap. For Wittgenstein, meaning and ontology run on different axes. When we are talking about meaning, we are investigating what it makes sense to say; when thinking about reality, we are thinking about what there is. Although the two are related, (one can only think about reality if one has a meaningful language in which to do so and hence there will be limits on how we can think about reality, constrained by the limits of our language) they do not form a single whole for Wittgenstein as they did for Carnap.

That Wittgenstein was prepared to both deny basic propositions the possibility of being mistaken, and at the same time affirm that they could be true or false shows that he conceded a gap between meaning and ontology. Not only can we find explicit examples of Wittgenstein conceding the gap, it should not surprise us to find him doing so because as I have already argued, it is a gap one finds already there in ordinary practice and therefore to deny it must be to commit oneself to a theoretical rather than a descriptive semantics. For Carnap, playing the game right was the only criterion we had for "rightness". Wittgenstein could not be more explicit about the difference between playing the game aright and saying something true. In *On Certainty* he writes:

> If I were to say 'I have never been on the moon - but that I may be mistaken' that would be idiotic. For even the thought that I might have been transported there, by unknown means, in my sleep, would not give me any right to speak of a possible mistake here. I play the game wrong if I do . . . I have a right to say 'I can't be making a mistake about this' *even if I am in error*.[29]

and again:

> Can I be making a mistake, for example, in thinking that the words of which this sentence

---

[29] Wittgenstein, L., *On Certainty*, §§662-3

is composed are English words whose meaning I know? . . . It is simply the normal case, to be incapable of mistake about the designation of certain things in one's mother tongue . . . 'I can't be making a mistake about it' simply characterises one kind of assertion.[30]

It could be objected here that there is an important difference between the logical status of empirical propositions that are exempt from doubt, and real grammatical propositions which don't seem to have anything to do with the empirical world. This objection requires that we acknowledge that there is a difference between propositions that are certain because no possible experience could bring us to doubt them (like mathematics) and propositions for which experience could be relevant but is in the present absent. But notice that Wittgenstein concedes no such difference:

> I cannot be making a mistake about 12×12=144. And now one cannot contrast mathematical certainty with the relative uncertainty of empirical propositions . . . can I prophesy that men will never throw over the present arithmetical propositions, never say that now at last they know how the matter stands? Yet would that justify a doubt on our part? [31]

Wittgenstein's distinction between "being mistaken" (understood as not playing the game right) and "being false" is important to keep in mind as we return to the debate between Plantinga and Phillips. Plantinga wanted to keep alive the possibility that we could be mistaken about which of our beliefs are basic and was criticised by Phillips on the grounds that it made no sense to think of us being mistaken about basicality. We can now see how both Plantinga and Phillips can be right. The possibility of being *mistaken* does not apply to basic propositions while they perform their role as basic propositions. As rules, they are the criterion for what counts as right and wrong in the game. This is what it is to belong on the meaning-axis. But there is nothing intrinsic to basic propositions that denies them truth-aptness. As grammar we cannot speak of them being either true and false. But from a non-grammatical perspective, the possibility of them being false is a real one. It could turn out for example, that everyone but me is an automaton. If it did, this would render false the proposition "the world is full of human beings" (a proposition which currently qualifies as a grammatical rule).[32] That proposition could even at this

---

[30] Wittgenstein, L., *On Certainty*, §630-1

[31] Wittgenstein, L., *On Certainty*, §§651-2

[32] "To adopt a proposition as unshakeably certain - I want to say - means to use it as a grammatical rule; this removes uncertainty from it." Wittgenstein, L., *Foundations of Mathematics*, p. 170

moment be false, but the possibility does not require that our language-game includes doubt. "Doubt gradually loses its sense. The language-game is just like that."[33]

Thus when Phillips accuses Plantinga of appealing to a metaphysical criterion of rationality in order to substantiate his view that basic beliefs could turn out not to be basic after all, we can see that there is a confusion in both accounts. Basicality isn't something we can be wrong about; on that Phillips is right. But basicality doesn't guarantee truth, nor are basic propositions in themselves devoid of truth-aptness; here Plantinga is right. That Phillips does not acknowledge the possibility of basic beliefs being true or false is not insignificant. Phillips' denial is motivated by a commitment he has to a particular understanding of the nature of grammar. It is an understanding more Carnapian than Wittgensteinian, as can be brought out by examining how Phillips characterises disputes between different grammatical systems. Again, his dialectic with Plantinga can help us bring out the nature of his view.

World Pictures and Pictures of the World

We have seen that in the absence of a criterion for rationality, Plantinga suggests that we can only trust that our epistemic practices (basic beliefs) are not wrong. Phillips is critical of the conception of "trust" Plantinga seems to employ, arguing that when it comes to our epistemic practices, we just have to accept them for what they are. The concept of "trust" here is idle as we have no idea of what it would be like to be wrong. "If showing that our practices are correct is confused, so is showing that they are incorrect."[34] Phillip's position here reflects Wittgenstein's suggestion that when we attempt to justify either our language or our practice, we reach the end of possible justifications by accepting the basic forms of life that give rise to such practices. It certainly makes no sense to speak of justifying our forms of life just because that would mean getting outside ourselves (another way of trying to "get outside meaning") and we have condemned that idea as unintelligible. But if we accept that there is no metaphysical meaning or "way things are in themselves", do we have to accept that there is no sense in which we can doubt our practices? The success of Phillips' critique of Plantinga depends on denying any such sense.

---

[33] Wittgenstein, L., *On Certainty*, §56
[34] Phillips, D.Z., *Faith after Foundationalism*, p. 25

In the previous section we saw how Wittgenstein was prepared to separate certainty from truth, thus suggesting the intelligibility of a gap between our ways of speaking and the way things are. Obviously it wasn't a metaphysical gap. In acknowledging the possibility that everyone might be an automaton except me, I am not slipping into metaphysics. In acknowledging that in future times, we may not accept that $12 \times 12 = 144$, I am not invoking a metaphysical gap between how we currently say things are and how things actually are. I am merely accommodating the ordinary sense in which we do come to reject the ways in which we speak about the world, and in doing so label the old ways "false". When Phillips argues that "Plantinga's purpose is the discovery of what is in fact true. He wants to give a correct picture of the world", we can accept that "this is very different from Wittgenstein's conception of philosophy"[35] if Plantinga is indeed trying to establish a metaphysically "correct picture of the world". Is that what Plantinga is trying to do? I think not and here is why I think not.

Plantinga is a religious believer. He believes certain things about the world - namely that there is a God who created it, and a God who cares about the human race and a God who can hear him when he prays and is interested in the details of his life and so on. Plantinga realises that although these beliefs are held with unconditional certainty by him (they are basic to his noetic structure), not everyone believes that there is such a God. He accepts that his religious beliefs may not be true. When an atheist enters into discussion with him therefore, he willingly concedes that one of them has the true belief. Either there is a God or there isn't. There is a truth at stake between them, even if neither can establish which truth it is.

Is there anything in these trivial remarks which suggests Plantinga is metaphysically confused? Yes! says Phillips. Thinking that there is a truth at stake between believer and unbeliever is to think that there is a reality that our language must answer to. This is confused because it fails to recognise that the language itself constitutes what is meant by reality. The problem says Phillips, is that "the Reformed epistemologist has faith that our practices refer to reality, and by so doing, misses the references to reality made within them".[36]

What is it that Plantinga, as a religious believer, fails to recognise when he worries that perhaps his beliefs are false? According to Phillips he fails to recognise that the language doesn't refer to reality but contains references to

---

[35] Phillips, D.Z., *Faith after Foundationalism*, pp. 54-5
[36] Phillips, D.Z., *Faith after Foundationalism*, p. 135

reality within it, and that it is confused therefore to think in terms of it possibly being false.[37] The only way to understand this criticism is to read Phillips here as arguing that religious language does not refer to anything independent of itself but that it constitutes what it means to speak of God. There is in fact no God about whom it speaks. Instead the statement "God is love" is part of what we mean by the word "God". In other words, religious language does not describe or refer to anything; it constitutes the realities that we call religious. That this is clearly Phillips' view is well evidenced by remarks such as "retaining the view of language as being in itself, a set of descriptions, is to retain at least half of the metaphysical picture . . . In speaking of God we are not confined to sets of descriptions which approximate to, but never capture his reality . . . On the contrary, our talk of God is constitutive of what we mean by divine reality".[38]

What Plantinga does wrong in thinking that his beliefs could be false therefore is to confuse rules of language with statements about reality. In treating the proposition "God is love" as a claim that refers to and describes (either truly or falsely) some powerful being, he misunderstands the nature of the claim.

We saw in the previous chapter that although the distinction between rules of grammar and statements about the world is evident in Wittgenstein's work, the distinction has no metaphysical substance. Wittgenstein's criterion for whether a proposition belongs to grammar is whether in its context of use it is being used to explain a meaning (define). He had no difficulty in accepting that a rule of grammar could both function as a meaning constituent and a statement about the world. We also saw how Wittgenstein's position on grammar differed to that of Carnap. For the latter, a proposition was grammatical if no experience could be directly appealed to in order to verify or falsity it, and yet it legitimately belonged to a scientific framework that had explanatory force. On Wittgenstein's view therefore, it would be quite intelligible to suggest that statements about God are both rules for the use of the word; they define what "God" means, and that they are propositions which could be true or false. Of course because such propositions are not able to be verified or falsified, we cannot know whether they are true or false. But this is only a concern for

---

[37] The way in which the denial works in Phillips' account can be seen also in Winch's: "The discussion of what it is for a name to function in a certain way in a symbolism is a discussion of what it is to have a reference." (Malcolm's summary of Winch in Malcolm. N., *Nothing is Hidden*, p. 33).

[38] Phillips, D.Z., *Faith after Foundationalism*, p. 146

theorists like Carnap who maintain that we must be able to decide on the truth value of a proposition in order for it to be meaningful. The important point here is that in calling a proposition grammatical, we have not removed it from the axis of ontology. We have simply pointed out the role it has with regard to meaning.

If, according to Wittgenstein, a proposition can take its place both on a meaning and an ontological axis, what is Plantinga doing wrong when he claims that his religious beliefs might be false? Certainly, if he is holding the *meaning* of religious language accountable to an independent reality, then he is engaged in a confused activity for as we have seen, meaning is constituted by practices and rules and there is no getting *outside* it in the sense required. But Plantinga is clearly not saying that religious language means what it does because it successfully refers. Given the meaning of the language, he wants to know whether it is true. To deny him that right, one must deny that the language speaks of anything about which it could be true. And that is what Phillips does. His argument runs like this:

If we are to treat our grammatical propositions as beliefs about reality, we need a conception of how things are which is independent of all human practices.[39] But we do not have such a conception because the conception of "how things are independent of all human practices" is confused. Therefore, we cannot treat our grammatical propositions as if they are beliefs about reality. We must treat them instead as constitutive of reality. The notion of them being mistaken or false is incoherent because they could only be so if there is a way things are independent of how we speak (which there can't be because that idea doesn't make sense). Because that idea doesn't make sense, we cannot speak of our practices being mistaken. He writes:

> What can 'mistaken' or 'incomplete' mean in this context? After all, what is discovered is also of necessity, in the context of an epistemic practice. But in that case, how do we know that this context or discovery takes us closer or further away from how things are? To know that we would need to know that the epistemic practice which we call correct or complete is nearer to reality than the one we are correcting . . . It is no good either saying that we simply trust that the new of modified epistemic practice is correct or more complete, since our problem is the prior one of giving any sense to the terms 'correct' or 'complete' . . . we need a relation to reality of the epistemic practices outside any context where we could speak of checking whether something is real or not.[40]

---

[39] Phillips, D.Z., *Faith after Foundationalism*, p. 56 and p. 59
[40] Phillips, D.Z., *Faith after Foundationalism*, p. 60

Phillips maintains that in order to make sense of possibility that our epistemic practices are unreliable or wrong, "we need a conception of 'how things are' which is independent of all human practices".[41] But this is false. We saw that Wittgenstein could freely entertain the possibility that some day we might come to reject mathematical propositions that are currently embedded in our practices. To do so he didn't need to articulate an alternative conception of mathematics. We can see that Phillips is just picking up on Wittgenstein's criticism of attempts to justify our language, claiming that idea is unintelligible because it implies a second language which can speak about the first and show it to be justified. Wittgenstein's second (ideal) language is the equivalent of Phillips' conception of how things are independent of all human practices; both can be shown to be empty as philosophical assumptions but we must be careful in how we characterise the consequences of rejecting such a notion.

What Phillips does not acknowledge is that it is a feature of ordinary practice to speak in terms of being mistaken when it comes to epistemic practices. The task for the Wittgensteinian philosopher is not to deny the intelligibility of such talk but to show (elucidate) what such talk amounts to. That Phillips' account is inadequate in accounting for the ordinary concept of "being mistaken" comes out most explicitly when he characterises the ordinary usage as a transcendental use. When Plantinga, as a religious believer, claims that the unbeliever is mistaken in not believing in God, Phillips claims that this is an illegitimate appeal to a transcendental/philosophical concept of mistake which mischaracterises our language as attempting to interpret an independent reality. Phillips writes:

> The difference between religious and non-religious perspectives is not a philosophical difference. What separates them in their beliefs and convictions is constitutive of their different ways of life. These different ways of living are not interpretations of anything more ultimate than themselves. It is one of the deepest temptations in philosophy to so regard them.[42]

Does Plantinga think that the difference between the believer and non-believer is a philosophical difference? He certainly thinks that there is a truth at stake between them, but what makes that belief a confused "philosophical" one? According to Phillips, it is the assumption that there is something more at stake between them than the mere fact that they have adopted different world

---

[41] Phillips, D.Z., *Faith after Foundationalism*, p. 59
[42] Phillips, D.Z., *Faith after Foundationalism*, p. 107

views or perspectives. Plantinga's commitment to the illegitimate philosophical position is shown in his willingness to accuse holders of non-religious perspectives of being mistaken:

> Since epistemologies are regarded as theories or hypotheses about the nature of reality which are either true or false, Reformed philosophers cannot tolerate a plurality of noetic structures. There is an issue of correctness or incorrectness involved. There can only be one true theory of knowledge . . . In some sense or other it is clear that, for Reformed epistemology, the non-religious structures have to be deficient.[43]

And Phillips continues:

> Can Reformed epistemologists say that the adherents to non-religious noetic structures are mistaken? . . . What common ground can be appealed to if neutral common ground is unavailable? The answer of Reformed philosophers is: the common ground which actually represents the situation accurately, namely, Christianity.[44]

Phillips' argument against Plantinga is as follows: For the disagreement between religious and non-religious perspectives to be genuine (have a truth at stake), they would need to share a common ground. But the notion of a common ground cannot be made intelligible because it implies a way things are independently of either of these perspectives. The Reformers give content to the empty philosophical notion by making Christianity itself the common ground. In doing so, they transform a religious perspective into a metaphysical one. The criticism is made explicit here:

> Reformed epistemology . . . [resists] the notion of a sovereign reason to which religious belief is answerable . . . At the same time, however, within the Reformed Epistemologists view of religious belief there is the conception of a God who is sovereign over all things, reason included. There is a tension therefore, between Plantinga's emphasis on negative apologetics and the temptation to think that belief in an all-embracing God should yield, in the Christian philosopher, an all-embracing metaphysical system.[45]

It is not clear how we are to cash in on the idea of a "common ground" however. This is important because it is what makes it possible for Phillips to accuse Plantinga of turning a religious system into a metaphysical one. The criterion for what counts as a neutral ground is what is problematic. The

---

[43] Phillips, D.Z., *Faith after Foundationalism*, p. 97
[44] Phillips, D.Z., *Faith after Foundationalism*, p. 99
[45] Phillips, D.Z., *Faith after Foundationalism*, p. 97

religious believer, for example, will consider it enough that the unbeliever is a human being who belongs to the world that they see as God's world. That the unbeliever doesn't see it this way is not enough for us to say that they do not share a common ground. The dispute between them surely gets its importance from the fact that the each one thinks that their way of life is the right one. Unbelievers think believers are mistaken when they think there is a God and believers think unbelievers are mistaken. The debate between them is over whether one should be religious or not and we do not have to load this dispute with transcendental normativity as Phillips accuses Plantinga of doing.

This idea that genuine disputes are only possible if disputants share a neutral conception of reality is problematic. We can see this particularly when we try to make sense of ordinary disputes between conflicting world views. Phillips thinks that even here, talk of being mistaken or being right is confused. Apparently, for an individual to believe that their world picture is the right one, they too require a conception of "how things are" independent of all practices. But this is just false. Not only is it false, by insisting on it Phillips betrays a philosophical bias towards a Carnapian stance on the relationship of language to reality. It contains an implicit assumption that the notion of "how things are" can be given no sense other than "how we say things are". Phillips clearly holds that the giving up of a framework belief is not the giving up of a belief about reality, but a giving up of a way of conceptualising reality (or the reality it constitutes). It is not to move from falsity to truth, but merely from one system (world) to another. Phillips' illustrative case is an example from Wittgenstein and it usefully brings out how he characterises such shifts:

> Wittgenstein says: 'Men have believed that they could make rain. Why should not a king be brought up in the belief that the world began with him? And if Moore and this king were to meet and discuss, could Moore really prove his belief to be the right one?'[46]

For Wittgenstein, the example is designed to bring out what is involved in the shifting from one world view to another. Because of the nature of world views, namely that their foundational propositions cannot be proven because they are what holds the view together, we cannot prove one view to be correct. In accepting an alternative world view, we are converted to a different way of seeing. There is nothing in Wittgenstein's account to suggest that Moore. has no right to think that the king has a false belief when he thinks that the world

---

[46] Phillips, D.Z., *Faith after Foundationalism*, p. 66

came into existence when he did, nor that Moore cannot think that his world view is the right one. Things are different with Phillips' however. He tells us that Moore would be trying to awaken the king to his way of looking at the world, not because Moore thinks that the king looks at it the wrong way but because "the way the king looks at it may seem awkward and cumbersome". In other words, Moore wants to persuade the king that the world didn't come into existence when he did because that view is too complicated. Really? Surely the only sense we can make of Moore persuading the king that the earth has been in existence much longer than he has is because he believes that to be true and therefore the king's belief false! Phillips denies that what we have between Moore and the king are contradictory accounts as to the age of the world. Rather, we have two different conceptions of "the world"; one which says it is very old and one which doesn't. Phillips writes:

> Wittgenstein cannot be read as meaning that in the case of this clash, 'the world' is what the two views have as their common topic, standing as competing hypotheses or descriptions of it. If that were the case, then Moore would be saying that he had already checked his way of looking at the world and found it more satisfying than the king's.[47]

Why don't Moore and the king have competing hypotheses about the world? Phillips' answer is that for Moore's belief to be a hypothesis, he would have to be able to check (confirm) it and this is not something he can do. Why? Because the possibility of confirming or disconfirming makes no sense here. Although "one wants to say 'all of my experiences show that it is so'",[48] this is precisely what makes it impossible for there to be a separate experience that could either confirm or disconfirm our belief that the world is very old. "The proposition to which they [our experiences] point itself belongs to a particular interpretation of them."[49] In other words, our belief that the world has existed for a long time is part of what it is for us to think about the world. It belongs to the grammar (the meaning) of "the world". The king has a different conception of "the world", thus, the two views do not have "the world" as their common topic.

The conclusion we are to draw from this is that the disagreement between the king and Moore is a disagreement in meaning, not in truth. Because they mean something different by "the world", their dispute is apparently, not about

---

[47] Phillips, D.Z., *Faith after Foundationalism*, p. 66

[48] Wittgenstein, L., *On Certainty*, §145

[49] Wittgenstein, L., *On Certainty*, §145, brackets mine

some feature of the world (its age). Phillips writes: "what Moore tries to do in relation to the king is not so much correct him, but initiate him into an interest in history."[50]

But isn't Moore trying to correct the king? Isn't initiating him into an interest in history part of what it means to correct him? The reason for Phillips' denial here takes us to the very heart of his philosophical bias. He denies that Moore's belief about the age of the world is a hypothesis because there is no evidence that can legitimately confirm or disconfirm it. All the evidence is simply part of Moore's understanding of "the world". We might agree with Phillips that a hypothesis is something that invites verification or falsification. Do we also have to agree that when a proposition cannot be so verified, it is not a hypothesis? Or alternatively, do we have to agree that for a proposition to be about the world, it must be a hypothesis? i.e. there must be some evidence that could confirm or disconfirm it? Phillips' argument takes the following form:

1. The belief that the world is very old cannot be verified or falsified.
2. If a proposition cannot be verified or falsified, it belongs to logic (meaning) rather than description.
3. Therefore, the proposition that "the world is very old" is part of the meaning of "the world" and not a statement about the world.
4. A proposition of meaning cannot be true or false.
5. Therefore the proposition that the world has existed for a long time cannot be true or false.
6. Therefore someone who denies that the world has existed for a long time is not denying a truth about the world. They either don't mean what we mean by "the world" or they haven't yet learnt what we mean by "the world".

To claim that Moore and the king mean different things by "the world" is to adopt a positive semantics. Phillips does so for reasons akin to Carnap's. He wants to rule out bad philosophical/metaphysical questions which imply that there is some way the world is independent of the ways in which we speak about it. He thinks that for there to be truth at stake between Moore and the king, we have to concede this. But do we? Surely it is perfectly intelligible to claim that the dispute between Moore and the king is over the age of the world. We do not need a conception of a world independent of all the ways in which

---

[50] Phillips, D.Z., *Faith after Foundationalism*, p. 67

we speak about it. Clashes take place within our ways of speaking. In his willingness to characterise disputes as clashes in meanings rather than beliefs, Phillips' position is more reminiscent of Carnap's than it is of Wittgenstein's.

We saw in the previous chapter how Wittgenstein's semantic commitments can be distinguished from Carnap's, most notably because Wittgenstein will not commit himself to the positive, theoretical assumptions embedded in Carnap's position. These include the provision of a strict criterion for when a proposition belongs to meaning (grammar). It was because of this that Carnap could adopt a meaning imperialism, claiming effectively that different grammatical rules represented the boundaries between different kingdoms of meaning. One can choose the kingdom one wants to live in, but it makes no sense to think that in doing so, one is choosing between competing kingdoms. Each brings promises of its own. So for Carnap, migrating from one kingdom to another amounted to rejecting a kingdom of meaning (perhaps because one no longer wanted what it offered), rather than giving up a particular belief.

When speaking of the disagreement between the religious believer and non-believer, it is hard not to recognise a similar theme when Phillips writes:

> the gap between what the believer wants to say and what the unbeliever denies is itself a grammatical gap. To reject religion, or to come to God, is not to reject or embrace a hypothesis within a common way of looking at things, but, rather, to reject or embrace a whole way of looking at things.[51]

Plantinga's mistake, then, is to think that his religious perspective is the correct perspective. According to Phillips, he can't think that unless he has access to an absolute criterion of "correct". But when Moore converted the king, did he need an absolute criterion of what counted as the correct world view? No. It is simply an ordinary feature of our commitments that we hold them to be correct, and here "correct" is not being used in a transcendental sense. It is this ordinary conception of correct which undermines the substantive nature of Phillips' distinction between grammar and beliefs. It suggests that there is a legitimate sense in which grammar may be construed as ontologically entailing, even while we acknowledge its privileged status as grammar. If this is the case then there is something suspect about Phillips distinction between grammar and truths, which in turn undermines his criticisms of the reformers. The distinction Phillips requires is gestured at here:

---

[51] Phillips, D.Z., *Faith after Foundationalism*, p. 80

Wittgenstein's conception of a world picture must be distinguished from Reformed Epistemology's conception of pictures of the world. At the heart of the disagreement is the conception of epistemic practices as descriptions or hypotheses concerning reality. To put the matter in Wittgenstein's terms, the issue is whether the different grammars of the ways in which we speak are to be understood as a set of beliefs or descriptions of how reality or the world really is.[52]

But in pointing out difficulties in providing criterion for world pictures, or different grammars, I have tried to make problematic Phillips' distinction between world pictures and pictures of the world. The distinction is of course just another way of distinguishing between rules of grammar and truths about the world. We can pursue its problematic nature further by examining the way in which Phillips connects religious language to religious experience.

The Reality of God

The Neo-Wittgensteinians maintain that it is the result of an investigation into language-use that one is forced to deny the intelligibility of God existing in any other sense than that the concept "God" has meaning. Words only have the meanings we give them and we cannot given the concept of God actually existing any sense because we cannot verify or falsify the claim that "God exists". It is no use claiming that we can make sense of God existing in an ontological sense if we cannot show what such a claim would mean. What they don't realise is that their commitment to the view that words only have the meanings we give them is itself a form of meaning imperialism. This is nowhere more evident than in their repeated motto that "the distinctions between real and unreal get their sense from within epistemic practices"[53] and that "what the 'existence' of whatever it is amounts to is expressed (shows itself) in the way people apply the language they speak".[54]

We have seen that when Wittgenstein insists that what is real and unreal (what is meaningful and meaningless) *shows* itself, he is not giving us a theory about what exists (is "real") but emphasising that the limits of language can only be seen and not theorised about. We can therefore distinguish two different senses of "real":

---

[52] Phillips, D.Z., *Faith after Foundationalism*, p. 56
[53] Phillips, D.Z., *Faith after Foundationalism*, p. xiv
[54] Winch, P., *Trying to Make Sense*, Oxford, Blackwell, 1987, p. 114

"x is real" = "'x' is meaningful."
"x is real" = "x exists."

The Neo-Wittgensteinians deny that the second sense of "real" applies in the God case because we cannot establish the connection between "God" and the existence of anything. The notion of God's reality therefore has no sense other than that "God" is meaningful. So God's existence is not an existential property but a relation to a meaning framework (language-game). Users of religious language are committed to the existence of God. Denying God's existence is the equivalent to rejecting God talk as unintelligible, and hence is not really a denial of the existence of anything in particular, but a rejection of the linguistic framework in which "God" gets its meaning.

Gareth Moore states the view clearly: "The question whether God exists is a question whether to adopt the concept 'God' (the word and its use) into the language, or retain it. For me, the question of the existence of God is the question whether I can find a use for the word 'God' in my talk . . . there is nothing, exists nothing, that can be called God."[55] And the connection with verificationism is made explicit as he continues: "The question whether God exists is not a factual question, a question about what we might *find*."[56]

Effectively the Neo-Wittgensteinians argue that the only sense in which "reality" can mean "ontological existence", is in the case of physical objects. The onus is on the believer or theologian to show that in the case of God, "existence" has the same sense as it does when applied to physical objects. But how do we show our language has content/meaning? By proving that it does? Because the believer can't show that "exists" applies to God, we cannot make sense of God "existing". To think that existence can apply to God is to confuse the grammar of God-talk with the grammar of physical objects as Rhees points out:

> We use 'it exists' chiefly in connection with physical objects and anyway we use it where we can ask whether it is exists or not. This goes with the sense of finding out whether it exists. Now the 'it', whatever it is, is something we could identify in such an investigation . . . - by, for example, finding out. [57]

Notice that there are ambiguities in the point made here by Rhees. Although

---

[55] Moore, G., *Believing in God*, pp. 39-40
[56] Moore, G., *Believing in God*, p. 39
[57] Rhees, R., *Without Answers*, London, Routledge & Kegan Paul, 1969, p. 131

he begins by suggesting that we use "exist" when we can ask of something whether it exists, he moves very quickly to qualify this, suggesting that "x exists" goes with a sense of whether we can "find out" whether x exists. The qualification is not surprising as it is obvious that in the God-case, which is the case Rhees wants to rule out, we *can* (and do) ask about the existence of x (God). That criterion alone will not do the work for Rhees. But his qualification has problems of its own. By connecting "exists" with "finding out" he jeopardises the sense in which we do speak of existence in connection with objects. We don't for example, "find out" that trees exist, or that chairs exist. Wittgenstein makes this point:

> Children do not learn that books exist, that armchairs exist, etc. etc. Later, questions about the existence of things do of course arise. 'Is there such a thing as a unicorn?' and so on. But such a question is only possible because as a rule no corresponding question presents itself. For how does one know how to set about satisfying oneself of the existence of unicorns? How did one learn the method for determining whether something exists or not?[58]

If "existence" is to be relevant only where "finding out" is possible then the ordinary sense in which we speak of objects like trees and chairs existing is jeopardised. We do not "find out" that they exist. The whole idea of finding out has no sense here. But if that is the case, it is not clear how Rhees can make the distinction at all. How can we rule that "existence" ontologically construed is only applicable when we can "find out" whether the object exists or not? Certainly it does not look as though a descriptive semantics will establish this. And if it will not, then Rhees is doing more than merely describing grammar. He is drawing substantive conclusions from it. A similar illegitimacy plagues Phillips' position when he too concludes that "talk of God's existence or reality cannot be construed as talk about the existence of an object. Neither can questions about whether we mean the same by 'God' be construed as whether we are referring to the same object".[59] We might want to ask why talk of God can't be construed as talk of the existence of an object (or being)? It could after all be argued that the way religious believers interact with God is not so very different to how we ordinarily interact with other people; they attribute actions to him, they talk to him, claim he can communicate with them and so on. Talking to God is not exactly like talking to another person but are the differences enough to warrant the Neo-Wittgensteinian denial that talking to

---

[58] Wittgenstein, L., *On Certainty*, §477

[59] Phillips, D.Z., *Religion Without Explanation*, p. 174

God is anything like talking to or about another person?[60] Their position rests on the assumption that because we cannot identify God as an existing being, coming to believe in him is not to come to believe in an existing being. The grammar of coming to believe in God is spelt out here by Phillips:

> Praising, thanking, confessing, asking, and adoring before God may have meant little to a man. Suddenly it means everything to him. He says that God has become a reality in his life. Has this come about by his discovering an object? Hardly. What has happened is that he has found God in a praise, a thanksgiving, a confessing and an asking which were not his before. And if coming to God is not coming to see that an object one thought did not exist does in fact exist, neither is losing faith in God coming to see that an object one thought existed does not in fact exist.[61]

As a description of religious conversion, there is nothing controversial in what Phillips says here. No one comes to believe that God exists by discovering that an object exists.[62] What is controversial is the conclusion that because God is not a discoverable object, God is not something that "exists" at all. Indeed the Neo-Wittgensteinians go further and rule it impossible that God could exist.[63] Is it impossible that God exists? How could we establish that it is impossible? The Neo-Wittgensteinians argue that it is impossible because it is meaningless; the concept of "existence" relevant here cannot be shown to have any content. I want to suggest that ruling out meaningfulness on the grounds that we cannot prove meaningfulness is itself a form of meaning imperialism. Like Carnap and Wittgenstein, the Neo-Wittgensteinians are keen to rule out incoherent metaphysical remarks. But like Carnap and unlike Wittgenstein, they are willing to define meaningfulness theoretically. What this means is that they are not merely content to describe grammar. They think that a grammatical investigation can yield more than a trivial result. It can seemingly yield truths about meaning. One such truth is that "existence" can only be applied to objects whose existence we can discover. Substantive conclusions do not follow from grammar however, unless one has a theory of meaning in place. Where their work shows most promise is where their grammatical reminders of the nature of religious language are used to show how philosophy of religion tends to be preoccupied with the wrong sort of

---

[60] Rhees, R., *Without Answers*, p. 132

[61] Phillips, D.Z., *Religion Without Explanation*, p. 181

[62] Where "discovering" is given the empirical gloss, as in the case of discovering that I have a half-sister, or we discover another planet.

[63] See Phillips, D.Z., *Religion Without Explanation*, p. 149

questions. It is certainly right to point out that the philosophical preoccupation with proofs for God's existence and the rationality of religious beliefs does little to increase our understanding of the nature of religious activity. The work done by the Neo-Wittgensteinians, because of their sensitivity to grammatical differences is a valuable contribution to that enterprise. If I am right about their theoretical assumptions, however, we must learn to distinguish between grammatical insights and the conclusions drawn from them by the Neo-Wittgensteinians.

Not only are the conclusions drawn by the Neo-Wittgensteinians theoretical, the meaning theory they seem to have adopted is suspiciously Carnapian. Their emphasis on "finding out" lends itself to a verificationist dichotomy between implicit and explicit meaning. Why, according to Phillips, is God's existence not like the existence of another person? Because "in the case of God, there is no question of anything like a material investigation to find out whether there is a God".[64] And because there is no material investigation, what we *mean* by God's existence cannot be the same as what we mean by the existence of another person. Notice the move Phillips makes, from the admission that God's existence cannot be verified, to the conclusion that we cannot mean by "God's existence" what we mean when we speak about existence in connection with objects whose existence we can verify. This move is central to their account of what "God" means. The argument seems to be that because we cannot verify that God exists, we cannot know what it would mean for God to exist independent of knowing what the word "God" means. God and his existence therefore become conceptually connected (implicitly defined because it cannot be made explicit). So when a believer claims that "God exists" they are really claiming that "God" has meaning. They are not claiming that that anything in particular exists. Existence or reality in relation to God is guaranteed by (is internal to) the meaning of religious language. It is the conflation of the two senses of "reality" that we can reject.

Conflating Grammar and Beliefs

Because of his uneasy alliance with a Carnapian semantics, Phillips' account of religious language as grammar is full of ambiguities. This is most notable in his conflation of two different senses of absolute. He tells us that "the reality

---

[64] Phillips, D.Z., *Faith after Foundationalism*, p. 203

of God is absolute - it decides what it makes sense to say: it is the common measure, not what is measured", apparently drawing a distinction between a metaphysically confused view which claims that our language about God attempts to match up to something (measure God) and the preferred view that our concept of God itself determines what we can and cannot say about God. According to Phillips, the wrong thing to say is that in calling God's reality absolute we are saying that some particular reality is absolute because this would involve particularising an absolute reality and thereby make it relative (in Phillips' jargon, we would be measuring a reality and calling it absolute which is impossible because no reality we can measure could be absolute). The right thing to say, according to Phillips, is that the concept of "God" functions as a rule and in doing so guarantees that "God" is the measure and not what is measured. In other words, Phillips seems to think that the only way of doing justice to the religious idea that God's nature is absolute, is to classify it as a grammatical rule. Grammatical rules decide what it does and does not make sense to say and in this way, God's reality can decide what it makes sense to say.

We can see the ambiguities in this position by comparing it with an uncontroversial grammatical rule. To call a rule absolute is to draw attention to its role as a rule ("absolute" is being used synonymously with "necessary" here). To call a rule necessary is to pick out its role in meaning. It is to make an a posteriori observation into language use. To call God absolute is to make a claim about God. Of course one can say that for the believer, "God" does operate as a standard in their lives. Their religious beliefs often provide them with their ideals on how to live and what they should do, so in this sense we can agree with Phillips that "the reality of God decides what it makes sense to say", and this would also be a harmless a posteriori observation about the place of religious beliefs in the lives of believers. But Phillips clearly doesn't mean to have made *that* observation. Remember we are enquiring into what determines the difference between sense and nonsense. So the proposition "the reality of God is absolute" may be construed as a rule when it is used to remind someone who perhaps says "the reality of God is one among many" that this is not true. That person is being reminded of what we say about God and to think of his reality as one among many is to say something unacceptable. In this context, we remind the offender what they should say about God's reality. We are reminding them what they must say if they are to speak of God. But in reminding someone what they must say if they are to speak about God, aren't we also reminding them what it is we think about God? Just as reminding someone that "every rod has a length" would be to remind them that this is how we speak about rods, but it would also tell them that this is what rods are like. Speaking about words and speaking about objects can come to the same thing. Grammatical rules can be understood as making statements about reality. Indeed, they must be understood as such if one is to do justice to how language operates in ordinary practice.

If the difference between grammar and description is as unstable as I have been suggesting, then there is something very wrong about dividing disputes into those which are about language and those which are about the world. The dispute between Moore and the king is about the age of the world and the dispute between believer and unbeliever is about the existence of a being who listens to them when they pray, who created the world and so on. Phillips' insistence therefore that "if doctrinal statements are seen as grammatical remarks, [doctrinal] capitulation would take the form of the admission that one had not been speaking properly about God" rather than the capitulation "where one man sees that a description of an object he has provided is incorrect"[65] is uninteresting. The distinction between "speaking properly" about an object and speaking truthfully about an object, does not emerge in ordinary discourse. The distinction has substance for the Neo-Wittgensteinians because they conflate ontology and meaning. Whether or not religious believers or theologians take themselves to be talking about the same object or different objects cannot be decided by concentrating on what it is for something to be an object because not everyone will agree even on that. The conflation is evident in the following passage from Rhees:

> If one lays emphasis . . . on the fact that 'God' is a substantive, and especially if one goes on . . . to say that it is a proper name, then the natural thing will be to assume that meaning the same by 'God' is something like meaning the same by 'the sun' or meaning the same by 'Churchill'. You might even want to use some such phrase as 'stands for' the same. But nothing of the sort will do here. Questions about 'meaning the same' in connection with the names of physical objects are connected with the kind of criteria to which we may appeal in saying that this is the same object – 'that is the same planet as I saw in the southwest last night', 'that is the same car that was standing here this morning'. Suppose someone said 'the word 'God' stands for a different object now'. What would that mean?[66]

Whether we can point to an object or not, does not determine whether we mean the same by our language. There is a conflation between "meaning the

---

[65] Phillips, D.Z., *Faith after Foundationalism*, p. 213
[66] Rhees, R., *Without Answers*, pp. 127-8

same" where meaning is a semantic notion and "meaning the same" where the emphasis is not on semantics but on reference. The word "car" for example, can mean the same and refer to different objects. Rhees denies that we can find intelligible the question of whether the word "God" means different things or stands for different objects. But surely inter-religious dialogue has just this question on its agenda. That we cannot easily settle it in no way makes the question unintelligible. Nor is it right to think we can settle it by looking at the place the language has in our lives unless we adopt a positive semantics. Newton and Einstein gave us conflicting accounts of "mass". Can we look to the use of these concepts to determine whether they meant the same thing by "mass"? The Greeks spoke about stars as holes in the sky. We speak about them as balls of burning gas. Do we mean the same thing as the Greek's meant by "star"? How is looking at the use going to answer that question? It will only do so if we bring to the question a theory of what constitutes meaning.

Is religious language grammatical? The answer to this depends on how we construe grammar. If my argument is successful then from a Wittgensteinian perspective, we can concede the grammatical nature of religious language without having to deny that it has ontological entailment. Thus when Phillips criticises Lindbeck for maintaining that theological doctrines are grammar whilst at the same time holding that they make ontological claims, his criticisms betray an unWittgensteinian bias. Lindbeck claims that:

> if the form of life and understanding of the world shaped by an authentic use of the Christian stories does in fact correspond to God's being and will, then the proper use of Christus est Dominus is not only intrasystematically but ontologically true. Utterances within any not totally incoherent religion can on this account be intrasystematically true, but this in no sense assures their ontological truth.[67]

Phillips denies that grammar, when properly understood, can coherently be seen as making ontological claims; and following Wittgenstein, we can see what Phillips might mean by this. If we were to say of grammatical claims that they were true, we would not be *saying* anything - such a remark would be idle because of the place a grammatical claim has in the game. To acknowledge this is to acknowledge something uncontroversial. What Lindbeck is saying here is that we may play the game according to the correct rules (this is what it means to be intrasystematically true) and yet the claims of the game may not actually be true. In other words, he is appealing to a genuine distinction

---

[67] Lindbeck, G., *The Nature of Doctrine*, Philadelphia, Westminster Press, 1984, p. 63

between "being a rule" ("being unable to be mistaken"), and being a statement which could turn out to be true or false. Phillips thinks the distinction requires a metaphysical conception of truth, but we have shown that this is false. Of course as a Wittgensteinian, it is right to be suspicious of appeals to "ontological" truth but in the context of the distinction Lindbeck wants to make, the concept need not be construed metaphysically, or need only be done so if one imposes a verificationist theory of truth. "Intrasystematic" and "ontological" are fancy names for two different aspects of our language; the former captures the sense in which playing the game requires that one adhere to the rules, the latter captures the sense that from within the game, we can ask whether the rules are the right ones. Both can be made intelligible without an appeal to metaphysical truth. In other words, we can understand the distinction Lindbeck wants from within the distinction between sense and nonsense.

In summary, we could say that a believer who uses religious language meaningfully is using it "correctly". Whether or not religious beliefs are true is an entirely separate question. An analysis of the language can have nothing to say here for it is part of the nature of religious belief that its truth cannot be guaranteed. This is what makes faith possible.

Chapter Five

Expressivism[1]

"Let us be human."[2]

I have argued that despite the claims made by Neo-Wittgensteinians, religious language can be defended from a Wittgensteinian perspective as making coherent metaphysical claims once we have distinguished it from the "metaphysics" he wanted to undermine. A person who believes in the existence of God is not trying to "get outside" religious language. They are not making the mistake made by a metaphysical philosopher who does (according to Wittgenstein) attempt to get outside meaningful language. Religious believers are simply *users* of ordinary language. It is precisely the God described by religious language that they believe in. I have argued that the attempt to take away the "fact-stating" or descriptive status of the language cannot be achieved via an appeal to the grammatical status of the language. This is because the concept of grammar necessary to sustain the appeal belongs to a Positivistic rather than Wittgensteinian way of casting the distinction between grammatical and descriptive propositions. It is now time to examine a third attempt to undermine the purported fact-stating nature of religious language; philosophical arguments that attempt to establish that it is expressive rather than descriptive. These arguments work essentially with the idea that religious language is not the right kind of thing to be fact-stating because of its *expressive* nature. Analogies with moral discourse are often invoked. Such language, it is claimed, cannot tell us how things are in the world because on investigation, it turns out that the properties or entities the language speaks

---

[1] In the course of this chapter, I will be examining expressivism as it is primarily considered in relation to moral discourse. In so doing, I am assuming certain parallels between moral and religious language. I do not wish to pre-empt any conclusion about their very real differences. In using ethics, I am merely picking up on how the discussion concerning expressivism in the religious case is often formed. I would not want to push the analogy too far.

[2] Wittgenstein, L., *Culture and Value*, p. 30

about are not there to be found. Failing to identify the objects of the language, philosophers move to explain the language in terms that save it from being "mistakenly" about objects that aren't really there by claiming that it never intended to speak about such objects in the first place. Error theorists are not so charitable, but we shall not detail the moves they make because we are more concerned with what it means to characterise a discourse as "expressive".

There are various ways in which we might want to make good on the claim that a statement or belief is expressive in nature. We do not necessarily have to be enforcing the classical distinction between cognitive and non-cognitive statements although this is most often what motivates expressivist accounts. We do not have to characterise what we mean by expressive in the same way either. Philosophers may agree that a statement or discourse is expressive but disagree over what it means for it to be expressive. Whether or not the consequences of such disagreement are serious or superficial, the fact remains that to predicate "expressive" of a discourse or a statement tells us very little in the first instance.

In this chapter I shall briefly sketch the cognitive/non-cognitive distinction as it is traditionally drawn and then examine the way the Neo-Wittgensteinian philosophers of religion characterise the expressive nature of religious belief. My intention is to show that in whatever way Wittgenstein was an expressivist about certain discourses, it was neither as an advocate of the traditional non-cogntivism, nor as an adherent to something resembling the Neo-Wittgenstein position on the exressive nature of religious language. In presenting and criticising these two positions, the reading of Wittgenstein I am defending will be more clearly open to view.

The chapter will proceed as follows. In Section One, I discuss what I call the traditional distinction between descriptive and expressive discourse; the cognitive/non-cognitive divide. It will be argued that this distinction is motivated essentially by explanatory concerns; that it is in the attempt to explain certain beliefs that we end up with a non-cognitive characterisation of them. The relevant difference between the cognitive and the expressive is that what causes the latter cannot be explained in terms of sense experience. Some kind of inner subjective state is then appealed to, losing the discourse its right, not necessarily to objectivity,[3] but certainly to truth-aptness. My discussion here will be critical. I intend to show not only that the distinction is unstable,

---

[3] The quasi-realist, for example, retains objectivity but not truth-aptness for the disputed discourse.

but that it wasn't a distinction to which Wittgenstein was committed.

In Section Two, I will examine what I am calling the orthodox Neo-Wittgensteinian view. Their position is most notably a reaction against the first because they reject the explanatory motivation behind it. Neo-Wittgensteinian expressivism could therefore be characterised as appealing to the expressive nature of a language as a way of indicating that the beliefs concerned *cannot* be explained. The Neo-Wittgensteinian critique of the former view will be examined and I will argue that although they attempt to overcome the shortcomings of orthodox non-cognitivism, the Neo-Wittgensteinians do not move very far away from it at all. Not surprisingly, given our discovery of their verificationist bias, the Neo-Wittgensteinian position is difficult to distinguish from that of the positivists once its implications have been examined. This view is itself dependent on distinctions that cannot be substantiated without revisionary consequences for the language concerned. For this reason, the view will not be accepted as Wittgenstein's own.

In Section Three, we will move towards an understanding of Wittgenstein's concept of the expressive role of language whilst avoiding the philosophical commitments of classical non-cognitivism. In characterising what I take to be a genuinely Wittgensteinian view, I will be emphasising that when it comes to moral or religious beliefs, we can concede that they are importantly different from scientific beliefs, but that we must also be careful in how we characterise the ways in which they are different. Aside from differences that can be described by looking at how they are used, any other claims made about the nature of the language must necessarily commit the claimant to a substantive position on moral and/or religious matters. I will show that it is a failure to recognise this that is responsible for many of the expressivist debates. It will become clear why Wittgenstein thought that ultimately in ethics and religion, everyone must speak for themselves and why a philosopher qua philosopher cannot speak at all.[4]

Section One: The Cognitive/Non-Cognitive Distinction

C.L. Stevenson perhaps most famously sums up what is involved in making a distinction between cognitive and non-cognitive judgements when he writes:

---

[4] Waismann, F., *Wittgenstein and the Vienna Circle*, New York, Barnes and Noble, 1979, p. 117

> What is the nature of ethical agreement and disagreement? . . . The disagreements that occur in science, history, biography and their counterparts in everyday life, will require only brief attention . . . In such cases one man believes that p is the right answer, and another that not-p, or some proposition incompatible with p, is the answer; and in the course of discussion each tries to give some manner of proof for his view, or to revise it in the light of further information. Let us call this 'disagreement in belief'. There are other cases differing sharply from these which may yet be called 'disagreements' . . . they involve an opposition not of beliefs, but rather of attitudes - that is to say, an opposition of purposes, aspirations, wants, preferences, desires and so on

> The two kinds of disagreement differ mainly in this respect; the former is concerned with how matters are *truthfully* to be described and explained; the latter is concerned with how they are to be *favoured* or disfavoured.[5]

In these two brief passages, we have all we need to understand the essential categories in which cognitive and non-cognitive judgements are placed. Stevenson brings out the nature of different judgements by emphasising that although we can have disagreements with regard to both of them, there is something very different about the nature of the respective disagreement. Notice Stevenson's language here. Disagreements in *belief* are those which have a *truth* at stake whereas disagreements in *attitudes* are those which have something *subjective* like "aspirations", "wants", "desires", and "purposes" at stake. Disagreements in belief are solved or at least a solution is attempted by appealing to further "information" or "proof." Disagreements in attitude cannot be solved that way because there is no further information one can appeal to. Ultimately, the disagreement is not about what is true, but what is preferred or favoured.

Emphasising the fact that the judgements in question are devoid of objective validity (which is what Stevenson implies by classing the disagreement in terms of what is "preferred" and "favoured"), A.J. Ayer continues the non-cognitivist credo:

> We can now see why it is impossible to find a criterion for determining the validity of ethical judgements. It is not because they have an 'absolute' validity which is mysteriously independent of ordinary sense-experience, but because they have no objective validity whatsoever. [6]

---

[5] Stevenson, C.L., *Ethics and Language*, New Haven, Yale University Press, 1944, pp. 2-4, emphasis mine

[6] Ayer, A.J., *Language, Truth and Logic*, Harmondsworth, Penguin, 1971, p. 144

Of course it would be wrong to imply here that Stevenson and Ayer are in total agreement over the nature of non-cognitive judgements. But they do stand together in distinguishing their positions from subjectivism, most particularly over the role of "feelings" in such judgements and the way we should talk about their validity. Bringing out the difference Ayer writes: "Whereas the subjectivist holds that ethical statements actually assert the existence of certain feelings, we hold that ethical statements are expressions and excitants of feeling which do not necessarily involve assertions."[7] The significant difference is that for the subjectivist, because moral statements are assertoric (they are statements about feelings) they can be true or false (if the feelings obtain or not), whereas the emotivist is keen to deny the assertoric nature of such judgements by maintaining that they are expressions of, or expressive of something. They are not *about* anything and therefore do not qualify as truth-apt.

It is not important for us to examine the individual criticisms directed at these views. Our concerns are not with the specific details but with the meta-philosophical assumptions underlying the possibility of making the distinction between cognitive and non-cognitive (or descriptive and expressive) judgements in the first place. What makes it so easy for Stevenson and Ayer to appeal to a distinction between beliefs and attitudes, or "objective validity" or "truths" and "preferences", concepts on which the intelligibility of the position depends? What is the nature of the contrast between cognitive and non-cognitive judgements and what is the philosophical content of the contrast?

Uncontroversially, we can say that characterising non-cognitive judgements is done by drawing a contrast with cognitive ones. Thus the stability of the position depends on there being a class of judgements rightfully classed as cognitive, against which the relevant class of non-cognitive judgements may be contrasted. The meta-philosophical assumptions therefore will primarily concern the nature of a cognitive judgement. This is the category doing the necessary substantive work. What then is it for a judgement to be "cognitive"?

The Nature of Cognitivity

We saw that Stevenson and Ayer used the concepts "objectivity", "truth" and "belief" in the same breath as "cognitive". This was not accidental. These are the concepts traditionally used to characterise judgements of a cognitive nature.

---

[7] Ayer, A.J., *Language*, p. 145

Broadly speaking we could say that this cluster of concepts suggest that a cognitive judgement is one that attempts to *state what is the case - to map or mirror an independent state of affairs*. Hume famously articulates the contrast between judgements that attempt to state what is the case and those which do not:

> The one discovers objects as they really stand in nature, without addition or diminution: the other has a productive faculty, and gilding and staining all natural objects with the colours, borrowed from internal sentiment, raises in a manner a new creation.[8]

Noting in passing that this distinction fails to tell the difference between judgements which *successfully* map an independent state of affairs (true judgements) and those which intend to do so but which fail (false judgements), we are still clearly in need of a criterion for telling when we have discovered objects as they really stand in nature and when we have merely gilded and stained, projected onto or into our judgements, sentiments of our own. Appealing to the objectivity, or truth-aptness of the judgement merely seems to be going around in circles. We can only know if it is genuinely truth-apt if we know that it purports to tell us how things are. So how do we know whether that is what the judgement aims to do? The question is not an easy one to answer and it is part of the purpose of this section to show that much is assumed in debates between cognitivists and non-cognitivists that cannot be clearly worked out without appealing to metaphysical notions of objectivity or philosophical distinctions of a seemingly arbitrary nature.

The distinction between cognitive and non-cognitive judgements finds most enthusiastic support from empiricist quarters and recognising this helps in our investigation for the criterion which might distinguish judgements that map and those that project. Empiricists tend to support meaning or truth theories with a verificationist bias and thus find it more natural to divide judgements into categories of those which are in principle capable of being verified or falsified and those which are not. Non-cognitive judgements are that class for which there is no possible verification or falsification; that fact is what denies them their status as cognitive. Of course qualifications had to be made by the positivists about the reliance of such statements on our language and the consequences this has for our ability to state how things are in nature, but the Positivists worked hard on this qualification and promised to give us a pretty

---

[8] Hume, D., *Enquiry Concerning the Principles of Morals*, in Selby-Bigge [ed], *Hume's Enquiries*, 2nd Edition, Oxford, Oxford University Press, 1902, Appendix 1

good idea of what nature looked like ungilded and unstained. In answer, then, to our question concerning the criterion for a cognitive judgement, the positivists claimed that a judgement proves itself to be cognitive by qualifying for verifiability (in principle if not in practice). If it couldn't meet this criterion, it was either consigned to the status of the non-cognitive or the metaphysically meaningless (tautologies belonged to a special class). Although the Positivism of the 1920s and 1930s did not survive, its spirit is very much alive, especially when it comes to distinguishing fact-stating propositions from those that express feelings, dispositions or preferences.

The positivists could assign to certain judgements a non-cognitive status just because they had a strict definition for what it was for a judgement to have cognitive content. Not all philosophers who support a distinction between the cognitive and non-cognitive operate with the verificationist criterion. Indeed, there are many ways to define a discourse as cognitive and the question at stake in this section does not so much concern the classical metaphysical positions such as realism, idealism, and so on, but the more local issue of characterising the distinction between cognitive and non-cognitive judgements. We are specifically concerned with the grounds on which the distinction might be drawn and legitimised.

What Motivates Non-Cognitivism or Expressivism?

Perhaps the most obvious motive behind expressivist (non-cognitive) theories is the desire to avoid the metaphysical and epistemological problems that can arise if the discourse is treated as cognitive. Having to appeal to some unnatural property of goodness in order to defend the cognitive status of ethical judgements, or of beauty for aesthetic judgements, for example, may not appeal to philosophers who decline the invitation to metaphysics. Indeed it is not clear that such appeals to qualities of that sort can help us "explain" the relevant judgements anyway. The idea that the invoking of moral facts will help explain moral beliefs falls to Wittgenstein's criticism of a circular and ultimately useless theory. We have not explained moral behaviour by appealing to moral facts. We have only given the impression of doing so. Thus in order to produce more satisfying explanations, philosophers prefer to work with what we can clearly see and in the case of moral discourse, that includes admitting that there is no sense-experience of a peculiar moral quality that can intelligibly be appealed to as the cause of our moral language.

In keeping with their Humean heritage, expressivists tend to hold that the disputed judgements express non-cognitive mental states such as emotions, desires, habits, or expectations; such states are spread or projected onto the genuine facts or states of affairs so we come to speak as if there were an extra layer of properties in the world. The problem of determining whether our thought is cognitive or expressive is often decided on explanatory grounds. Simon Blackburn brings this out:

> The projectivist holds that our nature as moralists is well-explained by regarding us as reacting to a reality which contains nothing in the way of values, duties, rights and so forth; a realist thinks it is well explained only by seeing us as able to perceive, cognise, intuit, an independent moral reality . . . [For the projectivist] moral 'states of affairs' play no role in causing or explaining our attitudes, their convergences, their importance to us.[9]

We should just note here the difficulty in keeping questions of analysis distinct from questions of explanation. Blackburn gets his distinction between "real" and "projected", not from an analysis of the kind of judgement involved but from the explanation we provide for the judgement. He is effectively claiming that only a real property can cause us to talk about it. What isn't real has trouble causing anything. Therefore, if no real property can be appealed to in our explanatory account, the property concerned is a projected property and the judgement is non-cognitive.

There are difficulties here in explicating the relationship Blackburn perceives between real properties and causal explanations. At first glance, it seems that the real property will be found when we look to explain our belief about that property and that is what makes the use of language cognitive rather than expressivist. But there is too much assumed here, both in terms of what it means for a genuine property to be found, and the kind of explanation Blackburn (and other non-cognitivists) take themselves to have provided. We can bring out the difficulties by considering scientific terms which even scientists admit have no properties that we can point to (phlogiston for example). We cannot appeal to phlogiston to explain our language about phlogiston and yet we do not intuitively want to say that scientific beliefs about phlogiston are non-cognitive. If we then make the move to explain phlogiston in terms of a broader scientific theory that does justify and explain our beliefs about phlogiston, we must allow such moves to users of moral and religious language also. And here lies the difficulty facing those who want to uphold a

---

[9] Blackburn, S., *Spreading the Word*, New York, Oxford University Press, 1981, p. 164 and p. 185

substantive difference between the two kinds of judgement. It concerns ambiguity over the kind of explanation of a judgement that is being provided. If the scientist is allowed phlogiston because of a broader scientific theory in which the term gains currency, the religious believer must be allowed the use of religious concepts which also can be explained (and often are) from within a religious perspective. When asked for an explanation of God-talk, believers themselves might appeal to God's interaction with the world, his communication with Moses and so on. If we are to disallow such an appeal because of its circularity, so too the scientist must be disallowed their justification of certain property terms (like phlogiston) by appealing to the broader context of scientific explanations.

These difficulties point to ambiguities in the kind of explanation Blackburn takes himself to be providing. The ambiguity comes out in examining the statement made by Blackburn that "moral states of affairs play no role in causing or explaining our attitudes, their convergences, their importance to us". Blackburn takes this to be obvious but it is exactly what moral cognitivists dispute and indeed it may be disputed by users of the language themselves. As we have seen, a religious believer may appeal to God's causal interaction with the world to explain religious practices. Thus they would claim (contra Blackburn) that religious states of affairs do play a role in explaining our religious attitudes. The clash between Blackburn and the believer is at the fundamental level of a clash of commitments between naturalism and supernaturalism. In order to justify his rejection of the religious (or moral) explanation, Blackburn must show us why naturalism is true. This cannot be easily achieved and certainly cannot simply be offered up as a philosophically neutral assumption. Blackburn's quasi-realism is not simply meant to be science. His endeavour is to offer up a philosophical explanation of our beliefs and practices. I think this shows in the following remarks where Blackburn appeals to the concept of a "true" explanation where the implication seems to imply a synonymity between "true" and "naturalistic". Projectivism, he says, holds that:

> we talk and think 'as if' the world contains a certain kind of fact whereas the true explanation of what we are doing is that we have certain reactions, habits and sentiments which we voice and discuss by such talk.[10]

---

[10] Blackburn, S., *Essays*, p. 216

The ambiguity in Blackburn's account concerns the kind of explanation he considers possible, which is in turn informed by his notion of "true" explanation. Although he claims to be picking out an uncontroversial feature of the relevant discourse, his own account demands that the users of that discourse accept that their own explanations may be confused (the believer is supposed to accept that the appeal to God's interaction with the world as an explanation for religious belief/language is illegitimate). What would legitimate that conclusion however? Blackburn holds that all aspects of the discourse in question can be explained without invoking the idea of a "genuine order of objective facts" to which we should think of the assertions within it as owing truth-conditional allegiance whilst at the same time being able to give an account of why the relevant discourse is realistic sounding in nature. In other words, Blackburn attempts to explain how a discourse that is not descriptive comes to look as though it were. His project is to license realist-sounding talk for that discourse, without invoking unnatural facts or unnatural states of affairs.

Blackburn does not think that moral statements (or statements of the relevant discourse) ever intend to map states of affairs and so are not mistaken beliefs. But what if the user of the discourse says that they are so intended? Blackburn claims that our own understanding of it can lead us to think so because we are confused by its surface grammar. We confusedly think of such judgements as analogous to scientific statements of fact. This is a confusion we can clear up whilst retaining the essential nature of moral judgements (their apparent objectivity). According to Blackburn, his project is to explain how a discourse can sustain a sense of objectivity whilst at the same time avoiding the errors of metaphysical realism. But the difficulties should now be clear. When Blackburn makes a claim about a judgement that is disputed by those who make the judgement, it is not obvious that he has established for himself a right to an explanatory priority. He effectively faces the same problems as emotivists. At the end of the day his position rests on an assumption which the ordinary language user has to be given a reason to accept. For the emotivists it was a verification bias. For the Blackburn and fellow quasi-realists it takes the form of a concept of "real property" which is established via an appeal to naturalistic explanation that is itself not without its own philosophical presuppositions.

What I have been suggesting is not that non-cognitivists have mischaracterised a discourse that is, in fact, cognitive. Rather, I have been suggesting that there is no way to draw up the contrast in the first place without prioritising some particular feature of the discourse in a philosophically substantial way. In addition, there is no limit to the variety of cognitivisms that might be articulated and seemingly no way of deciding between them. The Positivists' appeal to verification, Blackburn's appeal to "real" property (which is further articulated in terms of causal explanation) and any other attempt to distinguish cognitivity from non-cognitivity cannot justify itself as the right way, or the true way to mark the difference between kinds of beliefs and judgements.

Wittgenstein is often taken to be an advocate of some version of either subjectivism or non-cognitivism. Brand Blanshard, for example, when speaking of such views writes: "This view has recently come into much favour. With variations of detail, it is being advocated by Russell, Wittgenstein and Ayer in England, and by Carnap, Stevenson, Feigl, and others in this country."[11]

It is easy to see why Wittgenstein was put into the same category as the positivists Ayer and Carnap. Blanshard claims that all the above thinkers belong to positivistic schools of thought and that it was because of their particular categories of judgement that they came to think the way they did about ethics. The success of Blanshard's argument against subjectivist theories is not important to us here. More interesting is his classification of Wittgenstein among the group named. Was Wittgenstein a non-cognitivist about ethics and religion? Reasons for thinking that he was have been insisted upon by Blackburn.

To support his view that Wittgenstein drew a philosophically substantial distinction between cognitive and non-cognitive judgements, Blackburn discusses Wittgenstein's remarks on ethical judgements and contends that if there ever was a clearly drawn distinction between about facts and values evident in Wittgenstein's work, it is to be found here. Just look at what he says in his *Lecture on Ethics*: "No statement of fact can ever be, or imply, a judgement of value." Blackburn points out that if Wittgenstein had changed his mind about this (as he changed his mind about some of his earlier philosophical commitments) we would have expected to find him later denying the distinction by admitting that each discourse has its own facts: "Of course my lecture was hopeless; ethics describes facts - ethical facts."[12] And we could

---

[11] Blanshard, B., *The New Subjectivism in Ethics*, in *Philosophiy and Phenomenological Research*, 1949, Vol. IX, No. 3, p. 505

[12] Blackburn, S., *Wittgenstein and Minimalism*, in Garrett, B., and Mulligan, K. [eds], *Themes*

perhaps add: mathematics describes mathematical facts, religion describes religious facts, psychology describes psychological facts and so on. I think Blackburn is right, both to point out that for Wittgenstein, the distinction between facts and values mattered and that the difference between doing mathematics, being religious and forming and testing scientific hypotheses also mattered. What is less clear is whether the differences Wittgenstein cared about are characterised the right way by Blackburn and his non-cognitivist colleagues. Take for example, Wittgenstein's lecture on ethics. Apart from the fairly innocuous remark on the difference between facts and values, Wittgenstein also says some remarkable things that are ignored by Blackburn. What are we to make of comments like: "If a man could write a book on Ethics, that really was a book on Ethics, this book would, with an explosion, destroy all the other books in the world"?[13] Or when commenting on what ethics is:

> it seems obvious that nothing we could ever think or say should be *the* thing, Ethics if it is anything, is supernatural, there is a reality outside the world . . . outside any sphere that is accessible to human faculties. Corresponding to this reality, at the centre of the human heart is the longing for an absolute good, a longing which is always there and is never appeased by any object in this world.[14]

Even this small selection of remarks should caution us against too hasty a reading of Wittgenstein as a non-cognitivist. Just looking uncritically at them, we could issue a compelling argument for moral realism (science describes empirical facts, ethics describes supernatural "beyond this world" facts), we could go the Positivists route and classify an ethical judgement as both expressive and meaningless (it is not difficult to see why so many thought Wittgenstein was a champion of Positivism) or we could be struck by the fact that whatever Wittgenstein is talking about here, it bears little resemblance to the concerns of meta-ethics. Wittgenstein's paradigm ethical experience was, for example, the feeling of absolute safety. It is not unreasonable to ask what this has to do with "goodness" or "rightness" - the usual raw material for ethical deliberations.

Although we may agree with Blackburn that "the thrust of the lecture must surely be that it is from a different standpoint than that of description that ethics

---

from Wittgenstein: Working Papers in Philosophy, No. 4, Canberra, Research School of Social Sciences ANU, 1993, p. 3

[13] Wittgenstein, L., *Lecture on Ethics* in *Philosophical Occasions*, p. 40

[14] Wittgenstein, L., *Lecture on Ethics*, p. 41

is found",[15] this observation amounts to very little on its own. Not only is the concept of "description" left unexamined, it is not obvious that success in articulating such a distinction will lead to non-cognitivism. In a later section I will suggest ways in which Wittgenstein's remarks might be understood which do not support Blackburn's interpretation. Before doing so, we must return to Wittgenstein's own remarks on ethics. Having these before us will help bring out the nature of the distinction I ultimately want to defend.

Speaking for Oneself

We saw that Blackburn insisted that Wittgenstein's position on ethics shows that he believed that values were not facts and that this is good evidence that some kind of non-cognitivism can be attributed to him. In other words, Blackburn holds not only that such a distinction is intelligible but that Wittgenstein himself was committed to it. In what follows I want to suggest an alternative way of understanding not only Wittgenstein's comments on ethics, but ways of framing the debate between cognitivists and non-cognitivists. My argument will be that each position rests on a grammatical truth. Confusions arise only when such truths are given a philosophically significant status. The illegitimate move is the lapse into metaphysics.

Our starting point is Wittgenstein's comment to Waismann that "at the end of my lecture on ethics, I spoke in the first person. I believe that is quite essential. Here nothing can be established. I can only appear as a person speaking for myself".[16] This comment suggests that understanding Wittgenstein's remarks in that lecture on ethics should be done in the context, not of discovering philosophical arguments, but of understanding Wittgenstein's own ethical views - not as a philosopher but as a person. What is most striking about the lecture is that it is almost propaganda for the importance of ethics. As a motive for why the most esteemed logician of the day would give such a peculiar lecture (and I think it is right to be struck by its peculiarity) we might set the remarks in a broader context; the mysticism of the *Tractatus* which confounded Russell but which Wittgenstein insisted was the most important part of the treatise, his own uncompromising struggle for moral purity (to Lady Ottoline: "Don't you want to be perfect? Then I'm afraid we cannot possibly be friends"), the odd connection he made between the moral

---

[15] Blackburn, S., *Wittgenstein and Minimalism*, p. 3

[16] Waismann, F., *Vienna Circle*, p. 117

identity of the thinker and what one can think about ("How can I be a logician if I am not yet a human being?"), his remark to Schlick that he would rather say that the Good is what God wills because it puts an end to further explanation and preserves what it important about Ethics and so on.

The distinction Wittgenstein invokes between facts and values therefore looks less like a philosophical distinction of the kind required by the cognitive/non-cognitive debate, and more like a characterisation of the *importance* of ethics. Reconstituted, his "argument" in the lecture looks something like this:

1. Ethics is about the absolute/necessary.
2. Facts can only describe what is contingent.
3. Therefore Ethics must be distinct from facts.

A similar argument is to be found in the *Tractatus*. The schema there runs as follows:

1. In the world everything is as it is, and everything happens as it does happen: in it no value exists - and if it did exist, it would have no value.
2. If there is any value that does have value it must lie outside the whole sphere of what happens and is the case. For all that happens and is the case is accidental.
3. What makes it non-accidental cannot lie within the world since if it did it would be accidental.
4. It must lie outside the world, so it is impossible for there to be propositions of ethics. Propositions can express nothing that is higher.

Notice how persistent Wittgenstein is in his insistence that anything you could identify in the world *cannot* have anything to do with Ethics. It is *because* Ethics is absolute that is must be kept distinct from facts. Wittgenstein's ethical seriousness is often seen as part of his eccentricity. This is not surprising as it is difficult to know quite what to do with it. What we must not do, and this is what Blackburn is guilty of, is to isolate the terminology from the seriousness as if it were somehow possible to separate philosophical insights from Wittgenstein's ethical passion. He warned us against doing that in the *Tractatus*. Blackburn seems to ignore the warning, content to neutralise Wittgenstein's comments, reducing what is in itself an expression of ethical passion to a philosophical position.

Wittgenstein's distinction between facts and values is designed to preserve what is important about ethics. That ethics can have nothing to do with the facts turns out to be analytic for Wittgenstein because anything to do with the facts is rejected as non-ethical: "I see at once clearly, as it were in a flash, not only that no description that I can think of would do to describe what I mean by absolute value but *I would reject every significant description that anybody could possibly make on the grounds of its significance.*"[17]

In all of Wittgenstein's deliberations on ethics, what comes out most clearly is not a philosopher wanting to understand ethics but a human being claiming that philosophy can only misunderstand it. Bouwsma recalls him speaking of "all the harm philosophers do in ethics. When a man is in deep earnest about what he ought to do then one can see how fantastic what philosophers do is",[18] and to Rush Rhees he remarked that: "It was strange that you could find books on ethics in which there was no mention of a genuine ethical or moral problem."[19]

Rhees here puts a different gloss on these comments by adding that "[Wittgenstein] wanted to speak of a problem only where you could imagine or recognise a solution".[20] It is true, of course, that Wittgenstein had in the *Tractatus* spoken of genuine questions as those which could be answered: "If a question can be framed at all, it is also possible to answer it."[21] On the other hand, he also spoke of a problem that is set by all the facts and to which they can play no part in finding the solution.[22] In the context of a broader view, we find Wittgenstein not ruling out ethical problems as impossible because solutions could not be imagined, but that ethical problems and their solutions are of an entirely different nature to scientific problems and their solutions. They necessarily involve ethical subjects. We can see this in Wittgenstein's reticence about the ethical status of Brutus's stabbing of Caesar. Rhees asked Wittgenstein whether the stabbing was a noble action (as Plutarch thought) or an evil one (as Dante thought), and "Wittgenstein said that this was not even something you could discuss. 'You would not know for your life what went on in his mind before he decided to kill Caesar. What would he have had to feel

---

[17] Wittgenstein, L., *Lecture on Ethics*, p. 44, italics mine

[18] Bouwsma, O.K., *Conversations*, p. 39

[19] Rhees, R., *Discussions*, p. 98

[20] Rhees, R., *Discussions*, p. 99

[21] Wittgenstein, L., *Tractatus*, 6.5

[22] Wittgenstein, L., *Tractatus*, 6.4321

in order that you should say that killing his friend was noble?'"[23]

The problem here is two-fold. Ethics is connected with agency and motive and we have no way of knowing what really motivated the killing. Second, even if we did, we have not determined what makes a motive a noble one. These questions are not scientific. It is necessarily the case that ethical concepts are not neutral. That is what makes them distinctively ethical. In answering ethical questions therefore, everyone must speak for himself or herself.

The problem with philosophical ethics according to Wittgenstein, then, is that it completely misunderstands the nature of its subject. For Wittgenstein, ethics *is* the struggle to be ethical. It requires an ethical subject confronted by the everyday problems of life. No statement of fact "can ever have the power of a coercive judge" because life itself - the facts relevant to the problem - merely set it up. And problems are problems *for* someone. The book of the world (see Lecture on Ethics) which contained nothing but facts would not contain the ethical subject nor any ethical propositions. It would not contain any ethical problems. If it attempted to talk about ethics, such talk *could* only be chatter. Kierkegaard's ironic journal entry "take the paradox away from a thinker - and you have a professor", could aptly be transposed into a Wittgensteinian intuition that if you "take the problem away from the ethical individual you have a philosopher".

We seem to have strayed a long way from our discussion of non-cognitivism. What has Wittgenstein's ethical passion got to do with the way we characterise ethical judgements? I realise that I have not yet developed an argument to show why I believe Wittgenstein would be suspicious of the distinction between cognitive and non-cognitive judgements. In order to properly do this, I want to first present the Neo-Wittgensteinian account of the expressive nature of religious language.

The Neo-Wittgensteinians promise to provide us with a genuinely Wittgensteinian alternative to the debate between cognitivists and non-cognitivists. Unfortunately, despite its promise, the Neo-Wittgensteinian account fails to deliver just because it turns grammatical distinctions into philosophical ones and so falls into illegitimate metaphysics. The result, therefore, is not so very different to the philosophical positions they claim to undermine. The advantage of the Neo-Wittgensteinian account is that it does contain a genuinely Wittgensteinian motivation and is therefore helpful for us in our pursuit of an understanding of what Wittgenstein meant by "expressive".

---

[23] Rhees, R., *Discussions*, p. 99

Section Two: Expressive as Primitive

The orthodox Neo-Wittgensteinians are suspicious of the cognitive/non-cognitive debate, especially when it is called on as a device to explain features of language and behaviour. Indeed, the Neo-Wittgensteinians do not offer expressivism as an explanation for a discourse. Rather, for them, "expressive" signifies that the language *cannot* be further explained. Hence the concept of the "primitive" plays a key role in their characterisation. As is well known, Wittgenstein made significant use of the concept himself and it is the Neo-Wittgensteinian thesis that they are carrying on where Wittgenstein left off. If this were so, we would expect their account to be truly devoid of philosophical assumptions. It turns out that despite their disclaimer to the contrary, even the Neo-Wittgensteinian view falls to the same kind of confusion suffered by our protagonists earlier. There is much that is right however, in their use of the "primitive" and the role played by the concept in Wittgenstein's own thought. In critically examining their view, we will be able to characterise an alternative which does not fall victim to the philosophical urge to say more than can be said whilst at the same time, more positively, highlighting important differences in the way we use language.

Language and Reality: Some Preliminary Remarks

We saw earlier that the cognitive/non-cognitive debate is driven in part by the assumption that we can separate real properties from projected ones. What is at stake is whether some conception of reality, or "real" property, can be identified and defended. The Neo-Wittgensteinians promise some kind of resolution to this debate by suggesting that conceptions of "real" or of "reality" are to be found within our uses of language and that different usages will produce different conceptions. So they agree that it is confused to give priority to empirical or scientific conceptions of reality (by insisting that only empirical properties are "real") but don't accept that there is nothing more to be said. They claim that language gets connected to reality via its application in our practices. Different applications will produce different conceptions of "real" and none of them can be used to sustain a uniquely philosophical concept of objectivity or reality. The Neo-Wittgensteinians question the non-cognitivist's assumption that cognitivity can be cashed out in terms of real properties. If different linguistic uses produce different conceptions of "real", then it becomes very difficult to draw and sustain a genuine distinction between "real" and "projected" properties. The Neo-Wittgensteinians campaign for the abandonment of the distinction between "real" and "projected" properties, although we shall see as we examine the details of their argument, that it is not easy, even for them, to do without it.

The Neo-Wittgensteinian argument against distinguishing philosophically between cognitive and non-cognitive judgements has various parts. They contest the philosophical nature of the debate, arguing that the required conception of "real" cannot be defended. Their reason is the Wittgensteinian one that the relationship between our symbols and reality is set up in different ways by our practices and we have no way of conceptualising reality (or "real property") independently of our practices. We make it in applying what we say and different ways of applying (different language games) produce different ways of making (connecting symbols to reality). They then try to make good on the idea that the way language is connected to empirical reality is different to the way language is connected to religious or moral reality. Because this is a claim that could conceivably belong to classical non-cognitivism, we must now try to explicate why they think their position is different.

Language as Expressive Behaviour

The central issue in all this is how we might understand the expressive role of certain statements and what this might tell us about the nature the objects of which they speak. The way in which the Neo-Wittgensteinians understand what it means for an utterance to be "expressive" is brought out clearly in the following passage from Norman Malcolm. He writes:

> I want to sketch the development in Wittgenstein's thinking, after his return to philosophical research in 1929 of a new idea about language, an idea that was a sharp break with the *Tractatus*. The new conception was that there are meaningful sentences of everyday language which are 'expressive', in the sense in which a gesture, an outcry, a frown or a laugh, can express, not a *thought*, but indifference, or fear, or displeasure, or amusement.[24]

The idea that gestures too can be meaningful came as a revelation to Wittgenstein who had, in the *Tractatus*, been under the influence of certain philosophical spells, (most notably, the idea that meaningfulness could only be a property of thoughts where "thoughts" had become idealised in a Fregean

---

[24] Malcolm, N., *Nothing Is Hidden*, p. 132

manner). Recognising that gestures and cries are meaningful was part of Wittgenstein's conversion process, the nature and significance of which have already been examined. What then, according to the new program of philosophical enquiry, should we make of the idea that language is often just a form of expressive behaviour where behaviour here is to be taken in the narrow sense of signifying primitive, spontaneous gestures like smiles and frowns? It is important to notice here that Malcolm explicitly distinguishes expressions of the kind outlined from "thoughts". Pursuing an understanding of what Malcolm might mean by this distinction takes us to the heart of the Neo-Wittgensteinian view. Our aim is to draw out how the Neo-Wittgensteinians think that "thoughts" are to be contrasted with expressive behaviour and the consequences this might have for our understanding of moral and religious beliefs and their relationship to reality.

The contrast between thoughts and expressions is implicit in the following remarks by Wittgenstein:

> A child has hurt himself and he cries: and then adults talk to him and teach him exclamations and later sentences. They teach the child new pain-behaviour. 'So you are saying that the word "pain" really means crying?' - On the contrary, the verbal expression of pain replaces crying and does not describe it.[25]

We might say that the expression "I am in pain" does not express a *thought* because it is interchangeable (synonymous) with a specific piece of behaviour. We could perhaps say that the statement and the cry are the same tool, or different tools which perform the same task. As Malcolm points out, it is in direct collision with the views he had held in the *Tractatus*, that Wittgenstein recommends that:

> we [must] make a radical break with the idea that language always functions in one way, always serves the same purpose: *to convey thoughts* - which may be thoughts about houses, pains, good and evil, or whatever.[26]

Leaving aside the specific controversies of the private language argument, what can we glean from these remarks that might be of interest in characterising an alternative to the cognitive/non-cognitive debate? Most obviously, Wittgenstein's remarks are designed to question one of the central

---

[25] Wittgenstein, L., *Philosophical Investigations*, §244

[26] Wittgenstein, L., *Philosophical Investigations*, §304, emphasis mine

assumptions of the cognitivist, notably their thesis that the best way to *explain* our language is to see it as *aiming* to refer to or describe some objective state of affairs. In answer to questions like "why do we talk about goodness?" "why do we talk about pains?" or "why do we talk about supernatural beings?", the cognitivist will answer "Because we think that there are such things." The cogntivist explains such behaviour in terms of us having "thoughts" about goodness, gods and pains. What's more, they then claim that such language is only justified if there are such things as pains, supernatural beings and goodness. We noted earlier in the context of the debate between Blackburn as a projectivist and his cognitivist opponent, that there is some ambiguity in the concept of explanation here. This ambiguity is fuel for Wittgenstein's critique. His emphasis on the primitive nature of language (or language as expressive behaviour) is designed to show that what I previously called "external" explanations are not so much wrong, but superfluous. The case of pain usefully brings out what Wittgenstein meant by calling language expressive behaviour and why drawing attention to this fact should make us more wary of our desire to explain such behaviour and the potential vacuity of such explanations. He writes:

> Being sure that someone is in pain, doubting whether he is, and so on, are so many natural, instinctive, kinds of behaviour towards other human beings, and our language is merely an auxiliary to, and further extension of primitive behaviour. (For our language-game is behaviour) (Instinct).[27]

We have already seen how central an idea it was for Wittgenstein that we understand our language (and its meaning) as intimately connected to natural behaviour. In its assumption that language *always* aims to represent an external state of affairs, realism makes our choice of concepts too deliberate, too rational. It is just because they are not that the idea of an explanation here is empty. For Wittgenstein, the concept of the primitive (often used interchangeably with "form of life") is appealed to as the ultimate resting-place for all attempted explanations of our language and practices. As we saw in an earlier chapter, what is primitive "can be explained [made clear] and cannot be explained".[28] The way in which it can be made clear is that we can acknowledge the role such behaviour has in the subsequent development of language and we can gain self-understanding in becoming more conscious of

---

[27] Wittgenstein, L., *Zettel*, §545
[28] Wittgenstein, L., *Remarks on Frazer*, p. 4

the fact that we are the kind of creature that behaves in just these ways.[29] As we saw earlier, Wittgenstein uses the concept "primitive" to combat idle philosophical theories which attempt to explain how our concepts acquire meaning by appealing to a reality that lies beyond their meaning. His criticism of such theories do not license non-cognitivism or expressivism as they would apply with as much force to judgements whose concepts would be considered cognitive.

Wittgenstein's remarks on the expressive nature of language do not limit themselves to the expression of sensations. Amongst other things, they also apply to properties that are traditional favourites for projectivists, like causation,[30] goodness and gods. This is clearly relevant to our desire to place Wittgenstein in the context of the cognitive/non-cognitive debate. On the nature of moral discourse Wittgenstein writes for example:

> If you came to a foreign tribe, whose language you didn't know at all and you wished to know what words corresponded to 'good', 'fine' etc., what would you look for? You would look for smiles, gestures, food, toys.[31]

and continuing the same theme:

> A child generally applies a word like 'good' first to food. One thing that is immensely important in teaching is exaggerated gestures and facial expressions. The word is taught as a substitute for a facial expression or a gesture . . . What makes the word an interjection of approval? It is the game it appears in, not the form of words. [32]

Wittgenstein is here suggesting that we learn "good" etc., like we learn pain; not by first forming the belief (or having the thought) that there is a property "goodness" we are describing when we say "this is good". We learn the concept "good" via gestures of approval and so on. Clearly the possibility of emotivism emerges here. It is after all, the emotivists thesis that "good" is synonymous with approving or clapping. That to say "x is good" is not to

---

[29] It is important to note that I am not ruling out empirical explanations of human behaviour. Nothing in what Wittgenstein writes is designed to rule out that kind of explanation. He is only interested in the confused attempt at a metaphysical explanation that gives the impression of getting outside that which it explains, as we saw in earlier chapters.

[30] See especially his notes on *Cause and Effect: Intuitive Awareness*, in *Philosophical Occasions*, pp. 371-411.

[31] Wittgenstein, L., *Lectures and Conversations*, p. 2

[32] Wittgenstein, L., *Lectures and Conversations*, p. 2

believe that x has the property of goodness but to express approval for x. The emotivist reading of the above remarks is particularly persuasive because of the apparent equivalence here between thinking something is good, approving of it and appreciating the taste of certain foods. Why I do not think the emotivist reading of Wittgenstein is the right one will emerge as we proceed.

I am currently suggesting that these remarks are best seen as part of Wittgenstein's polemic against metaphysical explanations which, it is argued, tend to distort or mischaracterise their explanandum. Seen in this context, these remarks would be making the point that there is something misguided in explaining moral discourse in terms of beliefs about the presence of a property of "goodness" in just the same way that explaining pain language in terms of beliefs about pain is misguided.

We now have a partial answer to our question concerning Wittgenstein's separation of language that expresses "thoughts" and language that doesn't. The distinction is designed to undermine philosophical explanations that model all language as the outcome of some enquiry. Language is seen as too spontaneous for that. Explanations of such language, which make it depend necessarily on "reasoning" are thus idle. We could say that the notion of "thoughts" belongs to speculative philosophy, or is a "super-concept".

In keeping with their Wittgensteinian heritage, the Neo-Wittgensteinians call on the primitive feature of our language as part of their polemic against the perceived confusions of metaphysical explanations. We have seen how they go about this in the preceding chapter. Their more positive move, however, is to emphasise that certain things follow from the fact that much of our language is really expressive behaviour. It is their positive thesis that is of interest to us here. What does follow, according to the Neo-Wittgensteinians, for our understanding of certain beliefs if we characterise the language in which they are couched as arising from primitive reactions and instincts? In answering this question, we shall see that their view contains commitments that look suspiciously "verificationist" in nature.

It is important to emphasise that for the Neo-Wittgensteinians, "primitive" is intended to signify a descriptive (and therefore uncontroversial) feature of the language that is merely being described. In characterising religious and magical beliefs as primitive, they appeal centrally to a certain reading of Wittgenstein's *Remarks on Frazer's Golden Bough*.

James Frazer's extensive observations on the rituals and practices of primitive cultures led him to conclude that they were motivated by an early attempt to understand the natural world. He claimed that primitive beliefs were primarily theories about causal connections and thus should be treated as primitive science. He suggests that instead of treating such practices as foreign forms of behaviour, we recognise the progress we have made in science is in part dependent on the errors made by our ancestors. He writes:

> But reflection and enquiry should satisfy us that to our predecessors we are indebted for much of what we thought most of our own, and that their errors were not wilful extravagances or the ravings of insanity, but simply hypotheses, justifiable as such at the time they were propounded, but which a fuller experience has proved to be inadequate. It is only by the successive testing of hypotheses and rejection of the false that truth is at last elicited. After all, what we call truth is only the hypothesis which is found to work best. Therefore in reviewing the opinions and practices of ruder ages and races we shall do well to look with leniency upon their errors as inevitable slips made in the search from truth, and to give them the benefit of that indulgence which we ourselves may one day stand in need of.[33]

In treating primitive beliefs as a form of failed physics, Frazer was offering an explanation of them. He was explaining why people come to believe in rain gods, or why they burn effigies. He concludes that these practices and beliefs are the *result* of attempts to explain and manipulate natural phenomenon. Their kinship with scientists of today is appealed to. If not hypotheses of the scientific kind, Frazer implies that they must be treated as "wilful extravagances or the ravings of insanity".

Wittgenstein read *The Golden Bough* with interest and increasing dissatisfaction. Frazer interpreted all the activities and beliefs as the result of rational thought. In effect, he claimed that the beliefs and practices were the product of early and uneducated Man looking around him and asking himself "What causes this?" "Where does this come from?" or "Why is this like it is?" and appealing to supernatural beings as the causal explanation of natural phenomena. Once they believed that a god was responsible for an event, it became pertinent to do what they could to influence the god - hence the development of ritualistic practices. The chronology is important here. On Frazer's model, the people first have the desire for an explanation, they come up with an answer and this results in practices of certain sorts. On this account, we may say that they were asking the "right" sort of questions, it is just that they didn't get any of the answers right and it is because we have gotten the answers right (or at least it seems so to us), we don't need to engage in the ritualistic practices which belonged to their kind of explanations.

---

[33] Frazer, J., *The Golden Bough* (Abridged Edition), London, Macmillan, 1922, p. 264

Leaving aside the difficulties with this "Intellectualism" (most notably, how one accounts for the fact that in the developed Western world people still engage in religious activities), there are real questions as to whether the practices should be characterised as the *outcome* of rational enquiry. Frazer's account suffers the same fate as the metaphysician who accounts for our belief that other people have pain in terms of reasoning by analogy from our own case, against which Wittgenstein writes: "'Putting the cart before the horse' may be said of an explanation like the following: we tend someone else because by analogy with our own case we believe that he is experiencing pain too."[34]

A clear theme in Wittgenstein's polemic against Frazer's account is the criticism that Frazer mischaracterises the nature of the beliefs and rituals he is recounting. This might be called Wittgenstein's negative thesis. Effectively it renders Frazer's so-called explanations superfluous in exactly the same way as the metaphysicians account of our beliefs is rendered superfluous - namely, because it misrepresents the nature of its explanandum and in so doing fails to explain it. Recognising their character as primitive or natural is, therefore, important both because it will stop us providing idle explanations and because our understanding of them will be a *just* one:

> One might begin a book on anthropology in this way: when we watch the life and behaviour of men all over the earth we see that apart from what we might call animal activities, taking food etc., etc., men also carry out actions that bear a peculiar character and might be called ritualistic. But then it is nonsense if we go on to say that the characteristic feature of these actions is that they spring from wrong ideas about the physics of things. (This is what Frazer does when he says magic is really false physics, or as the case may be, false medicine, technology etc.) What makes the *character* of ritual action is not any view or opinion.[35]

Notice that Wittgenstein is here defending the character of rituals. To call them primitive is to characterise them in a certain way; it is to point out that they are not the result of an enquiry. To characterise something as primitive, we have of course, said nothing yet about it except that explanations which do not take this particular feature of it into account should be rejected.

Are there more positive things to be said about the belief/behaviour under consideration? What, for example, are the implications for the content of the

---

[34] Wittgenstein, L., *Zettel*, §542
[35] Wittgenstein, L., *Remarks on Frazer*, p. 7, italics mine

beliefs concerned? One obvious approach is to move from acknowledging that the belief is not the product of a rational enquiry, to the conclusion that it is devoid of cognitive content. When people believed that a king could make rain, did they really believe that he could make rain? The distinction between a cognitive and non-cognitive belief in this sense is nicely brought out by Wittgenstein's own example:

> If I, who do not believe that somewhere or other there are human-superhuman beings which we might call gods - if I say, 'I fear the wrath of the gods', then this shows that with these words I can mean something or express a feeling that need not be connected with that belief.[36]

Here the contrast between those who really believe in the gods and Wittgenstein who doesn't, but who can nevertheless use the terminology, might be understood, loosely, as the distinction between a cognitive belief, and a non-cognitive belief. The question we have now set is whether a belief that arises out of primitive behaviour must necessarily be understood as non-cognitive (in the sense loosely defined above). Another way to put it is to ask whether a belief has to be scientific (in Frazer's sense), in order to be about the way the world is. The Neo-Wittgensteinian answer to these questions is extremely interesting but ultimately to be rejected on the grounds that they develop a substantive philosophical account of the distinctions under review. This comes out most clearly in their gloss on the relationship between primitive behaviour and beliefs.

Concept-Formation, Behaviour and Beliefs

Emphasising the apparent spontaneity of religious behaviour may tempt us to conclude that religious language does not make claims about the world. This temptation arises because in calling religious behaviour/language primitive, we are denying that it *aims* to describe or represent (and so criticising philosophical theories which characterise it as such). But in so characterising the belief, are we also committed to the denial that it *can* be cognitive? Equating "primitive" with non-propositional or non-cognitive certainly seems to be part of the Neo-Wittgensteinian plan, as Malcolm makes clear when he writes:

---

[36] Wittgenstein, L., *Remarks on Frazer*, p. 8

> In likening the utterance 'I'm in pain' to a cry of pain, Wittgenstein was not declaring that it *is* a cry of pain . . . though it may be conceded that the first-person psychological utterances are part of expressive behaviour, one may want to insist that nevertheless they are radically different from non-verbal expressive behaviour. Of course they are different. But why radically? Behind this emphasis is the persisting urge to view them as 'statements' or 'propositions' and to hold that they are put forward as 'corresponding with reality'.[37]

The ambiguity of the Neo-Wittgensteinian position can be seen here. Malcolm is denying that the utterance "I am in pain" is a statement about reality (or at least suggesting that there is something confused in treating it as such). But when a person says that they are in pain, don't we naturally take them to be making a statement about reality (namely, that they are in pain)? What can Malcolm mean when he denies this? It is important to pursue this question because the subtlety of the Neo-Wittgensteinian position depends on it. Malcolm makes Wittgenstein's point that the criteria for first person psychological utterances are different to third person utterances. "I infer that he needs to go to the doctor from observation of his behaviour; but I do not make this inference in my own case from observation of my behaviour",[38] and it is tempting to think that Malcolm wants to deny first person psychological utterances a correspondence with reality because there is no criterion for determining whether they correspond or not. The obvious danger in this reasoning is that it lends itself to a verificationist interpretation. Malcolm might be trying to emphasise Wittgenstein's point that:

> To call the expression of a sensation a statement is misleading, because 'testing', 'justification', 'confirmation', 'refutation' of a statement are connected with the word 'statement' in the language-game.[39]

However, it is not clear that he is content to treat this as the trivial claim that the concept of verification does not apply to the statement "I'm in pain" in the way it applies to "He is in pain". Malcolm seems to make the further point here that because verification doesn't apply, neither can the statement be treated as a statement about reality.

It is not just Malcolm who leans dangerously towards verificationism. We have already seen how it emerges for the Neo-Wittgensteinians in our discussion of grammar and religious language. The relevance here is that non-

---

[37] Malcolm, N., *Nothing is Hidden*, p. 143

[38] Wittgenstein, L., *Zettel*, §539

[39] Wittgenstein, L., *Zettel*, §549

cognitivists also claim that statements which express are not statements about reality and yet the Neo-Wittgensteinians deny that they are non-cognitivists. How then is their position different?

Malcolm contends that "Of utterances such as 'I'm afraid', 'I'm in pain', 'I intend to go to Vienna', we have a powerful inclination to say: 'They are propositions; and when I utter them they are assertions or statements about myself. And I know whether they are true or false. This knowledge must be based on my observations of myself . . . all of these remarks are either misleading, confusing, or nonsensical."[40]

The reason the utterances "I'm afraid" or "I'm in pain" are not statements about myself is apparently because they are *expressions* of fear and of pain, not descriptions or hypotheses. The Neo-Wittgensteinians argue that matters are the same for the religious case. The utterance "God loves me", for example, is not a statement but an *expression* of love and trust. Rhees writes: "'God exists' is not a statement of fact. You might say also that it is not in the indicative mood. 'There is a God', though it appears to be in the indicative mood, is an *expression* of faith."[41] Phillips echoes: ". . . that a man says that God cares for him in all things is the *expression* of the terms in which he meets and makes sense of the contingencies of life."[42] It is perhaps an illustration from Winch that makes the point most explicit. Winch asks us to:

> imagine a tribe whose speech includes nothing that we want to identify as the expression of religious beliefs. They have, however, certain striking practices. Let us suppose they live among the mountains. When one of their number dies, he is buried or burned with a certain ceremoniousness. The ceremony includes perhaps some moment of silent contemplation of the mountains, perhaps prostration of their bodies before the mountains. Similar things are done at other important moments in the life of the tribe - at a marriage, on the occasion of a birth, when an adolescent is initiated into adult life . . . Now we are told to imagine that there is also talk of 'gods who inhabit the mountains . . . the rituals are explicitly regarded as showing reverence towards the mountain gods'.[43]

Winch might just as well say that the belief that there are gods in the mountains is an *expression* of awe and reverence at the mightiness of the mountains. His denial that the ritual of looking towards the mountains can be explained by belief in the mountain gods can be happily conceded as we have

---

[40] Malcolm, N., *Nothing is Hidden*, p. 142
[41] Rhees, R., *Without Answers*, p. 131
[42] Phillips, D.Z., *Religion without Explanation*, p. 114
[43] Winch, P., *Trying to Make Sense*, pp. 111-2

already agreed that behaviour/practices often precede beliefs. Winch however, wants to make the further point that the belief is connected to the practice in the way the utterance "I am in pain" is connected to the expression of pain in behaviour. We have already seen Malcolm treading on dangerous ground here. Winch goes the same way. It surely does not follow that because a religious belief may express something (awe and wonder perhaps), that the language is synonymous with religious gestures. Nor is it the case that a statement cannot both be expressive and cognitive - a point Mackie makes in his criticisms of Phillips position when he writes that:

> it suggests a false antithesis, that since this language is expressive it cannot also be literal and descriptive. Why should it not be both? In fact it most naturally would be both. Meeting the contingencies of life in a spirit of what we might call ultimate confidence and security would very naturally both support and be supported by a literal belief in an almighty and caring power and in a world beyond the one we know.[44]

Mackie's point is valid because he is not suggesting that the feeling of confidence and security is explained by or explains the belief that there is a caring power. We can accept that there is an internal connection between them (indeed for those who incline towards metaphysical realism it is important they do so) without having to draw the conclusion that the belief has the same semantic status as the behaviour. Malcolm gestures towards an awareness of this when he writes:

> What Wittgenstein seems to be saying is that the verbal utterance, for example, 'I'm in pain' is *like* a natural, non-verbal expression of pain such as a groan or a grimace. The word 'akin' should prepare us to note differences as well as similarities. An obvious difference is that the utterance 'I'm in pain' is a sentence, whereas a groan or facial contortion is not.[45]

Clearly the interesting question here is what we might be willing to concede as a difference between *sentences* and *grimaces* or groans. Remember that for an emotivist or non-cognitivist, there is no relevant difference. It is difficult to think that Winch believes that there is an important difference either in his account of the mountain tribe and their beliefs in the mountain gods. Unfortunately Wittgenstein himself made some remarks which suggest this false antithesis and which have been uncritically adopted by the Neo-Wittgensteinians. The most glaring case is his declaration that the people who

---

[44] Mackie, J.L., *The Miracle of Theism*, Oxford, Oxford University Press, 1982, pp. 223-4
[45] Malcolm, N., *Nothing is Hidden*, p. 139

engage in the ritual of the Rain King clearly do not believe that the king can actually make rain. The relevant passage from Frazer is as follows:

> the Kings of the Rain, Mata Kodou, are credited with the power of giving rain at the proper time, that is, in the rainy season. Before the rains begin to fall at the end of March, the country is a parched and arid desert . . . when the end of March draws on, each householder betakes himself to the King of Rain and offers him a cow that he may make the blessed waters of heaven drip on the brown and withered pastures. [46]

Wittgenstein's response is interesting but extremely controversial:

> I read . . . of a rain-king in Africa to whom the people appeal for rain *when the rainy season comes*. But surely this means that they do not actually think that he can make rain, otherwise they would do it in the dry periods when the land is 'a parched and arid desert'.[47]

The reason these remarks are controversial is that further on in Frazer's text we find out that if the rains failed to appear, the king *was* held responsible and gruesome punishments were often meted out for his failure to produce the rain.[48] Such behaviour is extremely difficult to understand if we don't concede, contrary to Wittgenstein, that the people *did* actually think that the king could produce the rain. I think this is clearly an example of Wittgenstein not listening to his own advice and looking to see how the practice is in fact carried out. Unfortunately it is not a small slip. It is Wittgenstein's remark here that underlies the Neo-Wittgensteinian distinction between the primitive/non-cognitive and scientific/cognitive. Interestingly, Wittgenstein's blindness here seems to be the result of his refusal to believe that anyone could be stupid enough to hold a human being responsible for the rain. He writes in a different passage, for example, that "it is, of course, not so that the people believe that the ruler has these powers, and the ruler knows very well that he doesn't have them, or can only fail to know it if he is an imbecile or fool".[49] Just what we should make of this remark in the context of Wittgenstein's apparent rejection of the intellectualism of Frazer is a question I want to put to one side. Of greater relevance, is the issue of whether the ritual of the rain king (which we may accept did not develop in answer to the scientific question "what causes the rain?") produces beliefs that have cognitive significance. I think we must

---

[46] Frazer, J., *The Golden Bough*, p. 107

[47] Wittgenstein, L., *Remarks on Frazer*, p. 12

[48] Frazer, J., *The Golden Bough*, p. 107 and p. 75

[49] Wittgenstein, L., *Philosophical Occasions*, p. 139

agree that it does and that this justifies Mackie's (and the common sense) intuition that a belief can be both expressive and cognitive. It doesn't automatically mean that all such beliefs *are* cognitive. Determining whether they are can only be done by looking at the surrounding practice as we did in the case of the rain king and the practice of punishment.

There is one other remark made by Wittgenstein which might lend support to the Neo-Wittgensteinian distinction between expressive and cognitive beliefs which must be discussed. It runs as follows:

> Does speech play an essential part in religion? I can well imagine a religion in which there are no doctrines, so that nothing is spoken. Clearly then, the essence of religion can have nothing to do with what is said - or rather if anything is said, then this itself is an element in religious behaviour, and not a theory. Further, no question accordingly arises whether the words are true or false or meaningless.[50]

This remark contains a variety of complex ideas. For the Neo-Wittgensteinians it is confirmation that religious language does no more than religious gestures and because of this it cannot be representational or cognitive. It is not difficult to see why these remarks are taken to support their interpretation. It is important however, to be careful about the status of this remark. Just as Blackburn was tempted to see a straightforward non-cognitivism in Wittgenstein's lecture on ethics, we can be tempted to think we have learnt the intended lesson from what Wittgenstein says here. And the temptation is made even stronger when we already have a theory about the nature of religious beliefs such as the Neo-Wittgensteinians do. For them, these remarks are like honey off Wittgenstein's tongue. The remarks support their theory that religious beliefs have the same semantic status as gestures and hence can say no more about the world than gestures can. Isn't that what Wittgenstein must mean here? On the interpretation of Wittgenstein that I am offering it is exactly what Wittgenstein can't mean. It either has to be a grammatical remark - a comment designed to combat theories that rationalise religious experience - or a reflection of Wittgenstein's personal beliefs. What it can't be (or what would be unacceptable from Wittgenstein's own philosophical stance) is for the remark itself to imply some kind of philosophical theory about religious language.[51] It we treat it as a grammatical

---

[50] Waismann, F., *Wittgenstein and the Vienna Circle*, p. 117

[51] And if Wittgenstein is saying that religious language cannot even be putatively fact-stating, or truth-apt, or cognitive, then he is contravening his own standards of philosophical enquiry

remark, we can see that it makes the standard point that we should not attempt to pin down philosophically the *essence* of religion and makes it particularly against the philosopher who assumes that beliefs (language) are essential to religion or that religion must spring from an intellectual source. In imagining, with Wittgenstein, a religion in which there were no doctrines and nothing was spoken, we should lose our desire to characterise speech as an essential element of religious behaviour. It doesn't of course follow from this that a religion without its language would be unchanged. If Wittgenstein means to imply that then he is saying something that is clearly false. So too is Wittgenstein saying something false if he is suggesting that in ordinary life, we cannot ask whether religious language is true, false or meaningless because clearly that is something we do. I do not think he is saying either of these things. These remarks, if taken as grammatical, are clearly directed towards philosophers and theorists, against whom it makes perfect sense to suggest both that religion need not necessarily contain propositional beliefs (these remarks would be good against Frazer for example), and that philosophers can have nothing to say on whether such language is true, false or meaningless because answering such a question presupposes some unique philosophical insight of the sort Wittgenstein denies makes sense. His claim that language is an element of religious behaviour allows that language may be essential to a particular religion and only suggests expressivism if one already has licensed that kind of theorising. The remark that language "is itself an element of religious behaviour and *not a theory*" must be handled with care however. It is central to the Neo-Wittgensteinian interpretation and provides a useful focus for where I think their interpretation goes wrong.

What the Neo-Wittgensteinians get right is that religious (or moral) language is mischaracterised when treated as if it *aims* to represent a state of affairs. What they do wrong is to conclude that it can't be understood as descriptive or representational because it isn't the result of an *intention* to describe or represent. We can see the influence of the Wittgensteinian point that the meaning of a statement is found in its purpose or its use. Effectively, the Neo-Wittgensteinians claim that because religious language is expressive (and they here gloss expressive as "primitive" or "spontaneous") it cannot be understood as making claims about the world. This in turn commits the Neo-Wittgensteinians to the view that language only gets to be about the world when we *intend* it to be so. But that is a very unWittgensteinian position to be

---

and what I say to the Neo-Wittgensteinian's would also apply to him.

committed to. It runs the risk of turning the notion of "intention" into a super-concept; a result the Neo-Wittgensteinian should be keen to avoid.

The Neo-Wittgensteinians are right to reject philosophical explanations that account for religious practices in terms of religious beliefs because as we have seen, when properly understood, this kind of explanation does no work. (An example of such an idle explanation from first person utterances would be "I cry because I have the belief that I am in pain"). The Neo-Wittgensteinians' implied dependence on the role of "intentions" in a so-called descriptive semantics could here remind us of the traditional cognitivist. We have seen that for the cognitivist, a cognitive judgement is one that aims at truth. The non-cognitive judgement has no such aim and is not the result of such intent. The Neo-Wittgensteinian position on religion moves even closer to a non-cognitivist interpretation because of the place that they award emotion in their account of the nature of religious beliefs. Although they want to undermine the explanatory motivation behind non-cognitivism, it is not clear that their own account is not itself committed to a connection between emotions and beliefs which leads to non-cognitivist conclusions.

The most obvious place to look for a disagreement with non-cognitivism is in the Neo-Wittgensteinian insistence that although religious language is expressive, this does not mean that the objects it speaks of are not real. They do not agree with the cognitivist that they are real, but neither do they say with the non-cognitivist that they are not. Instead they claim that both cognitivist and non-cognitivist are working with a misleading notion of "real". The truth in non-cognitivism is that religious reality is different to scientific reality but this does not mean that religious objects have no reality. What it *means* for anything to be real, claim the Neo-Wittgensteinians, is given in the application of language. Against the non-cognitivist who accounts for the relevant beliefs in terms of emotions and attitudes (and deny that the object of the beliefs have any reality), the Neo-Wittgensteinians appear to differ on only one substantial point: that emotions can't be called on to explain the beliefs.[52] The Neo-Wittgensteinians claim that religious objects are real, (it is just that their reality is of a different kind) does not offer us anything uniquely different to the classical non-cognitivist because that remark is one the non-cognitivist could

---

[52] It is better to construe the relationship this way: "When [Frazer] explains to us for example, that the king must be killed in his prime because according to the notions of the savages, his soul would not be kept fresh otherwise, we can only say: where that practice and these views go together, the practice does not spring from the view, but both of them are there." (Wittgenstein, L., *Remarks on Frazer*, p. 2)

easily accept. It is offered by the Neo-Wittgensteinians, however, as if it were a contribution to the debate, so to conclude our critical discussion of the Neo-Wittgensteinian view, this claim must now be examined.

Language, Beliefs and Reality - Concluding Remarks

Perhaps the biggest difficulty facing the Neo-Wittgensteinians is that of making good on their claim that what we mean by "reality" is given in applications of language. The difficulty is two-fold: they must identify these so-called different applications and show how the meaning of "real" is different in each of them. If they could do this successfully, we would be presented with a genuine alternative to the cognitive/non-cognitive debate. We would have a solution to our problem of identifying "real" as opposed to "projected" properties by being forced to admit that no such distinction can be made without illegitimately promoting one of its applications as *the* meaning of "real". There is nothing in principle to rule out the success of the Neo-Wittgensteinian view. The problem lies in the actual application of it to language and belief. Do we find the meaning of "real" relevantly different in each discourse? I think not. Certainly when we look at language use, we find different applications of the term, but the difference is not where the Neo-Wittgensteinians claim to have found it.

When we look at how the Neo-Wittgensteinian distinguish different applications of language, we find them talking, for the most part, in terms of "science", "religion", "aesthetics" and so on. They are particularly insistent that scientific conceptions of "real" are distinct from religious conceptions of "real". In asking the Neo-Wittgensteinians what counts as a scientific conception of real however, their answer appears to amount to a "look and see". This won't do. If you ask a scientist whether quarks are real, you will probably get a variety of different answers. The fact that there is no consensus here is important. It is no use saying that we can look at the application of language to find the relevant conception of real. There will be disagreements even amongst those who use the language. The Wittgensteinian philosopher is not in a position to adjudicate between them. The Neo-Wittgensteinians attempt to make the distinction by pointing out that in religion we cannot test or verify our beliefs and imply by this, that in science, real properties are those whose existence we can verify. There is enough being done by contemporary philosophers to raise questions about the legitimacy of that claim. When it is used to rule that religious objects must have a different *kind* of reality, it becomes particularly precarious. By conflating ontology and semantics as

Winch does when he suggests that "what is real and unreal shows itself in the sense language has", the Neo-Wittgensteinians are not looking at the ways in which "real" is understood in ordinary use at all. They are insisting on distinctions that are only there for substantive philosophical theorists. Here is Winch for example, trying to illustrate the difference between making requests of God and making requests of a person, with the aim of showing that the *kind* of existence God has is different to the kind of existence a person has:

> Philosophers who say that praying to God makes sense only if it is presupposed that God exists seem to be offering the following account. There is the practice of talking to people and making requests of them and the rationality of this practice is not in question. Particular instantiations of the practice may be criticised on the ground, for example, that the person addressed does not exist, is in no position to hear what is said, or in no position to fulfil the request. Praying is a particular instantiation of this practice and can, therefore be treated in a similar way . . . Against this I want to argue that there is a difference in grammar between 'asking something of God' and 'asking something of the Yugoslav ambassador' . . . I mean that what constitutes asking (and also answering) is different . . . 'Making requests of x' is not a function which retains the same sense whether 'God' or some name or description of a human being is substituted for 'x'.[53]

Winch goes on:

> It would certainly be wrong to say that the existence of the addressee is presupposed in one case and not in the other. But this does not mean that the existence of the addressee is presupposed in both cases. It would be better to say that this question of 'existence' cannot arise in the one case in the way it can in the other.[54]

The fact is that the existence of God *can* be questioned, even by a believer and even whilst she is engaged in prayer. The question is not so very different to asking whether in ordinary conversation, the addressee is listening. In wanting to insist that it is, Winch is not describing a feature of religious language. He is applying a particular meaning thesis that requires philosophical presuppositions, not unlike those recommended by the positivists. (The parallels between them have already been discussed). The most problematic aspect of the Neo-Wittgensteinians' distinction between the empirical and religious notion of "real" is that they can only make good on it by returning to some sort of verificationism. Winch insisted that the mountain tribe couldn't be taken to believe that there were actual gods who lived in the mountains

---

[53] Winch, P., *Trying to Make Sense*, p. 119
[54] Winch, P., *Trying to Make Sense*, p. 119

because they (and we) have no idea of what it would mean for there to be mountain gods.[55] He implies that this is because we can't *find out* what it would be like for them to exist. In contrast, we know what it is like for empirical objects to exist because, well, what other criterion can Winch appeal to here but that we can point to them? We can verify the existence of empirical objects and so know what it means for them to exist whereas we can't verify the existence of God or goodness and so we don't know what it would mean for God or goodness to exist. The conclusion drawn by Winch is that because users of religious language do know what they mean by God's existence, they cannot mean that he exists in the problematic sense. I want to strongly suggest that when a believer claims that God exists it is precisely in the problematic (unverifiable) sense that they mean it.

We seem to be back where we started. The cognitive/non-cognitive disagreement turned on explicating a notion of "real" that could be attributed to the properties of some beliefs and not others. The Neo-Wittgensteinians promised to cut through the debate altogether by showing that what we mean by "real" is different in each discourse. It turns out, however, that there is nothing in their account to make this statement by the emotivist Ayer, unacceptable. Ayer writes:

> In saying that a certain type of action is right or wrong, I am not making a factual statement . . . I am merely expressing certain sentiments. And the man who is ostensibly contradicting me is merely expressing his moral sentiments. So there is plainly no sense in asking which of us is in the right. For neither of us is asserting a genuine proposition.[56]

We can hear the Neo-Wittgensteinian echo; "In saying that there will be a Last Judgement, or that God exists . . . I am merely expressing certain religious sentiments. And the man who is ostensibly contradicting me is merely expressing his religious sentiments. So there is plainly no sense in asking which of us is in the right. For neither of us is asserting a genuine proposition".

There are also clear parallels between the Neo-Wittgensteinians and Ayer when it comes to the confusion succumbed to by believers in thinking that "God" is a name. Ayer writes:

> it is when the theist claims that in asserting the existence of a transcendent god he is expressing a genuine proposition that we are entitled to disagree with him . . . the mere

---

[55] Winch, P., *Trying to Make Sense*, p. 113
[56] Ayer, A.J., *Language, Truth and Logic*, p. 142

existence of the noun is enough to foster the illusion that there is a real, or at any rate a possible entity corresponding to it. It is only when we inquire what God's attributes are that we discover that 'God' in this usage, is not a genuine name.[57]

We have seen that Phillips, Rhees and Winch are also happy to disagree with believers if they insist that their beliefs express genuine propositions or that "God" is a name. The difference between Ayer as an emotivist and the Neo-Wittgensteinians, although intended by them to be a substantial one, is in the end, hard to find.

Section Three: Wittgenstein and Expressivism

The difficulty facing any philosophical position that requires a distinction between expressive and descriptive statements is to make good on the notion of a descriptive statement against which the expressive may be contrasted. We have so far examined two attempts to draw this distinction, which although motivated by different concerns, end up with similar results. The classical non-cognitivist recognises that the properties spoken of in the relevant discourse are somehow different in kind to those we identify empirically and concludes from this that the properties are not real but projected. The Neo-Wittgensteinians also recognise that the properties spoken of are different in kind but deny that the right conclusion to draw from this is that they are not real. They argue that we cannot bias the concept of "real" in that way. I have suggested that their argument contains a piece of philosophical theorising however and this goes against what we would expect to find in a genuinely Wittgensteinian account. Their flirtation with a metaphysical stance lies in their apparent drawing of boundaries between different discourses and the connected claim that what we mean by reality can be found within them. I have tried to point out that their position has an end result not unlike classical non-cognitivism. Both produce revisionary consequences for our ordinary understanding of the discourse concerned. The non-cognitivist tells the ethical individual that goodness is not real and that moral judgements cannot be true or false. The Neo-Wittgensteinians tell the religious believer that "God" cannot be a referring term and that it is confused of them to think that anyone is listening when they pray. Given that Wittgenstein is often thought of as a non-cognitivist, it is now time to place Wittgenstein in some relation to these debates.

---

[57] Ayer, A.J., *Language, Truth and Logic*, pp. 153-4

Grammatical Differences and Substantive Disputes

We have seen that it is Wittgenstein's contention that metaphysical disputes are essentially over matters of grammar. The cognitive/non-cognitive debate is no exception. Both parties have picked up on legitimate features of the relevant beliefs. What makes these positions metaphysical is the attempt to explain or theorise about these features that can only be described and that cannot be explained from a philosophical stance.[58] To explain or draw uniquely philosophical conclusions from grammatical features requires that we get outside them and we saw in chapter three that the very concept of getting outside grammar is confused.

The non-cognitivist, in asserting that ethical (or religious) beliefs don't state what is the case, picks up on an important and genuine feature of these beliefs. An ethical question isn't straightforwardly about a state of affairs. It concerns how we should act and what we should consider valuable. A religious question likewise, is less about a state of affairs (or isn't merely so) than it is about the meaning and telos of human life. Where there are various courses of action available (or various religious systems to choose from) the individual does not "investigate reality", or carry out empirical experiments in order to find out what to do. She reflects on her convictions on how people should act or what it means to be good. She may ask others for their advice and this could be called an "investigation" of a sort, but it is importantly different from a scientific investigation. What the individual decides to do will ultimately reflect their own moral position, which is a position on how people should act. Thus in ethical deliberations, it makes no sense to speak of appealing to reality as a way of justifying one's stance. To note this is simply to note that in an ethical dilemma, the question is not answered by finding something out. One has to make a decision. This is the point Wittgenstein is making when he ways that "no amount of factual knowledge can make a man good".

Ethics has to do with agency, with meaning. Thus, in the natural world, where we talk of causes rather than reasons, there is nothing of value. This is Wittgenstein's point in the *Tractatus*. Ethics can be no science because of what ethics is. To say this is to make a grammatical point. When Ayer wrote that "there can be no such thing as an ethical science, if by ethical science one

---

[58] Of course I am perfectly happy with scientific explanations, just so long as they don't masquerade as philosophical ones.

means the elaboration of a 'true' system of morals",[59] he was not pointing out a *failing* of ethics. He was elucidating its nature. This applies also to his position on ethical disputes that "one never really does dispute about questions of value". His remark merely betrays the fact that Ayer only accepted one kind of dispute; that disputes over empirical matters of fact (which could be resolved by appealing to natural facts) was all he was prepared to call a *genuine* dispute.

In pointing out that we cannot look to the natural world to uncover the nature of ethics, Ayer is making a grammatical point. The natural world is what we might call "motivationally inert".[60] What the non-cognitivist does wrong is to move from the fact that the concepts of goodness and God do not have empirical manifestations (which can be called upon to explain or justify our beliefs in them) to the conclusion that ethics (or religion) can be (must be?) accounted for in terms of our dispositions, emotions, desires and so on. This is the move from a grammatical to what I want to call a substantive position. Bernard Williams makes explicit the non-cognitivist's reasoning when he writes:

> Since moral judgements do not track the truth, we must instead understand them as expressions of dispositions society's members have.[61]

The non-cognitivist denies that there are moral standards independent of an individual's or society's dispositions.[62] The cognitivist objects to this conclusion and asserts that there are moral standards. They are effectively reclaiming the objectivity that appears to belong to ethical judgements; an objectivity they perceive the non-cognitivist has denied. The tension between knowing the apparent truth about ethical judgements (that they are a matter of dispositions) but also experiencing the categorical nature or objectivity of such judgements is one admitted to by Williams.

Having assumed that morality is essentially a matter of dispositions, Williams has to reconcile the two views: that of the internal, or the ethical individual themselves with the external, the "truth" about one's ethical beliefs. This leads him into the following difficulties:

---

[59] Ayer, A.J., *Language, Truth and Logic*, p. 148

[60] See Johnston, P., *Wittgenstein and Moral Philosophy*, London, Routledge, 1989

[61] Williams, B., *Ethics and the Limits of Philosophy*, London, Fontana/Collins, 1985, pp. 199-200

[62] So too does the subjectivist and relativist, neither of whom are non-cognitivists. Hence I mean this only in the narrow sense in which I have been characterising non-cognitivism.

The difference between the inside point of view, the view from one's dispositions, and the outside view of those dispositions shows how it is that in the most obvious sense it is not true that all ethical value rests in the dispositions of the self, and yet, in another way, it is true. It is not true from the point of view constituted by the ethical dispositions - the internal perspective - that the only thing of value are people's dispositions . . . If we take up the other perspective however, we may ask the question 'what has to exist in the world for the ethical point of view to exist?' The answer can only be 'people's dispositions'. There is a sense in which they are the ultimate supports of ethical value.[63]

Wittgenstein's injunction that we should look at a discourse like morality or religion and in order to see how beliefs are acquired and disputes settled (or not), if taken seriously, ought to lead to a cessation of the cognitive/non-cognitive debate because in coming to understand the nature of the relevant beliefs, we will see that there is something confused about the debate. Cavell brings this out nicely when speaking of Stevenson's analysis of the difference between scientific and moral disagreements writes:

But what have we actually been told? That some disagreements between people can be settled in obvious ways and that some cannot be. Nothing could be clearer. Some disputes are factual and some are not. To say a dispute is about a matter of fact is exactly to say that there are certain ways of settling it. Just as, to say that something is a fact is to say that it can be or has been discovered in certain ways. To say that other sorts of disputes (for example, moral ones) cannot be settled in such ways is not a 'hypothesis' and requires no 'psychological generalisation' but is a point of grammar. So where does the rush of associations with 'science', 'ethics', 'beliefs', 'attitudes', and 'psychology' come in?[64]

The cognitive/non-cognitive debate is fuelled by a false dichotomy. It assumes that if moral judgements do not "track truth",[65] they cannot be right or wrong. Given that it is a feature of moral discourse to believe that one's judgement is either right or wrong, the non-cognitivist must be revisionary about the discourse. Similarly the religious believer who comes to see that God is just the product of people's dispositions and desires (perhaps in something like a Feuerbachian sense) will also undergo a radical shift in how they understand their religious commitments. It will be hard for them to go on praying to God, for example, when they no longer think of God as an independently existing being. To place the absolute demand of morality in a contingent feature of our psychology is to deny it; so too for the God-case.

---

[63] Williams, B., *Ethics*, p. 51

[64] Cavell, S., *The Claim of Reason*, Oxford, Oxford University Press, 1979, pp. 259-60

[65] Where a particular gloss is given on what it is to "track truth".

The consequences of Williams' position helps us recognise why Wittgenstein insisted that in ethics and religion, everyone must speak for themselves. To try to explain the grammatical features of these beliefs commits one to a substantive position. Underneath the philosophical gloss, the non-cognitivist is denying that moral values exist, just as Phillips and Winch are denying what religious believers assert: that the objects of religious language could possibly exist.[66] These denials, because they are conclusions drawn from features of grammar rather than mere grammatical insights, commit both the non-cognitivist philosopher and Phillips to a *stance* on the existence of God (or of goodness) which will be rejected by believers themselves. They make the mistake Wittgenstein speaks of when he writes:

> It is a mistake to explain something in terms of something else. It lies at the back of Russell's definition of a number which we expect to tell us what a number is. The difficulty with these explanations in terms of something else is that the something else may have an entirely different grammar.[67]

That Wittgenstein himself refuses to conflate two grammatically different items can be seen in the following remarks from his lectures on religious belief. Referring to someone who was about to embark on a long journey and who said to a friend: "We might see each other after death", Wittgenstein writes: "Would I necessarily say that I don't understand him? I might say [want to say] simply, 'Yes, I understand him entirely'." One of the students present at the lecture made the not unreasonable suggestion: "In this case, you might only mean that he expressed a certain attitude", to which Wittgenstein replied: "I would say, 'No, it isn't the same as saying 'I'm very fond of you' - and it may not be the same as saying anything else. It says what it says. Why should you be able to substitute anything else?"[68]

We are now in a position to see how a non-subjectivist or non-relativist reading of the following remarks is possible.[69] Wittgenstein can be seen to be

---

[66] Notice that I have identified this claim as an assertion. I have said nothing about whether it is true or not.

[67] Wittgenstein, L., *Cambridge Lectures*, p. 29

[68] Wittgenstein, L., *Lectures and Conversations*, p. 59

[69] A common enough reading of these remarks, epitomised by Roger Trigg. He mistakes a grammatical insight for a philosophical position. He accordingly responds: "If . . . it is denied, and it is suggested that there are no such things as reasons for commitment, it must follow that it does not matter what we commit ourselves to . . . Not only will it be impossible to produce reasons why a fanatical Nazi is wrong, but we must be forced to admit that it does not matter

doing two things. He is pointing out the *substantive* nature of ethics and showing how we can understand the place of truth-talk in ethics. He famously remarks:

> Someone might ask whether the treatment of such a question in Christian ethics is right or not. I want to say that this question does not make sense. The man who asks it might say: 'Suppose I view his problem with a different ethics - perhaps Nietzsche's . . . surely one of the two answers must be the right one. It must be possible to decide which of them is right and which of them is wrong.'

> But we do not know what this decision would be like - how it would be determined, what sort of criteria would be used, and so on. Compare saying that it must be possible to decide which of two standards of accuracy is the right one. *We do not even know what the person who asks this question is after.*[70]

> Or suppose someone says, 'One of the ethical systems must be the right one - or nearer to the right one.' Well suppose I say Christian ethics is the right one. Then I am making a judgement of value. It amounts to adopting Christian ethics. It is not like saying that one of these physical theories must be the right one. The way in which some reality corresponds - or conflicts - with physical theory has no counterpart here. [71]

Blackburn argues that Wittgenstein is here rejecting any appeal to a moral reality that will justify one moral opinion over another. I am suggesting that this is not a remark about the cognitive status of ethics at all. The point of philosophical interest is that the "gounds" for adopting an ethical position are different to the grounds for adopting a scientific theory. The notion of it "corresponding to reality", if construed in the scientific sense of *"explaining experience"*, has no counterpart in ethics. This means not that ethical judgements fail to correspond to reality but that such talk is inappropriately applied to ethics. Both cognitivists and non-cognitivists are doing something confused when they fight over the issue of the relationship of an ethical judgement to reality.

It is tempting to think that ruling out such talk commits Wittgenstein to the view that there is no such thing as proper conflicts and contradictions in ethics. Wittgenstein appears to fuel that interpretation when he remarks:

---

what he believes. To suggest that it does matter would be to imply that there are reasons for believing one thing rather than another." (Trigg, R., *Reason and Commitment*, p. 121)

[70] Rhees, R., *Discussions*, p. 100, italics mine

[71] Rhees, R., *Discussions*, p. 101

If you say that there are various systems of ethics you are not saying that they are all equally right. That means nothing. Just as it would have no meaning to say that each was right from his own standpoint. That could only mean that each judges as he does.

Someone may say, 'There is still the difference between truth and falsity. Any ethical judgement in whatever system may be true'. Remember that 'p is true' simply means 'p'. If I say: 'Although I believe that so and so is good, I may be wrong': this says no more than what I assert may be denied.[72]

Both the Neo-Wittgensteinians and the non-cognitivists deny that sense can be given to the notion of a contradiction between believer and unbeliever (or disputes between ethicists), but Wittgenstein very clearly makes the point that it is not that there is no contradiction; rather, what it means to speak of a contradiction is different:

Suppose I say that the body will rot, and another says 'No. Particles will rejoin in a thousand years, and there will be a Resurrection of you'.

If someone said: 'Wittgenstein, do you believe in this?' I'd say: 'No'. 'Do you contradict the man?' I'd say: 'No'.

If you say this, the contradiction already lies in this.[73]

Wittgenstein's final remark is what is important here. He allows that there is a kind of contradiction, even though it may not be of the same kind that we find between straightforward disagreements (those that can be settled). That Wittgenstein makes this point is important. He is effectively saying that the contradiction lies in the *stance* one has taken on a matter (here it is a religious matter, although it could be moral or aesthetic, etc.) For disagreements that we can settle, the disputants must agree on something, hence they can be said to occupy the same stance. The contradiction in these cases does not lie in the stance but over the evidence (re: the German aeroplane).[74] Reading his remarks this way also helps to explain Wittgenstein's next point that the disagreement between believer and unbeliever is not one of being "fairly near"- but of being "on an entirely different plane".[75] This contrast makes the point that religious disagreements are substantive and here it is important not to gloss

---

[72] Rhees, R., *Discussions*, p. 101
[73] Wittgenstein, L., *Lectures and Conversations*, p. 53
[74] Wittgenstein, L., *Lectures and Conversations*, p. 53
[75] Wittgenstein, L., *Lectures and Conversations*, p. 54

"substantive" as "not meaning the same" as the Neo-Wittgensteinians do. Wittgenstein points out that "the difference might not show up at all in any explanation of the meaning";[76] a point Putnam shows sensitivity to in his recent work on Wittgenstein. Putnam argues that Wittgenstein should be understood as rejecting all talk of incommensurability. The doctrine of incommensurability requires that one can explain the meanings concerned and this is exactly what Wittgenstein denies is possible to do in the religious case. Putnam writes "that two speakers aren't able to communicate because their words have different meanings is precisely the doctrine of incommensurability" and here Wittgenstein "is warning us against supposing that talk of 'meaning the same' and 'not meaning the same' will clarify anything".[77] Although we can recognise that the atheist and believer talk past each other, it is impossible to analyse philosophically what this talking past each other amounts to. The doctrines of incommensurability and non-cognitivism claim to provide an explanation of this talking past each other. Instead of succeeding in this, they bring out grammatical features of the disagreements.

The philosophical preoccupation with the truth or the rightness of religious or ethical beliefs is what is misleading, although this in no way implies that truth or rightness doesn't matter. What it means is that the philosophical preoccupation blinds us from the character of such beliefs and thereby encourages us, when we think about them philosophically, to misrepresent or misunderstand them. As a domain of human behaviour and language, religion is just as vulnerable to philosophical injustices as any other and gaining a perspicuous understanding of the many ways in which religious concepts operate in human life can only be done philosophically by not holding them accountable to standards that themselves can only be legitimated through philosophical injustices. The philosopher, who has no unique standpoint, can only describe the differences and be content with that:

> Religious truth? ... Of course it isn't botany, it isn't anything about eclipses, it isn't economics or history ... *But what is one to say besides that?* The man in Christ Church will very likely talk about Christian dogmas. And one might make some sense in this way, each believer talking about what he believes. But there is no sense talking about religious truth in general.[78]

---

[76] Wittgenstein, L., *Lectures and Conversations*, p. 53
[77] Putnam, H, *Renewing Philosophy*, p. 152
[78] Bouwsma, O.K., *Conversations*, p. xxvi, italics mine

Conclusion

If we lose our philosophical preoccupation with facts, values, and whether or not Wittgenstein thought that religious beliefs were really beliefs or not, we will be able to appreciate his remarks for what they are. At times, they will be descriptive with the aim of undermining illegitimate philosophical judgements and at other times they will reflect Wittgenstein's own position on religious matters. It is important to recognise this because treating a personal stance as a grammatical one might suggest all kinds of illegitimate philosophical conclusions.

An example of how easy it is to confuse the two can be seen in Roger Trigg's interpretation of the following remarks. In *Culture and Value*, Wittgenstein writes:

> Christianity is not based on a historical truth; rather, it offers us a (historical) narrative and says; 'now believe!' But not believe this narrative with the belief appropriate to historical narrative, rather; believe through thick and thin, which you can only do as a result of a life. Here you have a narrative, don't take the same attitude to it as you take to other historical narratives. Make a quite different place in your life for it.[79]

He goes on: "the historical account in the Gospels might, historically speaking, be demonstrably false and yet belief would lose nothing by this". Trigg takes this to be a denial that the historical basis of Christianity matters, that Wittgenstein is saying that we could find out that Christ never lived, etc., and it would make no difference to Christian believers. I want to suggest that we can read these remarks a different way. Wittgenstein could be seen to be making the more interesting (descriptive) point that the place these historical claims have in the context of the Christian message is completely different from normal historical claims. To treat them as purely historical, is to be blind to a central feature of Christianity, namely, that "this message (the Gospels) is seized on by men believingly (lovingly). That is the certainty characterising this particular acceptance-as-true, not something else".[80]

Denying that Christianity makes historical claims, or that the truth of such claims matters, is not something Wittgenstein does here. Indeed it would be impossible to square such a denial with the following confession: "What inclines even me to believe in Christ's resurrection? . . . If he did not rise from

---

[79] Wittgenstein, L., *Culture and Value*, p. 32
[80] Wittgenstein, L., *Culture and Value*, p. 32

the dead, then he is decomposed in the grave like any other man . . . In that case, he can no longer help."[81]

Wittgenstein is not suggesting that a believer could both accept the gospel as false and still believe it. They could however, reject what everyone else accepts as a demonstration of its falsity. That this is much more likely is brought out by Wittgenstein's emphasis on religion being a different game to the "historical proof game".[82] Religious believers might reject what historians accept as proof, rather like a Catholic might reject the scientific analysis of the consecrated communion bread and wine,[83] The conflict between the historian and the believer (or the scientist and the Catholic) is a genuine one. It cannot be solved by the philosopher. Each individual must decide for themselves.

Wittgenstein greatly admired the Danish philosopher, Soren Kiekegaard and so it is fitting, I think, to conclude with one of Kiekegaard's parables which captures what I take to be the spirit of Wittgenstein's distrust of philosophy, particularly when it attempts to theorise about ethics and religion. Kierkegaard writes:

> Imagine a country. A royal command is issued to all the office-bearers and subjects, in short, to the whole population. A remarkable change comes over them all: they all become interpreters, the office-bearers become authors, every blessed day there comes out an interpretation more learned than the last more acute, more elegant, more profound, more ingenious, more wonderful, more charming, and more wonderfully charming. ... Everything became interpretation - but no one read the royal command with a view to acting in accordance with it. And it was not only that everything became interpretation, but at the same time the point of view for determining what seriousness is was altered, and to be busy about interpretation became real seriousness . . . What do you suppose this almighty king would think about such a thing? Surely, he would say, 'The fact that they do not comply with the commandment, even that I might forgive; moreover, if they united in a petition that I might have patience with them, or perhaps relieve them entirely of this commandment which seemed to them too hard - that I could forgive them. But this I cannot forgive, that they entirely alter the point of view for determining what seriousness is'.[84]

---

[81] Wittgenstein, L., *Culture and Value*, pp. 32-3

[82] Wittgenstein, L., *Culture and Value*, p. 32

[83] Wittgenstein, L., *On Certainty*, §239

[84] Kierkegaard, S., *For Self-Examination*, Princeton, Princeton University Press, 1990, pp. 58-9

Chapter Six

Some Concluding Remarks

"That man will be revolutionary who can revolutionise himself."[1]

The picture of Wittgenstein that has emerged is that of a revolutionary: someone who wanted to change the way we think about ourselves. His motives were ethical. He worried about the pictures which bewitch us, especially in philosophy but also in everyday life. As we saw, the picture of *progress* was one of the bewitching pictures of the day. As with any picture, this one was particularly dangerous because it took responsibility away from the individual with the false promise that everything was alright, whereas the way Wittgenstein saw it, there was no reason to think that this was so at all. Pictures beguile us into losing sight of how things *actually* are, by providing us with an image of how we think things must be or how we want them to be. The particular and real is hidden by the general and ideal:

'Yes, that's how it is', you say, 'because that's how it *must* be!
'Of course, that's how it must be!' It is just as though you have understood a creator's *purpose*. You have grasped the *system*.[2]

I think it is important to realise that behind these remarks lies Wittgenstein's *concern* for the consequences of failing to understand the role our pictures play. His work is not merely designed to show the confusion that lies in treating the normativity of our pictures (their necessity) as a feature of reality. The important thing for Wittgenstein is not to distinguish pictures from truths, but to understand better the nature and the limits of our pictures. So although Wittgenstein certainly wanted to restore integrity to our pictures, he did so, not by marking a distinction between ways of seeing and that which is seen, but by restoring to them their status as *our* pictures. That is to say, Wittgenstein was

---

[1] Wittgenstein, L., *Culture and Value*, p. 45

[2] Wittgenstein, L., *Culture and Value*, p. 26

concerned with the way our pictures blind us, beguile and bewitch us. Hence his need to remind us of their role and the place they have in our practices. The best antedote for bewitchment is a dose of reality; a *reminder* of how things actually are. The following observation by Edwards is relevant here:

> To give an image its own integrity is to use it in a particular fashion. It is to use it as a way of seeing; the image becomes a way to see through the object to which it is applied . . . to give an image its own integrity is to keep it constantly in mind as an image. It is not to lose sight of the lenses, so to speak, through which we are always looking.[3]

The idea that Wittgenstein wanted to restore integrity to our pictures is an important one but we must understand what this means. As I have already said, the point is not to distinguish pictures from truths (grammar from facts). It is to combat the apparent necessity of this particular image: the metaphysical placement of the picture as a super-fact, as an image of how things *must* be. Wittgenstein combats that kind of activity because it leads to injustice and blindness. Hence, the emphasis in Wittgenstein's work on the pursuit of self-knowledge; the pursuit of a just conception, or an accurate understanding: what Wittgenstein called *perspicuity*. It is not that we must see our images *as* images, as opposed to the facts (a misleading distinction), but we must see our images as *our* images. Philosophers like Trigg who are made immediately anxious ("but what about objective Reality?") have not yet come to the realisation that the ideal of an objective reality is itself an ideal *we* have; they have not yet seen *themselves* in their philosophical pursuits. Self-understanding does not require that we resign ourselves to the fact that we are epistemically inferior to the task of knowing what Reality is really like. Nor does it demand we accept some form of relativism. It shows us that it is not that there is something we have to admit that we cannot know, but that what we are in pursuit of (the ideal of Knowledge and of the World) is unintelligible. "The aim of philosophy is to erect a wall at the point where language stops anyway."[4] It is because of our difficulty in recognising the unintelligible or the unjust, that "work in philosophy is actually more of a kind of work on oneself. On one's own conception. On the way one sees things. (And what one demands of them.)"[5] The work done by providing reminders therefore, is to help turn our

---

[3] Edwards, J.C., *Ethics Without Philosophy: Wittgenstein and the Moral Life*, Gainsville, University of Florida Press, 1982, p. 212

[4] Wittgenstein, L., *Big Typescript*, p. 187

[5] Wittgenstein, L., *Big Typescript*, p. 163

gaze from pictures onto ourselves. They are reminders of who and what we are.

In Chapter Two, I criticised Kenny for failing to realise how intimately connected in Wittgenstein's work are the themes of therapy and perspicuity. Kenny's difficulty had come out in the following remarks:

> Wittgenstein seems at first sight to have two rather different views of philosophy. On the one hand, he often compares philosophy to a medical technique, to a therapy, a method of healing. On the other hand, he seems to see philosophy as the giving overall understanding, a clear view of the world.[6]

I argued that the healing lies in the gaining of perspicuity. I want now to qualify that slightly. For it would be a mistake to think that Wittgenstein believed that once one had been cured of metaphysics, there was nothing more to be done. On the contrary, the real struggles begin right there. Perspicuity does not bring with it a static seeing of the world. The world of everyday life comes back into view. And that kind of seeing, just because it is unglamorous, is the most difficult to sustain. Wittgenstein brings this out most clearly in the following passage that was part of a longer letter written to Norman Malcolm in 1944:

> What is the use of studying philosophy if all that does for you is to enable you to talk with some plausibility about some abstruse questions of logic, etc., if it does not improve your thinking about the important questions of everyday life, *if it does not make you more conscientious than any . . . journalist in the use of the dangerous phrases such people use for their own ends.* You see, I know that it's difficult to think *well* about 'certainty', 'probability', 'perception', etc. But it is, if possible, still more difficult to think, or *try* to think, really honestly about your life & other people's lives. And the trouble is that thinking about these things is *not thrilling*, but often downright nasty. And when it's nasty then it's *most* important.[7]

These remarks help us to understand, I think, why Wittgenstein believed that one paid for thoughts with *courage*.[8] The emphasis on courage is not an eccentricity on Wittgenstein's part. It is intimately connected to the pursuit of perspicuity, which is the rendering of the world and ourselves as we *actually* are. Self-knowledge requires courage; it is not easy to face the facts about oneself. So, although Wittgenstein admired Schopenhauer and was clearly

---

[6] Kenny, A., *Wittgenstein on Philosophy*, p. 2

[7] Malcolm, N., *Ludwig Wittgenstein: A Memoir*, Oxford, Oxford University Press, 1958, p. 39, italics mine

[8] Wittgenstein, L., *Culture and Value*, p. 52

influenced by him, he nonetheless could see the lack of depth in Schopenhauer's work. And how is the depth of a writer to be gauged? For Wittgenstein it was their courage; by their ability to know and live with the truth.[9] Wittgenstein writes:

> Schopenhauer is quite a *crude* mind, one might say . . . where real depth starts, his comes to an end . . . one could say of Schopenhauer: he never searches his conscience.[10]

And:

> Courage, not cleverness; not even inspiration, - this is the grain of mustard that grows into a great tree. To the extent that there is courage there is a link with life and death.[11]

This link with life and death is the link between the thinker and their thought, the artist and their creation. It is the mark of being *present* in the thought or in the work. A distinction made by Edwards is perhaps helpful here. Arguing in a relevantly similar fashion to my argument here, Edwards draws an analogy between Wittgenstein and the poet. The essential feature of the analogy is the distinction Edwards makes between *presenting* the world and *re-presenting* it. According to Edwards, "the poet wants to *present* the world not re-present it".[12]

The distinction between presenting the world and re-presenting it, captures Wittgenstein's essential distinction between perspicuity - seeing things as they are (and that includes seeing the truth about ourselves), and obscurity - the hypostasising and thus the hiding of the world. We could say that the poet presents us with the world, confronts us with it, whereas the metaphysician separates us from it. The re-presentations of metaphysics exclude the representer. The presentations of poetry are of ourselves and our world. The poets' images, Edwards tells us, "are not statements, but reminders".[13] They are reminders of who we are. (This of course, makes interesting a possible reading of Wittgenstein's remark that his preferred form of philosophical expression was poetic composition.[14]) The poet has to speak the truth however:

---

[9] Wittgenstein, L., *Culture and Value*, p. 35

[10] Wittgenstein, L., *Culture and Value*, p. 36

[11] Wittgenstein, L., *Culture and Value*, pp. 38-9

[12] Edwards, J.C., *Ethics*, p. 214

[13] Edwards, J.C., *Ethics*, p. 214

[14] Wittgenstein, L., *Culture and Value*, p. 40

A poet too has constantly to ask himself; 'but is what I am writing really true?' [15]

The importance of provoking an examination of our pictures is not to undermine them, or to realise that they are *only* pictures (as opposed to truths - the fallacy we criticised earlier). The value in seeing our pictures as pictures is that doing so encourages a restoration of the relationship between ourselves and our pictures. We then have a better chance of seeing other pictures more justly and we are less likely to fall back into the self-forgetfulness of metaphysics. Such concerns are the concerns of someone for whom selves matter. Hence we return again to the indisputable fact that underlying Wittgenstein's work is an ethical motivation: a *concern*, not with the abstract representation of the world, but with an honest ("realistic") understanding of *who we are*.

The sense in which we are present in the world is, therefore, not lost in Wittgenstein's work, but emphasised. On the metaphysical model however, the person, the human subject, is necessarily the representer, never the subject of representation, and is therefore never *seen*. Of course it is not just metaphysics which can obscure us from ourselves. We are very good at doing so because, as Wittgenstein puts it, honesty is *not* thrilling. We can (and will) use almost anything to hide behind. Wittgenstein's particular concern with metaphysics however, can perhaps be understood by recognising that metaphysics *must* eliminate the individual and their life. It must posit mankind in general because its posits are always of generalities. It is concerned with the universal, not with the particulars. But as Spengler points out:

Mankind is a zoological expression, or an empty word. Mankind? It is an abstraction. There are, always have been, and always will be, men and only men. (Goethe to Luden, quoted by Spengler) What is real is the hard reality of living, not the *concept* of life. [16]

Importantly, therefore, it wasn't merely that Wittgenstein saw metaphysics as confused. It completely trivialises his work to see it merely as providing a corrective for a harmless activity. He saw the confusions as *dangerous*, just as he saw the gaining of perspicuity (the overcoming of confusion) as the philosophical ideal. The numerous references to illness, therapy and medicine in Wittgenstein's work cannot be ignored:

---

[15] Wittgenstein, L., *Culture and Value*, p. 40
[16] Spengler, O., *Decline of the West*, p. 21, and p. xiv

The philosopher is the man who must cure himself of many intellectual diseases in himself before he can arrive at the notion of sound human understanding.

If in life we are surrounded by death, so too in the health of our intellect we are surrounded by madness.[17]

It is probably no exaggeration to say that Wittgenstein worried that in excluding the individual from the world altogether, the illness of metaphysics threatened to be terminal. In his work there is a double vision: of restoring the individual to the world and confronting them with who they are. So, against the image of illness, it is probably fair to say that Wittgenstein must have had a vision of what it was to live a healthy human life.[18] The vision is a moral vision and it has something to do with the ability to "think honestly about your life and about other people's lives". It is a life lived in the pursuit of justice and truth.

So what does all this mean for religious belief? Clearly we can also use religious pictures to hide behind. The promise of heaven, of another world, can be (and is) used to obscure us from this one. Whenever it does so, we can imagine Wittgenstein engaging those pictures too in his critical cogs. Such criticisms are not directed at a technical fault of the language that takes itself to be speaking about realities that are not there. It is a failure to see *how things are*; it is an ethical failure. If I am right about this, most of what the Neo-Wittgensteinian philosophers of religion say on behalf of Wittgenstein about the nature of religious belief and the nature of religious language, completely misses its mark. And this is because they are not revolutionaries; they turn Wittgenstein's ethical perspective into a philosophical one. Their claim, for example, that it is confused to think of God as an ontologically existing being, rests on trivialising into a linguistic or grammatical claim, Wittgenstein's deeper (and Kierkegaardian influenced) insight that God exists for subjectivity. This is surely the way to understand Wittgenstein's perplexing and controversial remark: "If Christianity is the truth then all the philosophy that is written about it is false."[19] Philosophy cannot talk about those things that confront an individual. Philosophical ethics is chatter in the face of any real ethical difficulty. Philosophy of religion is completely inappropriate for the answering of the question of God's existence. Ethics and religion are

---

[17] Wittgenstein, L., *Culture and Value*, p. 44

[18] See Edwards, J.C., *Ethics*, for a lengthy discussion of the idea

[19] Wittgenstein, L., *Culture and Value*, p. 83

concerned with the meaning and value of life; but not with the general concept of *life*. Metaphysics objectifies the individual out of existence altogether. It is, one might say, *disinterested*. All value and meaning require interest however. They must be value and meaning *for* someone. Wittgenstein makes the point when speaking about Englemann's manuscripts: "It is right that . . . manuscripts should lose their value when . . . regarded *disinterestedly.*"[20]

Religious and ethical questions cannot be answered by philosophy just because it must be disinterested. Questions such as "Does God exist?" or "Will there be a Last Judgement?" if asked disinterestedly, lose their meaning. Philosophy has no authority to answer them. We could say, they have no answer except for those who answer them with faith, although such a claim must not be identified as the Neo-Wittgensteinian position that rejects the idea that the *truth* of the answer depends on how things are.

So why have so many been tempted to develop Wittgenstein's remarks into a most unWittgensteinian philosophy? There are probably many answers to that question, although I suspect that the penetrating insights Wittgenstein offers and at times the sheer force of his expression, drives the philosophical desire further. If taken in isolation from Wittgenstein's ethical vision, his remarks seem to license all sort of philosophical conclusions. But such a treatment of his work, is, I have argued, necessarily a misunderstanding of it. To separate Wittgenstein's remarks from their place in the broader context of Wittgenstein's conception of the nature of philosophy as the pursuit of perspcuity is, of course, the archetype philosophical mistake. Developments in a Neo-Wittgensteinian philosophy are, therefore, entirely (and ironically) to be expected. But to truly understand Wittgenstein's vision rather than to simply use his remarks to perpetuate further philosophical theorising means to understand his remarks in relation to their purpose. It means, to use his own metaphor, that we do not take the raisins out of the cake. For although raisins may be the best part of a cake, "a bag of raisins is not better than a cake; and someone who is in a position to give us a bag full of raisins still can't bake a cake with them, let alone do something better. A cake - that isn't as it were: thinned out raisins".[21]

---

[20] Wittgenstein, L., *Culture and Value*, p. 4
[21] Wittgenstein, L., *Culture and Value*, p. 66

Bibliography

Ackerman, F., *Does Philosophy Only State What Everyone Admits?*, in *Midwest Studies in Philosophy*, Vol. XVII, Notre Dame, University of Notre Dame Press, 1992, pp.246-254.

Aidun, D., *Wittgenstein on Grammatical Proposition*, in Shanker, S. (ed), *Ludwig Wittgenstein: Critical Assessments*, Vol. 4, Beckenham, Croom Helm, 1986.

Albritton, R., *On Wittgenstein's use of the term 'Criterion'*, in *The Journal of Philosophy*, 1958, Vol. LVI, pp.845-857.

Ambrose, A., *The Changing Face of Philosophy*, in Shanker, S. (ed), *Wittgenstein: Critical Assessments*, Vol. 4, Beckenham, Croom Helm, 1986.

Anscombe, E., *The Question of Linguistic Idealism*, in *Essays on Wittgenstein in Honour of G.H.von Wright*, ACTA Philosophica Fennica, Vol. XXVIII, Issues 1-3, Vol. 28, North Holland Publishing Company, Amsterdam,1976.

Anscombe, E., *Wittgenstein: Whose Philosopher?* in Griffiths, A.P. (ed), *Wittgenstein: Centenary Essays*, Cambridge, Cambridge University Press, 1991, pp.1-10.

Antony, L., *Can Verificationists Make Mistakes?*, in *American Philosophical Quarterly*, 1987, Vol. 24, No.3, pp.225-236.

Armstrong, D., *A Materialist Theory of Mind*, London, Routledge, 1968.

Ashdown, L., *D.Z. Phillips and his Audiences*, in *Sophia*, 1993, Vol. 32, No.3, pp.1-31.

Ayer, A.J., *Language, Truth and Logic*, Harmondsworth, Penguin, 1971.

Ayer, A.J., *Ludwig Wittgenstein*, Harmondsworth, Penguin, 1986.

Baker, G.P. and Hacker, P.M.S., *Wittgenstein: Meaning and Understanding*, Oxford, Basil Blackwell, 1984.

Baker, G.P. and Hacker, P.M.S., *Language, Sense and Nonsense*, Oxford, Basil Blackwell, 1985.

Baker, G.P. and Hacker, P.M.S., *Wittgenstein: Rules, Grammar and Necessity*, Oxford, Basil Blackwell, 1988.

Barrett, C., *Wittgenstein on Ethics and Religious Belief*, Oxford, Basil Blackwell, 1991.

Bartley, W.W., *Wittgenstein*, London, Quartet, 1977.

Beattie, J.H.M., *On Understanding Ritual*, in Wilson, B.R. (ed), *Rationality*, Oxford, Basil Blackwell, 1970.

Bell, R., *Theology as Grammar: Is God an Object of the Understanding?* in *Religious Studies*, 1975, Vol. 11, No.3, pp.307-317.

Bell, R., *Understanding the Fire Festivals:Wittgenstein and Theories in Religion*, in *Religious Studies*, 1978, Vol. 14, No.1, pp.113-124.

Black, M., *Wittgenstein's Language-Games*, in Shanker, S. (ed), *Ludwig Wittgenstein:Critical Assessments*, Vol. 2, Beckenham, Croom Helm, 1986, pp.74-88.

Blackburn, S., *Rule Following and Moral Realism*, in Holtzman and Leich (eds), *Wittgenstein:To Follow a Rule*, London, Routledge & Kegan Paul, 1981.

Blackburn, S., *Spreading the Word*, New York, Oxford University Press, 1984.

Blackburn, S., *Errors and the Phenomenology of Value*, in Honerich, T. (ed), *Morality and Objectivity*, London, Routledge & Kegan Paul, 1985.

Blackburn, S., *Manifesting Realism*, in *Midwest Studies in Philosophy*, Vol. XIV, Notre Dame, University of Notre Dame Press, 1989, pp.29-47.

Blackburn, S., *Wittgenstein and Minimalism*, in Garrett, B., and Mulligan, K. (eds), *Themes from Wittgenstein* (Working Papers in Philosophy No. 4), Canberra, Philosophy Program, Research School of Social Sciences, 1993, pp.1-14.

Blackburn, S., *Essays in Quasi-Realism*, New York, Oxford University Press, 1993.

Blanshard, B., *The New Subjectivism in Ethics*, in *Philosophy and Phenomenological Research*, 1949, Vol. IX, No.3, pp.504-511.

Boltzmann, J.L., *Theoretical Physics and Philosophical Problems*, Boston, Reidel, 1974.

Bouveresse, J., *The Darkness of this Time:Wittgenstein and the Modern World*, in Griffiths, A.P. (ed), *Wittgenstein Centenary Essays*, Cambridge, Cambridge University Press, 1991, pp.11-39.

Bouwsma, O.K., *Wittgenstein:Conversations 1949-51*, Indianapolis, Hackett Publishing Company, 1986.

Braithwaite, R., *An Empiricist's View of the Nature of Religious Belief*, in Mitchell, B. (ed), *The Philosophy of Religion*, Oxford, Oxford University Press, 1971, pp.72-91.

Brown, S., *Do Religious Claims Make Sense?* Bristol, SCM Press, 1969.

Carnap, R., *Philosophy and Logical Syntax*, London, Routledge, 1935.

Carnap, R., *The Elimination of Metaphysics through the Logical Analysis of Language*, in Ayer (ed), *Logical Positivism*, Connecticut, Greenwood Press, 1959, pp.60-81.

Carnap, R., *The Logical Structure of the World*, London, Routledge & Kegan Paul, 1967.

Carnap, R., *Meaning and Necessity*, Chicago, University of Chicago Press, 1967.

Carroll, L., *Through the Looking Glass*, London, Dent, 1976.

Cavell, S., *Must We Mean What We Say?* New York, Cambridge University Press, 1976.

Cavell, S., *The Claim of Reason*, Oxford, Oxford University Press, 1979.

Chesterton, G.K., *The Everlasting Man*, London, Hodder & Stoughton, 1930.

Cioffi, F., *Wittgenstein and the Fire Festivals*, in Block, I. (ed), *Perspectives on the Philosophy of Wittgenstein*, Oxford, Basil Blackwell, 1981, pp.212-237.

Cioffi, F., *Aesthetic Explanation and Aesthetic Perplexity*, in Shanker, S. (ed), *Ludwig Wittgenstein:Critical Assessments*, Vol. 4, Beckenham, Croom Helm, 1986, pp.334-359.

Cioffi, F., *Wittgenstein on Freud's Abominable Mess*, in Griffiths, A.P. (ed), *Wittgenstein Centenary Essays*, Cambridge, Cambridge University Press, 1991, pp.169-192.

Cioffi, F., *Congenital Transcendentalism and "the loneliness which is the truth about things"*, in Griffiths, A.P. (ed), *The Impulse to Philosophise*, Cambridge, Cambridge University Press, 1992, pp.125-138.

Coffa, J.A., *The Semantic Tradition from Kant to Carnap*, Cambridge, Cambridge University Press, 1991.

Conant, J., *Must We Show What We Cannot Say?*, in Fleming, R., and Payne, M. (eds), *The Senses of Stanley Cavell*, Lewisburg, Bucknell University Press, 1989, pp.242-283.

Conant, J., *Kierkegaard, Wittgenstein and Nonsense*, in *Pursuits of Reason*, Texas, Texas Tech University Press, 1993, pp.195-224.

Cook, J.W., *Notes on Wittgenstein's On Certainty*, in Shanker, S. (ed), *Ludwig Wittgenstein:Critical Assessments*,Vol. 2, Beckenham, Croom Helm, 1986, pp.328-351.

Cook, J.W., *Wittgenstein's Metaphysics*, Cambridge, Cambridge University Press, 1994.

Davidson, D., *Actions,Reasons and Causes*, in *Essays on Actions and Events*, Oxford, Oxford University Press, 1980.

Diamond, C., *The Realistic Spirit*, Cambridge, Massachusetts Institute of Technology, 1991.

Dilman, I., *Can Philosophy Speak About Life?* in Griffiths, A.P. (ed), *The Impulse to Philosophise*, Cambridge, Cambridge University Press, 1992, pp.109-123.

Drury, M.O'C., *Some Notes on Conversations with Wittgenstein* and *Conversations with Wittgenstein*, in Rhees, R. (ed), *Recollections of Wittgenstein*, Oxford, Oxford University Press, 1981, pp.76-171.

Drury, M.O'C., *Letters to a Student of Philosophy*, in *Philosophical Investigations*, 1983, Vol. 6, No. 2, pp.76-102.

Dummett, M., *Wittgenstein's Philosophy of Mathematics*, in *Philosophical Review*, 1959, 68, pp.324-48.

Dummett, M., *Truth and Other Enigmas*, London, Duckworth, 1986.

Dummett, M., *What does the appeal to use do for the theory of meaning?* in Moore, A.M. (ed), *Meaning and Reference: Oxford Readings in Philosophy*, Oxford, Oxford University Press, 1993.

Edwards, J.C., *Ethics Without Philosophy: Wittgenstein and the Moral Life*, Gainsville, University of Florida Press, 1982.

Eldridge, R., *Hypotheses, Criterial Claims and Perspicuous Representations: Wittgenstein's Remarks on Frazer's The Golden Bough*, in *Philosophical Investigations*, 1987, Vol. 10, No.3, pp.226-245.

Englemann, P., *Letters from Ludwig Wittgenstein with a Memoir*, Oxford, Oxford University Press, 1967.

Ernst, P., *Nachwart*, in Grimm, J., and Grimm, W., *Kinder-und Hausmarchen*, Vol. 3, Propylaen, Verlag, 1910, pp.271-314.

Fogelin, R., *Wittgenstein, The Arguments of the Philosophers*, London, Routledge & Kegan Paul, 1987.

Fogelin, R., *Appendix B: Two Wittgensteins*, in *Pyrrhonian Reflections on Knowledge and Justification*, New York, Oxford University Press, 1994, pp.205-222.

Frazer, J., *The Golden Bough* (Abridged edition), London, Macmillan, 1992.

Gaita, R., *Language and Conversation:Wittgenstein's Builders*, in Griffiths, A.P., *Wittgenstein Centenary Essays*, Cambridge, Cambridge University Press, 1991.

Hacker, P.M.S., *Insight and Illusion*, Oxford, Oxford University Press, 1972.

Haller, R., *Questions on Wittgenstein*, London, Routledge, 1988.

Hallet, G., *A Companion to Wittgenstein's Philosophical Investigations*, Ithaca New York, Cornell University Press, 1977.

Hepburn, R., *From World to God*, in *Mind*, 1963, Vol. LXXII.

Hertz, H., *The Principles of Mechanics*, New York, Dover, 1956.

Hertzberg, L., *Primitive Reactions - Logic or Anthropology*, in *Midwest Studies in Philosophy*, Vol. XVII, Notre Dame, University of Notre Dame Press, 1992, pp.24-39.

High, D., *Language, Persons and Belief*, New York, Oxford University Press, 1967.

Hick, J., *Sceptics and Believers*, in Hick (ed), *Faith and the Philosophers*, London, Macmillan, 1964.

Hintikka, J., *Language-Games*, in Shanker, S., (ed) *Ludwig Wittgenstein: Critical Assessments*, Vol. 2, Beckenham, Croom Helm, 1986.

Hintikka, M., and J., *Investigating Wittgenstein*, Oxford, Basil Blackwell, 1986.

Hollis, M., *The Limits of Irrationality*, in Wilson, B. (ed), *Rationality*, Oxford, Basil Blackwell, 1970, pp.214-20.

Hollis, M., *Reason and Ritual*, in Wilson, B. (ed), *Rationality*, Oxford, Basil Blackwell, 1970, pp.221-239.

Hudson, W.D., *Ludwig Wittgenstein:The Bearing of his Philosophy upon Religious Belief*, London, Lutterworth Press, 1968.

Hudson, W.D., *Wittgenstein and Religious Belief*, London, Macmillan, 1975.

Hudson, W.D., *The Light Wittgenstein Sheds on Religion*, in *The Southwestern Journal of Philosophy* (Philosophical Topics), 1977, Vol. VIII, No.1.

Hume, D., *Enquiry Concerning the Principles of Morals, Appendix One*, in Selby-Bigge (ed), *Hume's Enquiries*, 2nd Ed, Oxford, Oxford University Press, 1902.

Hunter, J.M.F., *Forms of life in Wittgenstein's Philosophical Investigations*, in Klemke, E.D. (ed), *Essays on Wittgenstein*, Chicago, University of Illinois Press, 1971, pp.273-297.

Hunter, J.M.F., *Wittgenstein on Words as Instruments*, Edinburgh, Edinburgh University Press, 1990.

Hurley, S., *Objectivity and Disagreement*, in Honerich (ed), *Morality and Objectivity*, London, Routledge & Kegan Paul, 1985.

Janik, A. and Toulmin, S., *Wittgenstein's Vienna*, New York, Simon & Schuster, 1973.

Janik, A. and Toulmin, S., *Wittgenstein, Ficker and Der Brenner*, in Luckhardt (ed), *Sources and Perspectives*, Sussex, The Harvester Press, 1975.

Johnston, P., *Wittgenstein and Moral Philosophy*, London, Routledge, 1989.

Kant, I., *Critique of Pure Reason*, London, Macmillan, 1933.

Keightley, A., *Wittgenstein,Grammar and God*, London, Epworth Press, 1976.

Kellenberger, J., *The Cognitivity of Religion*, London, Macmillan, 1985.

Kenny, A., *Wittgenstein on the Nature of Philosophy*, in McGuiness, B. (ed), *Wittgenstein and his Times*, Oxford, Basil Blackwell, 1982, pp.1-26.

Kerr, F., *Theology After Wittgenstein*, Oxford, Basil Blackwell, 1986.

Kierkegaard, S., *The Point of View for My Work as an Author*, London, Oxford University Press, 1939.

Kierkegaard, S., *Concluding Unscientific Postscript*, Swenson and Lowrie (trans), Princeton NJ, Princeton University Press, 1945.

Kierkegaard, S., *Soren Kierkegaard's Journals and Papers*, Bloomington, Indiana University Press, 1975.

Kierkegaard, S., *Parables of Kierkegaard*, Princeton, Princeton University Press, 1978.

Kierkegaard, S., *Philosophical Fragments*, Oxford, Princeton University Press,1985.

Kierkegaard, S., *For Self Examination*, Princeton, Princeton University Press, 1990.

Kiesel, G., *Wittgenstein's Theory and Practice of Philosophy*, in *British Journal for Philosophy of Science*, 1960, Vol. II, pp.238-52.

Kripke, S., *Wittgenstein on Rules and Private Language*, Cambridge Mass, Harvard University Press, 1992.

Lazerowitz, M., *The Structure of Metaphysics*, London, Routledge, 1955.

Lazerowitz, M., *Philosophy and Illusion*, London, George Allen & Unwin, 1968.

Lear, J., *Transcendental Anthropology*, in Pettit and McDowell (eds), *Subject, Thought and Context*, Oxford, Clarendon Press, 1986, pp.267-298.

Leavis, F.R., *Memories of Wittgenstein*, in Rhees, R. (ed), *Personal Recollections*, Oxford, Basil Blackwell, 1981.

Lindbeck, G., *The Nature of Doctrine*, Philadelphia, Westminster Press, 1984.

Lichtenberg. G., Mautner and Hatfield (Trans & Eds), *The Lichtenberg Reader*, Boston, Beacon Press, 1959.

Lukes, S., *Some Problems About Rationality*, in Wilson, B. (ed), *Rationality*, Oxford, Basil Blackwell, 1970, pp.194-213.

MacIntyre, A., *The Idea of a Social Science*, in Wilson, B. (ed), *Rationality*, Oxford, Basil Blackwell, 1970, pp.112-130.

Mackie, J.L., *Ethics: Inventing Right and Wrong*, London, Penguin, 1977.

Mackie, J.L., *The Miracle of Theism*, Oxford, Oxford University Press, 1982.

Malcolm, N., *Ludwig Wittgenstein:A Memoir*, Oxford, Oxford University Press, 1958.

Malcolm, N., *Wittgenstein's Philosophical Investigations*, in *Knowledge and Certainty: Essays and Lectures*, New Jersey, Englewood Cliffs, 1963, pp.96-129.

Malcolm, N., *Is it a Religious Belief that God Exists?* in Hick (ed), *Faith and the Philosophers*, London, Macmillan, 1964, pp.103-110.

Malcolm, N., *Moore and Ordinary Language*, in Rorty, R. (ed), *The Linguistic Turn*, Chicago, Chicago University Press, 1967.

Malcolm, N., *The Groundlessness of Belief*, in *Thought and Knowledge*, Ithaca, Cornell University Press, 1977, pp.199-216.

Malcolm, N., *Ludwig Wittgenstein:A Memoir*, Oxford, Oxford University Press, 1984.

Malcolm, N., *Wittgenstein: Nothing is Hidden*, Oxford, Basil Blackwell, 1986.

Malcolm, N., *Wittgenstein: A Religious Point of View?*, London, Routledge, 1993.

Marett, R., *The Threshold of Religion*, London, Methuen, 1914.

McDowell, J., *Non-Cognitivism and Rule Following*, in Leich and Holtzman (eds), *Wittgenstein: To Follow a Rule*, London, Routledge & Kegan Paul, 1981, pp.141-62.

McDowell, J., *Wittgenstein on Following A Rule*, in *Synthese*, 1984, Vol. 58, pp.325-63.

McGuiness, B., *Freud and Wittgenstein*, in McGuiness (ed), *Wittgenstein and his Times*, Oxford, Basil Blackwell, 1982, pp.27-43.

Midgley, M., *Philosophical Plumbing*, in Phillips Griffiths, A. (ed), *The Impulse to Philosophise*, Cambridge, Cambridge University Press, 1992, pp.139-152.

Monk, R., *Ludwig Wittgenstein: The Duty of Genius*, London, Vintage, 1991.

Moore, G., *Believing in God*, Edinburgh, T & T Clark, 1988.

Moore, G.E., *Wittgenstein's Lectures 1930-33*, in Klagge and Nordmann (eds), *Ludwig Wittgenstein:Philosophical Occasions 1912-51*, Indianapolis, Hackett Publishing Company, 1993, pp.46-114.

Murdoch, I., *The Sovereignty of Good*, London, Routledge, 1970.

O'Hear, A., *Wittgenstein and the Transmission of Traditions,* in Phillips, A.P. (ed), *Wittgenstein:Centenary Essays*, Cambridge, Cambridge University Press, 1991, pp.41-60.

Palmer, A., *Beyond Representation*, in Griffiths, A.P. (ed), *The Impulse to*

Philosophise, Cambridge, Cambridge University Press, 1992, pp.153-163.

Pascal, F., *Wittgenstein: A Personal Memoir*, in Rhees, R. (ed), *Personal Recollections*, Oxford, Basil Blackwell, 1981, pp.26-62.

Pears, D., *Wittgenstein*, London, Fontana, 1985.

Pears, D., *The False Prison, Volume One*, Oxford, Clarendon Press, 1987.

Pears, D., *The False Prison, Volume Two*, Oxford, Clarendon Press, 1987.

Phillips, D.Z., *The Concept of Prayer*, London, Routledge & Kegan Paul, 1965.

Phillips, D.Z. (ed), *Religion and Understanding*, Oxford, Blackwell, 1967.

Phillips, D.Z., *Death and Immortality*, London, Macmillan, 1970.

Phillips, D.Z., *Faith and Philosophical Enquiry*, London, Routledge & Kegan Paul, 1970.

Phillips, D.Z., *Religious Belief and Language Games*, in *Ratio*, 1970, Vol. 12, No.1, pp.26-46.

Phillips, D.Z., *Religion Without Explanation*, Oxford, Basil Blackwell, 1976.

Phillips, D.Z., *Belief, Change and Forms of Life*, London, Macmillan, 1986.

Phillips, D.Z., *Faith After Foundationalism*, London, Routledge, 1988.

Phillips, D.Z., *Religion in Wittgenstein's Mirror*, in Griffiths, A.P. (ed), *Wittgenstein Centenary Essays*, Cambridge, Cambridge University Press, 1991.

Pitcher, G., *The Philosophy of Wittgenstein*, Englewood Cliffs NJ, Prentice-Hall Inc, 1964.

Pitcher, G., *Wittgenstein, Nonsense and Lewis Caroll*, in *The Massachesetts Review*, 1965, Vol. 6, pp.561-611.

Pitkin, H., *Wittgenstein and Justice*, Berkeley, University of California Press, 1972.

Plantinga, A., *Is Belief in God Rational?* in Delaney (ed), *Rationality and Religious Belief*, Notre Dame, University of Notre Dame Press, 1979.

Plantinga, A., *Is Belief in God Properly Basic?* in *Nous*, 1981, Vol. 5.

Plantinga, A., *Reason and Belief in God*, in Plantinga and Wolterstorff (eds), *Faith and Rationality*, Notre Dame, University of Notre Dame Press, 1983, pp.16-93.

Price, Huw, *Facts and the Function of Truth*, Oxford, Basil Blackwell, 1989.

Price, Huw, *Metaphyscal Pluralism*, in *The Journal of Philosophy*, 1992, Vol. LXXXIX, No.8, pp.387-99.

Putnam, H., *Renewing Philosophy*, Cambridge, Harvard University Press, 1992.

Quine, W.V., *Word and Object*, Cambridge, Mass, MIT Press, 1960.

Quine, W.V, *Theories and Things*, Cambridge, Mass, Harvard University Press, 1981.

Ramsey, F., *Facts and Propositions*, in *The Foundations of Mathematics*, London, Routledge, 1931.

Ramsey, I., *Prospect for Metaphysics*, London, George Allen & Unwin, 1961.

Redding, P., *Anthropology as Ritual,Wittgenstein's Reading of Frazer's Golden Bough*, in *Metaphilosophy*, 1987, Vol. 18, No. 3 & 4, pp.253-268.

Rhees, R., *Without Answers*, London, Routledge & Kegan Paul, 1969.

Rhees, R., *Discussions of Wittgenstein*, London, Routledge & Kegan Paul, 1970.

Rhees, R. (ed), *Ludwig Witgenstein, Personal Recollections*, Oxford, Blackwell, 1981.

Rhees, R., *Wittgenstein on Language and Ritual*, in McGuiness, B. (ed), *Wittgenstein and his Times*, Oxford, Basil Blackwell, 1982, pp.69-107.

Russell, B., *The Philosophy of Logical Atomism*, in Blackman, L. (ed), *Classics of Analytical Metaphysics*, University Press of America, 1984.

Russell, B., *On Scientific Method in Philosophy*, in *Collected Papers*, Vol. 8, London, George Allen & Unwin, 1986.

Ryle, G., *The Concept of Mind*, Harmondsworth, Penguin, 1963.

Schlick, M., *General Theory of Knowledge*, Blumberg, A.E. (trans), New York, Springer Verlag, 1974.

Schlick, M., *Philosophical Papers*, Heath, P. (trans), Vols 1 and 2, Dortrecht, Reidel, 1979.

Schopenhauer, A., *The World as Will and Idea*, 2 Vols, London, Routledge & Kegan Paul, 1964.

Schopenhauer, A., *The World as Will and Representation*, E.F.J. Payne (trans), 2 Vols, New York, Dover, 1966.

Schwyzer, H., *Thought and Reality: The Metaphysics of Kant and Wittgenstein*, in Shanker, S. (ed), *Ludwig Wittgenstein: Critical Assessments*, Vol. 2, Beckenham, Croom Helm, 1986, pp.150-62.

Sherry, P., *Is Religion a Form of Life?* in *American Philosophical Quarterly*, 1972, Vol. 9, No.2.

Sherry, P., *Religion, Truth and Language-games*, London, Macmillan, 1977.

Shields, P., *Logic and Sin in the Writings of Ludwig Wittgenstein*, Chicago, Chicago University Press, 1993.

Soskice, J.M., *Metaphor and Religious Language*, Oxford, Clarendon Press, 1987.

Spengler, O., *The Decline of the West: Form and Actuality*, London, George

Allen & Unwin, 1926.

Spengler, O., *The Decline of the West: Perspectives on World-History*, London, George Allen & Unwin, 1928.

Staten, H., *Wittgenstein and Derrida*, Oxford, Basil Blackwell, 1984.

Stern, J., *Lichtenberg: A Doctrine of Scattered Occasions*, Bloomington, Indiana University Press, 1963.

Stevenson, C.L., *Ethics and Language*, New Haven, Yale University Press, 1944.

Tanner, M., *Metaphysics and Music*, in Griffiths, A.P., *The Impulse to Philosophise*, Cambridge, Cambridge University Press, 1992, pp.181-200.

Trigg, R., *Reason and Commitment*, London, Cambridge University Press, 1973.

Trigg, R., *Wittgenstein and Social Science*, in Griffiths, A.P., *Wittgenstein Centenary Essays*, Cambridge, Cambridge University Press, 1991, pp.209-222.

Waismann, F., *How I see Philosophy*, London, Macmillan, 1968.

Waismann, F., *Philosophical Papers*, Dortrecht, Reidel Publishing Company, 1977.

Waismann, F., *Wittgenstein and the Vienna Circle*, New York, Barnes & Noble, 1979.

Williams, B., *Wittgenstein and Idealism* in *Moral Luck*, Cambridge, Cambridge University Press, 1974.

Williams, B., *Ethics and the Limits of Philosophy*, London, Fontana/Collins, 1985.

Wilson, B.R., *Rationality*, Oxford, Basil Blackwell, 1977.

Winch, P., *The Idea of a Social Science*, in Wilson, B. (ed), *Rationality*, Oxford, Basil Blackwell, 1970, pp.1-17.

Winch, P., *Understanding a Primitive Society*, in Wilson, B. (ed), *Rationality*, Oxford, Basil Blackwell, 1970.

Winch, P., *Trying to Make Sense*, Oxford, Basil Blackwell, 1987.

Wisdom, J., *Foreword*, in Lazerowitz, M., *The Structure of Metaphysics*, London, Routledge & Kegan Paul, 1955, pp.vii-xii.

Wittgenstein, H., *My Brother Ludwig*, in Rhees, R. (ed), *Personal Recollections*, Oxford, Blackwell, 1982, pp.1-13.

Wittgenstein, L., *Tractatus Logico-Philosophicus*, London, Routledge & Kegan Paul, 1922.

Wittgenstein, L., *Philosophical Investigations*, Oxford, Basil Blackwell, 1958.

Wittgenstein, L., *Notebooks 1914-16*, Oxford, Basil Blackwell, 1961.

Wittgenstein, L., *Tractatus Logico-Philosophicus*, Pears and McGuinness (trans), London, Routledge, 1961.

Wittgenstein, L., *A Lecture on Ethics*, in *The Philosophical Review*, 1965, Vol. 74, No.1, pp.3-12.

Wittgenstein, L., *Lectures and Conversations on Aesthetics, Psychology and Religious Belief*, Oxford, Basil Blackwell, 1966.

Wittgenstein, L., *The Blue and Brown Books*, Oxford, Basil Blackwell, 1969.

Wittgenstein, L., *Notes for Lectures on 'Private Experience and Sense Data'*, in Jones, O.R. (ed), *The Private Language Argument*, London, Macmillan, 1971, pp.232-275.

Wittgenstein, L., *Letters to C.K. Ogden*, London, Routledge & Kegan Paul, 1973.

Wittgenstein, L., *Philosophical Grammar*, Oxford, Basil Blackwell, 1974.

Wittgenstein, L., *Letters to Russell Keynes and Moore*, Oxford, Basil Blackwell, 1974.

Wittgenstein, L., *Philosophical Remarks*, Oxford, Basil Blackwell, 1975.

Wittgenstein, L., *Cause and Effect: Intuitive Awareness*, in *Philosophia*, 1976, Vol. 6, Nos 3-4, pp.409-445.

Wittgenstein, L., *On Certainty*, Oxford, Basil Blackwell, 1977.

Wittgenstein, L., *Remarks on Colour*, Oxford, Basil Blackwell, 1977.

Wittgenstein, L., *Remarks on the Foundations of Mathematics* (Third edition), Oxford, Basil Blackwell, 1978.

Wittgenstein, L., *Remarks on Frazer's Golden Bough*, Miles, A.C. (trans), Doncaster, Brynmill Press, 1979.

Wittgenstein, L., *Letters to Ludwig Von Ficker*, in Gillette, B. (trans & ed), *Janik in Wittgenstein: Sources and Perspectives*, Sussex, The Harvester Press, 1979, pp.82-98.

Wittgenstein, L., *Culture and Value*, Oxford, Basil Blackwell, 1980.

Wittgenstein, L., Lee, D. (ed), *Wittgenstein's Lectures: Cambridge 1930-32*, Oxford, Basil Blackwell, 1980.

Wittgenstein, L., *Remarks on the Philosophy of Psychology*, Vol. One, Oxford, Basil Blackwell, 1980.

Wittgenstein, L., *Remarks on the Philosophy of Psychology*, Vol. Two, Oxford, Basil Blackwell, 1980.

Wittgenstein, L., *Zettel*, Oxford, Basil Blackwell, 1981.

Wittgenstein, L., *Last Writings in Philosophy of Psychology*, Vol. One, Oxford, Basil Blackwell, 1982.

Wittgenstein, L, Ambrose, A. (ed), *Wittgenstein's Lectures: Cambridge 1932-*

35, Oxford, Basil Blackwell, 1982.

Wittgenstein, L., Diamond, C. (ed), *Wittgenstein's Lectures on the Foundations of Mathematics*, Chicago, Chicago University Press, 1982.

Wittgenstein, L., *Last Writings on Philosophy of Psychology*, Vol. Two, Oxford, Basil Blackwell, 1992.

Wittgenstein, L., *Philosophy (sections 86-93 of the "Big Typescript")*, in *Philosophical Occasions 1912-51*, Indianapolis, Hackett, 1993, pp.158-99.

Wittgenstein, L., *Remarks on Frazer's Golden Bough*, in *Philosophical Occasions 1912-51*, Indianapolis, Hackett, 1993, pp.119-155.

Wittgenstein, L., *Lecture on Ethics*, in *Philosophical Occasions*, Indianapolis, Hackett, 1993, pp.37-44.

Wittgenstein, L., *Lectures on Freedom of the Will*, in *Philosophical Occasions*, Indianapolis, Hackett, 1993, pp.429-444.

Wittgenstein, L., *Notes for the "Philosophical Lecture"*, in *Philosophical Occasions 1912-51*, Indianapolis, Hackett, 1993, pp.447-458.

Wright, C., *Misconstruals made Manifest: A response to Simon Blackburn*, in *Midwest Studies in Philosophy*, Vol. XIV, Notre Dame, University of Notre Dame Press, 1989, pp.48-67.

Wright, C., *Truth and Objectivity*, Cambridge Mass, Harvard University Press, 1992.

Wright, G.H. von, *The Origin and Composition of Wittgenstein's Investigations*, in Luckhardt (ed), *Wittgenstein: Sources and Perspectives*, Sussex, The Harvester Press, 1979, pp.138-160.

Wright, G.H. von, *Wittgenstein in Relation to his Times*, in McGuiness, B. (ed), *Wittgenstein and his Times*, Oxford, Basil Blackwell, 1982, pp.108-120.

Zangwill, N., *Quietism*, in *Midwest Studies in Philosophy*, Vol. XVII, Notre Dame, University of Notre Dame Press, 1992, pp.160-176.

Index

For Product Safety Concerns and Information please contact our EU
representative GPSR@taylorandfrancis.com
Taylor & Francis Verlag GmbH, Kaufingerstraße 24, 80331 München, Germany

www.ingramcontent.com/pod-product-compliance
Lightning Source LLC
Chambersburg PA
CBHW070446100426
42812CB00004B/1219